THE WRECK OF THE MEDUSA

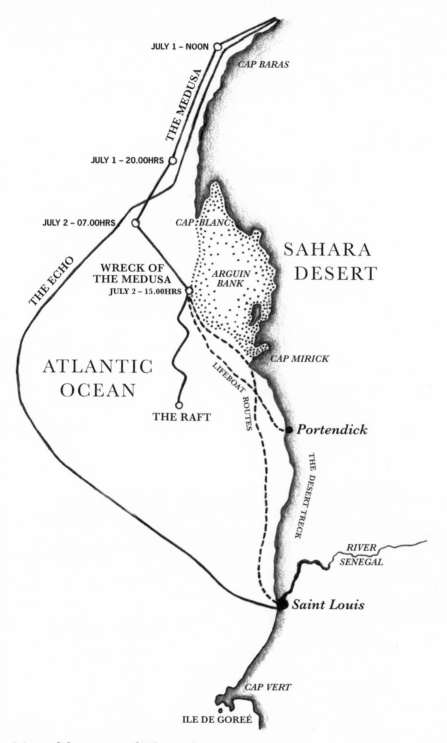

JULY 1 – NOON

CAP BARAS

THE MEDUSA

JULY 1 – 20.00HRS

JULY 2 – 07.00HRS

CAP BLANC

THE ECHO

SAHARA
DESERT

WRECK OF
THE MEDUSA
JULY 2 – 15.00HRS

ARGUIN
BANK

ATLANTIC
OCEAN

CAP MIRICK

LIFEBOAT ROUTES

THE RAFT

Portendick

THE DESERT TRECK

RIVER
SENEGAL

Saint Louis

CAP VERT

ILE DE GOREÉ

Map of the route of *The Medusa*

THE WRECK OF THE MEDUSA

JONATHAN MILES

THE WRECK OF
THE MEDUSA

The Most Famous Sea Disaster
of the Nineteenth Century

Atlantic Monthly Press
New York

Printed in the United States of America
Published Simultaneously in Canada

FIRST EDITION

ISBN-10: 0-87113-959-6
ISBN-13: 978-0-87113-959-7

Atlantic Monthly Press
an imprint of Grove/Atlantic, Inc.
841 Broadway
New York, NY 10003

Distributed by Publishers Group West

www.groveatlantic.com

07 08 09 10 11   10 9 8 7 6 5 4 3 2 1

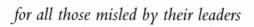

for all those misled by their leaders

Contents

CONTENTS

Illustrations

Théodore Géricault. Possible likeness of *Alexandrine-Modeste Caruel,* in Zurich sketchbook, Kunsthaus, Zurich, f° 47 r°.

Alexandre Colin. *Portrait of Géricault in 1816*-Lithograph, Musée de Rouen.

Théodore Géricault. *Le Chasseur de la Garde,* Musée du Louvre.

Anon. *The Frigate, The Medusa,* from *Le Petit Journal, Militaire Maritime,* Musée nationale de la Marine.

Alexandre Corréard. *Plan of the Raft of the* Medusa, in Corréard, Alexandre, et Henri Savigny, *Naufrage de la frégate la Méduse faisant partie de l'expédition du Sénégal en 1816,* 5th edition (Paris: Chez Corréard, Libraire, 1821), between pp. 52–53.

Anon. Sketch on ms. report showing order of boats towing the raft, in *Service historique de la Défense,* Vincennes: Dossier BB⁴393.

Anon. *Shipwreck of the Frigate, Medusa,* Musée nationale de la Marine.

Léon Antoine Morel-Fatio. *The Abandoning of the Raft of the Medusa,* in *France Maritimes,* Vol. IV, 281 mid-C19, Musée nationale de la Marine.

Anon. *The Finding of the Raft by the Argus,* in *Recueil d'événements maritimes,* 14, Musée nationale de la Marine.

Anon. *Saint-Louis in Senegal,* in René-Claude Geoffroy de Villeneuve, *L'Afrique ou Histoire, moeurs, usages et coutumes des Africains. Le Sénégal.* 4 Vols. Paris: Nepveu, 1814. Vol. I facing p. 63.

Théodore Géricault. *An Execution at Rome,* École nationale supérieure des Beaux Arts.

Théodore Géricault. *The Race of the Riderless Horses,* Musée du Louvre.

Théodore Géricault. *Fualdès being dragged and shoved into the Maison Bancal,* Private Collection.

Sébastien Cœuré. *Fualdès being dragged and shoved into the Maison Bancal,* Bibliothèque Nationale de France.

Théodore Géricault. *Studies of a Dancing Couple and a Centaur Abducting a Nymph,* London, Private Collection.

Théodore Géricault. *The Embrace,* Musée du Louvre.

Théodore Géricault. *The Kiss,* Thyssen-Bornemisza Collection, Madrid.

Théodore Géricault. *Lovers Reclining,* Private Collection.

Théodore Géricault. *Anatomical Fragments,* Musée de Montepellier.

Théodore Géricault. *Severed Heads,* Nationalmuseum, Stockholm.

Théodore Géricault. *Study for Cannibalism,* Private Collection.

Théodore Géricault. *Drawing for the Mutiny on the Raft,* Stedelijk Museum, Amsterdam.

Théodore Géricault. *Study for the figure of Corréard,* Zurich Sketchbook Kunsthaus, Zurich, f° 52 r°.

Théodore Géricault. *The Raft of the Medusa.* Musee de Louvre.

C. Motte. "Valade the Police Commissioner Confronting Corréard in Prison," in Corréard, Alexandre et Henri Savigny, *Naufrage de la frégate la Méduse faisant partie de l'expédition du Sénégal en 1816,* 5th edition (Paris: Chez Corréard, Libraire, 1821), p. 442. Bibliothèque Nationale de France.

Anon. *The Shape and dimension of the places for the slaves in the English slave-ship, Brookes,* in Thomas Clarkson, *The Cries of Africa to the Inhabitants of Europe; or, a Survey of that Bloody Commerce called the Slave-Trade* (London, 1822).

Théodore Géricault. *Study for the Slave Trade,* École nationale supérieure des Beaux Arts.

Alexandre Corréard. *Posthumous study of Géricault,* Musée de Rouen.

Théodore Géricault. *Shipwreck,* Musées Royaux des Beaux-Arts, Brussels.

NOTE

Four ships left France in June, 1816 to repossess Senegal from the British:

The *Medusa,* a frigate and flagship of the expedition

The *Echo,* a corvette

The *Argus,* a brig

The *Loire, a* supply vessel

On board the *Medusa* were the following boats used during its evacuation:

The captain's barge, commanded by Midshipman Sander Rang

The Senegal boat, commanded by Ensign Maudet

The longboat, commanded by Lieutenant Espiaux

The pinnace, commanded by Ensign Lapeyrère

The governor's barge, commanded by Lieutenant Reynaud

There was also a small skiff and a raft constructed out of debris from the *Medusa.*

Although many facts are consistent in the various narratives and fragments left by the survivors of these harrowing events, there are, at times, discrepancies. Memories severely tested by the ordeal, weak-ened by the interval between the events and their chronicling, weighted by guilt or by passionate political agendas account for these differences. In the few cases that it has not proved possible to corroborate, the most probable or trustworthy source has been used.

Acknowledgments

I would like to thank the staff of the *Bibliothèque nationale* in Paris who are always most kind and helpful, providing an environment in which it is a joy to work. The staff of the Bodleian Library in Oxford, the British Library, the U.K. National Archives, the *Bibliothèque du Musée national de la Marine, Les Archives nationales, Les Archives départmentales,* Gap, and *Le Service historique de la Defense* at Vincennes have been likewise helpful.

I am much indebted to the vision, guidance, and dedication of John Saddler, my agent in London, and the energy, counsel, and enterprise of George Lucas, my agent at InkWell Management in New York.

I feel a deep gratitude for the enormous enthusiasm, editorial acuity, and care of Joan Bingham at Grove/Atlantic, Inc. and Will Sulkin at Jonathan Cape who have, in very different ways, contributed so much to the text, as have their alert and sensitive copy editors.

I would like to thank John and Claire Rickard, Amélie Louveau, Dr. Eric Martini, Dr. Michel Martini, Dr. Patrick Chariot, Iradj Azimi, Jean-Yves Blot, Lucienne Ruellé, Claire Lemouchoux, and Mark Mullen. Immeasurable gratitude is due to my lovely Catherine, whose help has been invaluable, whose kindness is supreme, and to my daughter, Marjotte, whose bubbling enthusiasm for just about everything makes life a delight.

Paris, 2006

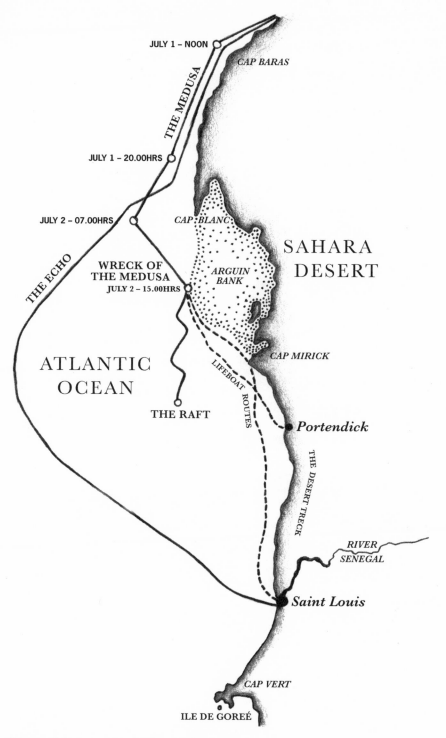

Map of the route of *The Medusa*

1

A Severed Head

An agitated young man with a recently shaven skull and piercing eyes emerged through a monumental portico that fronted the hospital and turned into the chilly shadow of the street. Hitherto unfocused, in this bitter winter of 1819 he had a newfound sense of determination, a resolve formed not a moment too soon: although only twenty-seven, this striking figure would, within the space of five years, be dead.

The street into which he turned was not busy. He had chosen to install himself in a working-class, northwestern suburb of Paris, close to the Beaujon hospital and away from society's babble. The district was scarred, as was every part of that damaged capital, by the bloodshed of a revolution turned vicious and, more recently, by the debris of an empire overthrown. A visiting English artist noted that there was "scarcely a driver of a fiacre, a waiter at a café, or a man in middle life, who had not been in battle, served in a campaign, or been wounded by a shot."[1] Mutilation was commonplace. Injured soldiers and amputees formed a macabre and lengthening procession that had dragged itself about the city since Napoleon's first conquests. Twenty years on, there were hoards of these invalids, retired on half pay after 1814, rejected victims of the restored monarchy's reduction of the once feared Grand Army. According to another English visitor, Paris was "a vast mourning family," where "three people out of five that one meets are habited in black."[2] Its citizens after a quarter of a century had, once again, been made royal subjects and discord grumbled round the capital.

Although the muslin parcel that he hugged in his arms was proving cumbersome, the young man attempted to quicken his pace. From his razored appearance and from the dark red staining the gauze, it would seem that his trade was perhaps butcher or that his guilty secret was murder. The fabric was proving far from impermeable and he was obliged to reposition his load in order to prevent his coat from becoming bloodied.

If it seemed like madness to parade in broad daylight with a severed head clutched closely to one's breast—and, indeed, neatly bound in the muslin sack was a human head that had, until recently, been attached to a living, breathing body—it was nothing to the folly of the world into which Théodore Géricault had plunged. His new friend Alexandre Corréard had promised to call. He was an excitable person with strong convictions, a frankly litigious man with a recently acquired sense of self-importance. Corréard had been on board the *Medusa*. He had survived the infamous raft and had much privileged information to impart.

The severed head was already putrid, but the stench that greeted the young man as he climbed the stairs to his lodgings was emetic. It was fortunate that he was living an almost reclusive existence, for the stink was overpowering as he opened his front door and beheld the carnage. Surely the domain of a homicidal maniac, the space was ornamented with portions of death. Arranged lovingly, like delicacies on a small table, were the amputated arms and legs of some unfortunate individual. If Géricault was no murderer, then surely he was a psychopath, a cannibal who had decided to feast upon the dead.

The sound of quick, purposeful steps could be heard on the stairs and the expected visitor, Corréard, burst into the room. He showed no sign of shock at the butchery, and neither did the reek of rotting flesh upset him. Corréard had, nigh on three years before, over a period of days while floating between life and death, eaten from the hacked-off limbs of dead companions. Since then, such sights had racked his dreams, but somehow, in the cold light of a winter's day, these scraps, arranged for purposes of research, seemed acceptable. Over the past few weeks his host Géricault had been living with putrefaction as fragments of bodies had decomposed all about him, helping the artist approach the horror precipitated by the wreck of the *Medusa*.

The flagship of a prestigious expedition to repossess the colony of Senegal, the *Medusa* had been driven onto a sandbank by its inept captain, a relic from the ancien régime, who had been appointed leader of the expedition not for any qualities of seamanship but in recompense for past political services. Corréard, as a member of that ill-fated expedition, had been the victim of an avoidable shipwreck and a self-ishly misconceived rescue plan. Adding insult to injury, when Corréard had sought compensation, he had been spurned by an indifferent government. Outraged by its callousness, he had publicized his misfortune, writing *The Shipwreck of the Frigate, the Medusa*—a best seller—and was visiting this stinking room to elaborate certain visual details that were absent from his text. He was here to help create an image, to act as adviser to this disturbed young artist who was deep in a painting with which he sought to make his name.

So gripping was the indictment of the French leadership in Corréard's book that it had been translated into English, German, and Dutch, with an Italian translation forthcoming. The work in its second French edition had become more politicized in scope and Corréard visited Géricault not only to reconstruct specific details of his terrifying days on the raft, but also to elucidate the sinister state of affairs. His argument, to which his own misfortune bore witness, offered a scathing appraisal of the Bourbon restoration, which, he claimed, was intent on betraying the positive gains of nearly three decades of French political struggle.

Host and visitor began to talk, exploring the labyrinth of issues that led out from that supreme act of cowardice, the release and cutting of the ropes that were supposed to tow the raft of the *Medusa* to safety. One hundred forty-seven people had been herded onto this makeshift platform because of a shortage of lifeboats. Abandoned by the leaders of the expedition, who fled in order to save themselves, all but fifteen died on board.

Swept along by Corréard's intense and penetrating diatribe, Géricault listened attentively. Géricault had begun to look about, in the streets and in the press, for something to excite his desire for relevance. He had come back early to Paris from his Italian painting trip, not with the usual copies of Michelangelo but with scenes of carnival upheavals, executions, and a fistful of tortured erotic drawings. He had returned searching for the kind of story that smacked of the moment, for an incident that thrilled the readers of the popular press of the day, one of those lurid news items that reported wide-ranging infamies from criminal and sexual scandals to suicides, shipwrecks, and cannibalism.[3]

Alexandre Corréard and Théodore Géricault, meeting in the midst of this butchery, had both suffered devastating setbacks, had scandals hounding them, had secrets to conceal and yet were determined to surmount misfortune. Corréard tireless in his struggles for retribution and justice; Géricault tackling his ambitious canvas with a fervor and single-mindedness that could be gauged from the hideous array of decomposing flesh with which he chose to populate his studio. It was a temporary space; he had rented it to paint the raft. Hence the strewn limbs, the sketches of the successive outrages in the drama, the small model of the platform, which had been assembled for him by the ship's carpenter, a man who had questioned aspects of Corréard's account of their thirteen days adrift.

Catching sight of a bundle of studies for which he himself had posed, Corréard pondered them for a moment and then turned to confront the large canvas on which Géricault had begun to work. He saw his own figure taking shape, center stage, in pride of place, the star of the nightmare.

2

Voyages Out

For Love and Loathing

Three fraught years earlier, in the summer of 1816, a summer that would change their destinies, Alexandre Corréard and Théodore Géricault appeared very different from the agitated, injured beings who would meet in that grisly studio during the winter of 1819. Both seemed, uncannily, so much younger. Géricault, in contrast to his later self, was very much the young man about town, handsome, well dressed, with an attractive head of reddish, light brown hair. Corréard was lithe and sinewy, excitable and alert. These two men, who would become important figures in each other's lives, had urgent reasons to leave France. Love would drive Géricault away; loathing for what was happening to his country would send Corréard, as a pioneer, to Senegal.

Despite the costly failures during the final months of his reign, Napoleon had boosted the self-esteem of a great many Frenchmen. In 1814, the twenty-six-year-old Corréard was by no means alone in feeling dismay at his emperor's defeat. Although a conciliatory constitutional monarchy was swiftly created, Louis XVIII was obliged to reward survivors from the ancien régime, counterrevolutionaries, and those who had been supportive to the crown in exile. Though the king was to preserve many of the improvements made in French administration since his elder brother, Louis XVI, had been forced from the throne and guillotined, the year 1814 saw ennoblement on an unprecedented scale and witnessed the restoration of that emblem of an all-powerful monarchy, the palace of Versailles.[1] Such conflicting signals were alarming to a country suffering from defeat and a formidable sense of collective loss.

During their childhood and youth, Alexandre Corréard and Théodore Géricault had known only the turmoils of revolution and the authoritarianism of the empire. Alexandre had been born into a class that had prospered since the French Revolution and grew up in one of the grandest houses in the precariously hill-hugging town of Serres in the mountainous region of southwestern France. On his father's side the family had been merchants since the Middle Ages and his mother's family were middle-class professionals. Elizabeth, the mother of ten children, of whom Alexandre was the sixth, was fervently religious. She kept to her faith throughout the revolution, which had, by turns, been unsympathetic or ambivalent toward the church. Just as Alexandre's flair for enterprise suggests some measure of paternal influence, so Elizabeth's tenacity was reflected in the ardor of her son's subsequent struggles against the injustices of the state. He attended a military school in the imperial city of Compiègne, coming to maturity when Napoleon was at the height of his power. In 1812, as the tide turned against the emperor, with food and anticonscription riots at home, defeat in Spain, and retreat from Russia, Corréard joined the Imperial Guard, in which he served until 1814.[2]

During those two years, the military and domestic situation in France deteriorated rapidly. With so many men conscripted, wounded, or dead, the women and children were to be found hard at work in the fields. Abroad, the unenthusiastic remnants of the French army in Spain were defeated at Vitoria-Gasteiz in June 1813, allowing the victorious Wellington to enter southern France. Napoleon was likewise defeated at Leipzig in October 1813, allowing the Prussians to push on toward the French frontier. By the early months of 1814, peasants had inundated Paris with their carts and cattle, seeking refuge from the invading armies. The mentally disturbed were turned out of asylums in order to provide quarters for the retreating troops; hospital patients were driven from their beds to make way for the wounded. In March, famine and pillage threatened the capital, presaging complete social breakdown.[3] Dead bodies were heaped up on the banks of the Seine and floated eerily in the river, a situation that the authorities duplicitously assured inhabitants would have no deleterious effect on drinking water. Mounds of the military dead were piled into mass graves and Paris took on the air of a sacrificial altar to a lost cause.

Then, at the end of March and the beginning of April 1814, it all changed. Throughout the city, Allied troops paraded. In the Tuileries, along the Champs-Elysées, and in the Palais Royal droves of curiously attired English tourists, along with a multitude of occupying troops, gave Paris the splendor of a fabulous extravaganza; a stroll through the capital would present the visitor with a

> savage Cossack horseman, his belt stuck full of pistols, and watches and hatchets . . . the Russian Imperial guardsman, pinched in at the waist like a wasp, striding along like a giant, with an air of victory that made every Frenchman curse within his teeth as he passed him . . . the heavy Austrian, the natty Prussian, and now and then a Bashkir Tartar, in the ancient Phrygian cap, with bow and arrows and chain armour, gazing about from his horse.

The cosmopolitan mayhem of the occupation flashed visions of "hopeless confusion . . . Russians, Poles, Germans, Italians, Jews, Turks and Christians, all hot, hurried and in a fidget."[4]

To secure peace and stability in Europe the Senate, at the behest of the provisional government and acting on the wishes of the Allied victors, summoned the Bourbon Louis Stanislas Xavier, king of France, to return home after his interminable exile and accept his rightful place on the throne. The event was heralded in a fast-selling pamphlet in which the royalist author vicomte de Chateaubriand celebrated the Allies as liberators, denounced Napoleon as having had "the sword of Atilla and the maxims of Nero," and hailed the royal family as healers.[5]

Returning to France in 1814, the Bourbons may have been thoroughbred French, with their line stretching back to the Middle Ages, but they were also an unprepossessing group who were coming to restore regal authority and order to a country that had run wild with bloodthirsty political experiment. Louis XVIII claimed that he had been de facto king since the death of his young nephew Louis XVII, in 1795. By 1814 he was aging, childless, and deteriorating with gout, yet his uncompromisingly absolute attitude, a reaction to the execution of his brother Louis XVI, had mellowed during his long exile. Not so, however, that of his younger brother, the dangerous and provocative duc d'Artois, who would succeed Louis as Charles X. Artois surrounded himself with extremists, "ultra-royalists" who had no intention of letting renegade republicans and Bonapartists have their say in restoration France. These ultras were to prove the most problematic of all the political factions, launching intimidating affronts to Louis's rule.[6]

The Senate called Louis XVIII to the throne as a constitutional monarch on April 7, 1814. The king arrived with a strong desire to heal his kingdom's wounds and to effect, as he put it, a "fusion of two peoples."[7] France was a nation in a state of shock and, as Louis's remark suggests, divided against itself. If a good number of people in many parts of the country welcomed the return of a king, the army remained loyal to Napoleon. Paris was split along political lines. Dangerously, factions were testy and likely to clash.

Remembering Napoleon's rule as a period of opportunity, Alexandre Corréard noted that, at the time of his fall, "I wanted to distance myself as far as possible from France and so I engaged as an engineer in the military expedition that was going to retake possession of the French establishments on the African coast."[8] As a geographical engineer, Corréard was appointed to identify a suitable location on Cap Vert, or its environs, for the establishment of a colony.[9] An expedition was set up in the late autumn of 1814 and participants began to assemble at Brest for a departure planned for the spring of 1815. The scheme for which Corréard enlisted was directed by the Philanthropic Society of Cap Vert and attracted a large number of republican, or Napoleonic, sympathizers who were seeking to start afresh in a French colony.[10] In order to gain official support, the Philanthropic Society presented itself as an organization that had been created to prevent disaffected people from taking their capabilities and capital off to other countries. With a schedule for reimbursing the crown for its initial support, the society was a properly structured commercial venture with shareholders, annual general meetings, a committee of directors, and projected profits.

As Corréard prepared to ship out, something unforeseen happened. On March 1, 1815, Bonaparte, who had been smoldering away on the island of Elba, landed in Golfe Juan on the south coast of France with the four hundred soldiers that he had illegally kept with him in exile. His reckless gamble seemed to be paying off when he entered Grenoble six days later, escorted by the very troops sent to check his advance. On March 10 in Lyon, Napoleon was greeted by crowds yelling, "To the scaffold with the Bourbons! Death to the royalists."[11]

Events followed swiftly. On March 14, the Crown Jewels were sent to England for safekeeping. Louis addressed the chamber of deputies, claiming that he stood for peace and liberty, whereas Napoleon brought war. However, on March 19 the king prepared to travel north into exile.

During the evening of the twentieth, Napoleon arrived in the capital, at the head of yet more troops who had been sent to oppose him.[12] Unwisely, Louis had replaced the ever popular tricolor, that rallying point for *liberté, égalité, fraternité,* with the white flag of the Bourbons. Upon Napoleon's return, the tricolor was unfurled with alacrity and shopkeepers exchanged their royal emblems for Napoleonic insignia, much as they had replaced Napoleonic eagles with fleur-de-lis only nine months before. It was as if Louis had never happened; the reconceived monarchy had been stillborn.

On June 12, Napoleon marched his army north to engage the Allied troops massed under Wellington and the Prussian field marshal Blücher. There were scores to settle and his new position to consolidate; although vast portions of the French population were loyal to the king, Louis now found himself in virtually unprotected exile. The future of the monarchy was, once again, in doubt until Napoleon's daring bid was, within the week, crushed by his defeat at Waterloo. By June 21 Napoleon was back in Paris, where, on the following day, he abdicated in favor of his son.[13] The period known as the Hundred Days was at an end. To prevent himself from being captured by his enemies, Napoleon made haste for Rochefort where two frigates would be waiting to enable his escape to America.

Forgetting earlier triumphs under Louis XIV against a united Holland and England, the French tended to undervalue their navy. In a pitiful state when Napoleon first came to power, its history during the previous forty years had been checkered, although the loss of most of France's first colonial empire at the end of the Seven Years' War in 1763 provoked a great period of naval reorganization, shipbuilding, and peaceful exploration, particularly in the Pacific. Louis XVI zealously sought a fleet that could wrest control of the high seas from the English and recover the French colonies lost under his grandfather Louis XV. By 1780 France possessed seventy-nine warships, eighty-six frigates, and about a hundred smaller ships. It was thus able to play a decisive but costly role in the American War of Independence. The French blockade of Chesapeake Bay in September 1781 prevented the Royal Navy from coming to the aid of Cornwallis, who was thus forced to surrender at Yorktown in mid-October. The Peace of Versailles in 1783 gave France minimal overseas territory, including Tobago and Senegal, yet the cost of helping the Americans free themselves from the yoke of unjust English taxation had been punishing. The deficit in the navy budget anticipated the ruin of the ancien régime itself.[14]

After the revolution, there had been a massive emigration and, by 1792, half of France's naval officers had disappeared. In 1793, when war broke out with England, the British sank the French fleet at Toulon. During the two following years France lost many vessels through bad seamanship as well as in combat, a sequence of disasters culminating, in 1798, with Nelson's crushing defeat of the French at Aboukir. Despite some reorganization under Napoleon, the navy was again beaten at Trafalgar on October 21, 1805, where the smaller but remarkably well trained English fleet beat the demoralized and badly equipped Franco-Spanish adversaries. The victors gained incontestable supremacy on the high seas and the subsequent blockade kept what was left of the French navy starved of materials and largely portbound.[15] After the restoration, that blockade ceased to exist but, toward the end of the Hundred Days, the English navy was again on hand to frustrate any attempt at escape.

The plan, in June 1815, was for Napoleon to set out for America on board the *Saale* while a frigate called the *Medusa* was to act as a decoy. This ship was the work of the acclaimed designer Jacques Noël Sané and construction began at Paimboeuf in April of 1807. She was to carry forty-four cannon, each capable of discharging a four-pound shot. The hull was reinforced to her waterline, with copper to protect it against mollusks and barnacles, and when ready for launch in July 1810 the *Medusa* was utterly up to date. Her maiden voyage in December of that year was the command of a small Franco-Dutch expeditionary force to Batavia.[16] It was an adventurous voyage out; the frigate was battered by high seas, lost her convoy, and was given chase by an English squadron. Shortly after her arrival in the Dutch East Indies, the islands were surrounded by British warships and Batavia surrendered. Julien Schmaltz, the quixotic adventurer who would later play such a shameful part in the *Medusa* scandals, was captured by the English. Meanwhile, the *Medusa* and her sister ship, the *Nymphe,* gave the enemy the slip, sailed off, and arrived safely back in Brest almost a year after they had left France.

The captain of the *Medusa* recorded that after various adventures during the voyage, he was in no doubt about the excellence of his ship. During 1812 and 1813 she put to sea a considerable number of times, given the blockade. Among her duties was the hunting of English merchant ships returning from the Far East. Her career was distinguished; by February 1814, along with the *Nymphe,* she had engaged and destroyed a dozen enemy ships. Under the restoration she serviced as a patrol vessel in the Caribbean, arriving back in Rochefort for a refit in February 1815. When the Hundred Days ended ignominiously for Napoleon, the *Medusa* was nominated to draw the fire of the English squadron moored off Rochefort, while the emperor fled on board the *Saale.* The captain of the frigate, le Chevalier Ponée, believed that he would be able to distract and deceive the English for about three hours. After that, his frigate would be finished, but by then the emperor would have put a little distance between himself and his pursuers. In the event, however, Napoleon gave himself up to the British captain Maitland on board HMS *Bellerophon* on July 14, 1815. Ponée, understandably, lost his command with the coming of the second restoration and, only months after its refit, the *Medusa* returned to Rochefort to be disarmed.[17]

With the unforeseen episode of the Hundred Days, Alexandre Corréard's departure for Senegal had been called off when the Philanthropic Society "momentarily suspended its activity." Feeling that there were grounds, once again, for hope at home, he was, in fact, left in France merely to witness the swift and final failure of his emperor and the subsequent eclipse of liberal prospects. After such an unexpected affront to European security, the occupation of France was more stringent than it had been in 1814, and the pressure on Louis to root out subversives even greater. With peace, however, the efforts of the Philanthropic Society recommenced, helping "peaceful men who were tired of exhausting their resources in conditions of social paralysis, and who, without ceasing to be French, wished to create a new country on land that is still untouched."[18] For Corréard, the expedition, a chance to escape to a land uncomplicated by conflicting ideologies, seemed overdue.

In the summer of 1816, the date of Alexandre Corréard's eventual departure for Senegal, Théodore Géricault also wished to leave France. He signaled no immediate dissatisfaction with the restoration; indeed, he played an active and positive part in the new regime. Born into a comfortable family in September 1791, Théodore spent his earliest years in Rouen, in a pro-royalist household that was threatened during that revolutionary period. In those early years the boy quite probably absorbed something of the violence that characterized the Reign of Terror under the Jacobins, and it is likely that the Géricaults left for Paris in order to escape from local revolutionary unrest. In the capital, Théodore's father, Georges-Nicolas Géricault, joined his brother-in-law Jean-Baptiste Caruel in his tobacco enterprise, while his son attended a nearby boarding school. Let out on Thursdays, the boy was much indulged by his grandmother, who lived with them in the faubourg Saint-

Germain, and he threw tantrums when it was time to return to school. In 1806 Théodore entered the Lycée Impériale, where it soon became evident that he had more enthusiasm for horses than for schoolwork; his eyes glazed over as he wrestled with Latin grammars while his "spirit was captivated by visions of imaginary cavalcades." However, early on, he did display artistic talent; a friend and fellow pupil, Théodore Lebrun, recorded Géricault's natural aptitude for drawing, commenting that he was already an artist without being conscious of the fact. Much of Géricault's recreation and study time was consumed by drawing, and as a result he appeared somewhat of a dunce and was frequently thrown out of class.[19]

In May 1807 a family event occurred that would have immense repercussions on Géricault's life and art. In a union not unusual for the period, Théodore's fifty-year-old uncle Jean-Baptiste Caruel married a young lady of twenty-two. His chosen, Alexandrine-Modeste de Saint-Martin, possessed a lively interest in the arts, and, within the confines of her new family with its narrow focus on business, it was inevitable that the artistic leanings of her personable young nephew would attract her. An animated friendship grew up between them, which benefited from the blessing of Alexandrine's busy husband. When she met with her nephew, she was keen to see his sketches and chat about art. He, at sixteen, was flattered, perhaps even a little embarrassed, by the attentions of an attractive young lady.

Within a year of Alexandrine's marriage, a death occurred that drew the young aunt and youthful nephew even closer together. In March 1808, Théodore's mother, a strong woman whom he had loved and by whom he had been much loved, died. While his father entertained practical and predictably safe ambitions for the boy, his mother had supported her son's budding artistic talent. After her death Théodore had even greater need of his aunt's understanding.

The boy and his father moved to the Right Bank, to a house only a stone's throw from the rich and luxurious establishment in the rue de la Grange-Batelière where the Caruels were installed. Alexandrine was particularly sensitive to the boy's grief, having lost her own immediate family during her childhood. She became a consoling presence who began to fill the emotional vacuum left by the death of Théodore's mother. He rejoiced in her sympathetic and vivacious spirit and she delighted in the vitality of someone close to her own age who was still sufficiently young enough to become a kind of protégé. Easily distracted by his eagerness to become a man about town, Théodore responded warmly to the relaxed atmosphere generated by Alexandrine in the Caruel home. The extent to which he had become an important part of her world is indicated by the fact that in December 1809, Géricault was named godfather of the Caruels' second son, Paul.

As the bond grew between Alexandrine and her elegant, tall, well-formed nephew, she became the most important woman in his life. They became so close that they started to hatch secret plots and deception became a part of their alliance. Géricault's father had continued misgivings about his son's desire to paint, so Alexandrine entreated her husband to provide a respectable cover for their nephew's artistic studies, persuading him to take the young man into his tobacco firm as a trainee accountant and to turn a blind eye to the boy's absences. During these escapades, Géricault went either to a riding school or to class at the studio of the anglophile and royalist Carle Vernet, an accomplished painter of history and horses. It was there that Théodore befriended Carle's son Horace, whose own studio would, by contrast, and within the first few years of the restoration, become a rendezvous for subversive Napoleonic and republican liberals.[20]

On the brink of maturity, and made financially independent by a substantial legacy from his mother, Géricault was much admired by women. Carle Vernet "asserted that he had never seen such a good-looking man," going on to remark that "his legs were, above all, superb." Géricault was fashionable and becoming careful in his dress to the point of affectation.[21] Yet any vain posturing was "tempered by a marked expression of gentleness." His eyes twinkled, and such a dashing and accomplished young man, exhilarated by the thrill of horseman-ship and beginning to take himself more seriously as an artist, proved a compelling companion for the youthful Alexandrine Caruel.[22]

One highly attractive place where he was welcome to stay and work was the magnificent property near Versailles that had been pur-chased by his uncle Jean-Baptiste Caruel in 1802. Adjoining the Parc de Trianon, the Château of Grand-Chesnay had once belonged to officers at the court of Versailles and was a typical purchase for a mem-ber of the bourgeoisie who had become rich after the revolution. The château's park and its dependent agricultural holdings were sizable and the house boasted a library of fourteen hundred classical texts and a collection of fifty pictures and engravings, mainly by minor Dutch and French artists.[23] Though these indifferent images had little to offer the young visitor, the large house and extensive grounds gave Géricault the opportunity to enjoy privileged moments with his young aunt. She was becoming more than a strong ally against paternal caution and the young man's attraction to her was developing into something more complicated than a mere replacement for maternal love and encouragement.

While at Grand-Chesnay, Géricault visited the nearby imperial stables to make paintings of three of the emperor's studs. He also fre-quented the Trianon Gallery where he would study the works of art, and it was there that he would meet and flirt with a certain Made-moiselle Montgolfier, who mistook the dalliance for a serious advance, a misunderstanding that Géricault was, as the months went by, more than happy to encourage. To be seen in the company of Mademoi-selle Montgolfier and to be talked about would provide a useful cam-ouflage for the serious, dangerous, and illicit adventure upon which he was embarking.[24]

Not wishing to become a victim of the disintegrating Napoleonic military machine, Géricault bought himself a replacement for his military service. This was perfectly legal and aboveboard and it meant that he could set out on a course of study that would prepare him for the competition for that year's prestigious Prix de Rome, a four-year scholarship to study at the French Academy in a city rich in classical statuary and artistic heritage. Whether or not Géricault entered the competition in 1812 has been argued by historians and biographers; what remains important is that, despite his youthful exuberance and dandyism, a new strain of seriousness appeared in his approach to his work. This, however, by no means suppressed his zest or volatility; in May he was banned from the Louvre after abusing and hitting a young student in the Grand Gallery. While the incident reveals his passionate nature, it also vouches for the fact that he was in the Louvre studying or copying. What is more, it was not the first time he had fallen foul of the museum authorities; Vivant Denon, director of a museum richly swelling with Napoleonic booty, had occasion to ban Géricault temporarily after he brutally resisted officials when they attempted to repossess his membership card. Perhaps the loss of his grandmother, in April 1812, and the stress of the developing triangle between himself, his kindly uncle, and his attractive aunt help to explain such outbursts.

Left even wealthier by the death of his grandmother, Géricault rented an empty shop on the boulevard Montmartre, and there he began work on the first of his few great projects, *The Officer of the Chasseurs*. Painted between September and October of 1812, at a time when Napoleon had rashly driven his army deep into Russia with its infamous winter coming on, the tensions in the painting reflect the moment at which and for which it was painted. It questioned imperial military hubris by pitting the officer's splendid uniform, so out of place and yet worn with such bravura, against the inferno of the battlefield. Resonating with fear, the painting registered the degenerating military situation and its insight was prized. Géricault won a gold medal worth 500 francs in the Salon of 1812 with what was, in fact, his first submission. By the time the Salon shut its doors on February 13, 1813, Napoleon had overreached his imperium and three hundred thousand of Géricault's compatriots lay dead in the Russian snow.

The Officer of the Chasseurs hinted at failure on a national scale, revealing that Géricault was already becoming sensitive to the political tensions that would transform him from the careless man about town into a shaven recluse, working with fanatical zeal, on *The Raft of the Medusa*. Eschewing Napoleonic mythmaking and contrasting what attracted him to the military—the fine horses, opulent saddle cloths, shimmering uniforms—with the reality of battle, Géricault began to engage with the truth.

During 1813, his uncle Jean-Baptiste Caruel became the mayor of the village of Chesnay and, with his young wife, began to spend more time at their château. As he added mayoral duties to his already demanding business schedule, relations between aunt and nephew developed into a full-blown love affair. The Château of Grand-Chesnay provided an ideal setting for secret meetings and intimate encounters. Yet despite their rapture the affair was understandably fraught. The underlying tension of deceits and stolen moments, along with the complication of Alexandrine's children and generous husband, the very man who had proved to be such an accommodating uncle, placed enormous pressure on the lovers. For every moment of elation, for every afternoon of delight, they suffered acute pangs of conscience. Nonetheless, their affair seemed unstoppable, their love uncontainable.

Perhaps in an attempt to distract himself from this complicated relationship Géricault decided to become a soldier. No sooner had Louis XVIII returned to France than the young artist joined the First Company of the Musketeers. By comparison with the dangers of Napoleonic conscription, the life of a soldier who was unlikely to be forced into battle pleased Géricault. The blade in him adored the red uniform and he was happy to be riding the fine gray chargers of the Musketeers.[25]

Embodying Louis XVIII's desire for unification and forgiveness, 41 out of the 176 Gray Musketeers had served in Napoleon's army, including Géricault's captain, the Comte de Nansouty. Others, such as Géricault himself, or the poets Lamartine and Alfred de Vigny, were veterans of no cause, but simply rich, idling young men who were attracted by the prospect of playing soldier. Their function was, however, taken very seriously by Louis XVIII, who believed that had his older brother surrounded himself with what was effectively a private army, he would not have fallen victim to the revolution.[26]

When the Hundred Days sent Louis into exile, Géricault, the toy-soldier musketeer, with his impulsive compassion for the underdog, followed the fleeing king through a dreary northern French landscape made even more depressing by an unrelenting downpour. Troops and wagons became bogged in the mud of Picardy and many followers took the opportunity to desert. Even well-mounted horsemen could advance only with great difficulty as the paths were reduced to muddy rivulets.[27] Ordered to disperse at Béthune, the Musketeers were free to return to their families or to follow the king into exile at Ghent.

There are several theories about where Géricault passed the remaining weeks of the short-lived insurrection. If he made for the Château of Grand-Chesnay, which would have been a likely destination, he would have been in contravention of the imperial decree of March 13, 1815, banning all the members of the royal household from residing in Paris, its outskirts, or near the imperial palaces at Saint-Cloud and Malmaison. However, Géricault needed Alexandrine and Napoleon had his mind on other things.

The Hundred Days substantially altered the political direction of the restoration. During his first year in power, Louis had proved a good strategist and, in attempting to rule over a radically divided country, he was prudent. He willingly submitted to Allied demands for a charter that would provide the basis for the country's constitution. Devised by the king himself, the document aimed to guarantee political liberties. But the charter was, in effect, a vague document that offered with one hand and took away with the other. Article Eight was just such a piece of chicanery and one that would create great problems for Alexandre Corréard and his fellow liberals: "Frenchmen have the right to publish and print their opinions, as long as they conform to the laws for repressing abuses of this liberty." Declaring that the charter was granted "by the free exercise of our Royal authority" in the "nineteenth year of our reign" was a gauntlet thrown down to the left as it effectively negated the political experiments that had changed the face of France over the previous twenty-five years.[28] Above all, however, the liberal tenor of the document and its intentions were detested by the extreme right.

After the final fall of Napoleon, the elections of August 1815 yielded a surprising result. Perhaps shaken by the swiftness and sureness of Napoleon's invasion, and manifesting their desire for stability, voters swung to the right, returning a chamber that was predominantly ultra-royalist. Louis retaliated by pointedly inviting the moderate duc de Richelieu to lead his ministers as president of the council. Nevertheless, the government included a strongly ultra military axis typified by the elderly vicomte DuBouchage, who had served as a minister under Louis XVI and who now became the minister of the Navy. By contrast Elie Decazes was a bright young politician who had so attracted Louis's admiration as the Parisian chief of police that the king appointed him minister of police. Decazes was an ambitious man of action who proved to be a strong moderate presence in the government, rapidly declaring his opposition to the extreme right.[29] This did not, however, prevent him from introducing rigorous legislation that safeguarded the survival of the king. During the autumn of 1815, a series of laws was introduced that suspended habeas corpus for those plotting against the royal family and the state, suppressed inflammatory acts against the crown, and set up temporary criminal courts without juries and any right of appeal.[30]

Although such menaces can only have provided confirmation for Alexandre Corréard about the desirability, if not the absolute necessity, of leaving France, the true political situation was even uglier than the election result and subsequent legislation indicated. Having received slight comfort from the first restoration, the nobility was full of bitterness and out for blood. Only two days after the abdication of Napoleon in favor of his son, the first major reprisal occurred in Marseille, where Napoleon's supporter General Verdier was removed from power. During the ensuing forty-eight hours, two hundred and fifty sympathizers were killed in an orgy of retribution. There was violence in Avignon and about one hundred Protestants were slaughtered in Nîmes as the new White Terror began. There were mass purgings of the public sector; between fifty thousand and eighty thousand members of the civil service, about a third of its total workforce, lost their jobs. Above all, untold numbers of people were murdered or tortured, particularly in the south where the ultra-royalists entertained dreams of southern secession. As the contemporary observer John Scott of Gala put it, "*Ultra-royalism* . . . has raised its monstrous head, professing to see in the last disturbance the necessity for giving a stronger hand to authority."

Politics descended into mob violence and looting as the White Terror weakened the Bourbons and their standing with the nation forever. The "demoralized state of the public character," wrote John Scott, rendered "it impossible for the King, whose inclinations and principles are decidedly moderate, to reckon on a substantial support."[31]

The relaunching of the French monarchy promised a turbulent passage fraught with conflict, and it was against such an unpropitious background of stormy division and strife that the newly repainted *Medusa,* with thirty cannon removed to make way for extra troops and stores, was about to set sail on her final voyage.

The Expedition Prepares

As a dangerous reminder of how things had turned against the liberal and republican cause at home, the crew, troops, colonists, and officers on board the flagship *Medusa* were to be under the command of a political appointee, the haughty Hugues Duroy de Chaumareys, a rusty relic from the ancien régime who had not put to sea for about a quarter of a century. Such ill-judged appointments were a hazardous fact of the restoration as the outmoded, old aristocrats, who had remained loyal to the crown, solicited just recompense. The absurdity of their appeals is amusingly underscored by a celebrated story of a petition brought to the government by an officer of the Royal Navy who had not served since 1789. At that time, the man had been a midshipman but now demanded the rank of rear admiral, arguing that this would have been his present position had his career evolved normally. "Tell him," said the secretary of state, "that we acknowledge the logic of his reasoning, but that he forgot a key fact—he was killed at the battle of Trafalgar."[32]

While the restoration government was forced to suspend more than six hundred officers and numerous enlisted men on half pay, or, worse still, make them redundant, the crown was obliged to reward loyal naval officers. Some of these had gone so far in their fidelity to the Bourbons as to fight against their own country; manpower shortages in England's Royal Navy had led to the recruitment of French royalists who had fought against republican and imperial France. Obviously, the readmission of such men would rankle as the restoration simultaneously checked the natural advancement of many of the officers who had distinguished themselves for the republic and empire. The situation was not only combustible, it was absurd. Veterans of great wars "are vegetating on half-pay in ports, while brilliant commissions are given to those whose only merit has been to remain faithful to the Bourbons," sniped Gicquel des Touches, one of the captains appointed to the Senegal convoy. Des Touches justly insists that fidelity "can be rewarded by pensions, court appointments, and not by commands of ships on which depend both the lives of men and the honour of the flag." Even the minister of the navy himself, the vicomte DuBouchage, the man who was organizing the expedition to Senegal, had been retired from public life for a quarter of a century when he was appointed.[33]

As for Chaumareys, the man who was made commander of the convoy, his credentials were acceptable, but twenty-five years out of date. On his mother's side, Hugues Duroy de Chaumareys was related to one of Louis XVI's great maritime strategists, Admiral d'Orvilliers, whose example determined the young man's choice of career and greatly facilitated his advancement in the service. Hugues Duroy embarked as a midshipman under d'Orvilliers in 1779 and on April 17 of the following year saw action in the American War of Independence. Wounded in the head but remaining at his post, he was subsequently promoted to ensign on the warship *Pegasus,* and then rose swiftly to the rank of captain of a transport ship. If it had not been for the revolution, it seems that Chaumareys, with that kick-start of a family connection and a demonstrable gift for advancement, would have made a tolerable career in the navy. However, in December 1790 he became an émigré, a royalist who fled the country. It was during this period as a refugee from the revolution that he fabricated the tale that he would use to obtain his captaincy of the *Medusa.*[34]

What is established fact is that Chaumareys participated in the royalist landing on the peninsula of Quiberon on June 27, 1795. The aim of the invasion was to rally support throughout Brittany and then march on Paris. It is likewise true that the insurgents were captured and transported to Vannes where Chaumareys, unlike so many of his fellow royalists, escaped being put to death. He avoided execution by lying. He swore that he was not a monarchist, that he had not taken up arms against the republic, and that he had had no military function at Quiberon. He was subsequently imprisoned in a tower at Vannes, from which he absconded, aided by sympathetic guards and by a local woman named Sophie de Kerdu. Chaumareys hid in the town for over two weeks before escaping to the English fleet and thence to England, where he was treated as a hero and given the Royal and Military Order of Saint-Louis on February 21, 1796.[35]

Lavish praise and recompense were prompted by a self-aggrandizing narrative that Chaumareys published while in London. Selling in both French and English bookshops, the story made assertions that would be guaranteed to serve its author admirably in any future restoration. Addressing those dead comrades who had, in fact, acquitted themselves more honorably than Chaumareys himself, he declares: "There are still tyrants in my country. . . . And you, touching victims of honour and fidelity, I saw your sublime devotion. . . . You're no longer here; but you spilt your generous blood for your King."[36] With sentiments worthy of a swashbuckling adventurer in the heat of escape, Chaumareys praises the courage of the young Sophie de Kerdu and, describing his leave-taking, swears that "I will do nothing but devote my life to you."[37] In the event, Chaumareys did not return to marry his brave, Breton peasant and live happily ever after; within two years he married another Sophie, a Prussian baroness named Sophie de Azentrampf. Obviously such a match was socially and politically more serviceable.

Making his bid for celebrity with a self-serving rewriting of the failed uprising, Chaumareys's distorted version of events, which ran into three editions, propagated the myths on which he would rebuild the wreckage of his career. Returning to France in 1804, he sat out the empire at his eighteenth-century family residence, the Château de Lachenaud in Limousin. During the first restoration, using his relation to Admiral d'Orvilliers, his service record, his inflated account of his participation in the Quiberon fiasco, and slightly adjusting his age, Chaumareys solicited a commission. In a torrent of letters to the minister of the navy, the story of his escape from Vannes was further distorted to his advantage. The part played by Sophie de Kerdu is excised from his new account, which simply foregrounded Chaumareys's own incontestable presence of mind. In light of such bravery and composure, the minister deemed him worthy of the command of a frigate and Chaumareys was expeditiously awarded the Légion d'Honneur in order to make amends for a ministerial gaffe in attempting to award him the Military Order of Saint-Louis for a second time.[38]

When, with testimonials from his noble friends that were mistaken in matters of character and not always accurate in matters of fact, Chaumareys eventually secured his command of the Senegal expedition on April 22, 1816, he was to face understandable suspicion and opposition from the other officers appointed to the convoy, most of whom had served France during the previous decades. Gicquel des Touches found him, on first meeting, to be snobbish and ill-informed.[39]

In the aborted 1815 expedition to Senegal under Captain Bouvet, Chaumareys was to have commanded a corvette.[40] Although this appointment would have given him ample time to familiarize himself with the potential hazards of the route, the minister of the navy urged Chaumareys to arrive in Rochefort well in advance of the June 1816 departure, in order to profit from the experience of sailors who had navigated the coasts of Senegal. It was a region badly charted and notoriously treacherous, but there was an account published in 1789 that documented some of the dangers. Sailing in the violent currents off the West African coast, the author observed that the water around the ship was becoming steadily clearer. He urged the captain of the *St. Catherine* to take a sounding but was rebuffed—"Why are you afraid, we're 80 leagues from the coast?" That very night they were beached and their tragedy was merely a prologue to attack and capture; when survivors from the frequent shipwrecks in the area managed to make it to shore, they found themselves on the edge of the interminable white sand plain of the Sahara Desert and prey to hostile Moors.[41]

Apart from the strong currents, there was an ill-defined and hazardous sandbank to contend with, but Chaumareys appears to have been too high-handed to take the opportunity to learn from those with knowledge of the region. Gicquel des Touches, in order to assert his superiority over this man who, on first meeting, had treated him so contemptuously, offered to give Chaumareys written instructions on how to circumnavigate the dangerous Arguin Bank. Upon receiving this offer of a helping hand, Chaumareys immediately altered his attitude toward des Touches, who observed that the commander of the expedition appeared much intimidated by the challenge of the perilous shoal.[42]

A legitimate source of Chaumareys's anxiety was the inadequacy of the available maps. Hydrography was in its infancy and charts were notoriously incomplete; many shoals, rocks, and reefs remained unrecorded because cartographers had an imperfect knowledge of the seas. This lack, coupled with a navigators's incapacity to correctly determine longitude, resulted in numerous shipwrecks.[43] In the case of the dreaded Arguin Bank, Bellin's map, which was supplied by the ministry, was known to be defective in its tracing of the western perimeter of the extensive shoal, a fact indicated in the *Nautical Description of the African Coast,* which was sent to Chaumareys before the convoy set sail. This text, printed in 1814, was a ninety-eight-page document written by Admiral de Rosily, director of the Navy Depot Hydrographic Service. It confessed that the French navy had minimal and imperfect knowledge of the West African coast, and a good deal of whatever information they did possess was the result of hearsay rather than serious study. It categorically stated that the "maps of the western coast in *Bellin's French Hydrography* are flawed and it would be dangerous to trust them." Above all, it claimed that "For the greatest safety, you must take soundings as often as you can and proceed according to the depth and the type of sea bed that you discover."[44] Such warnings would surely alert an insecure commander—if only his insecurity was not hedged by blinding arrogance.

A further source of concern for the leaders of the expedition was that Geoffroy de Villeneuve, in his authoritative history of West Africa, published in 1814, urged that all Europeans "who want to visit the African coast must aim to get there during November in order to acclimatize themselves before the onset of the rainy season which commences at the end of June and lasts until October."[45] With an unpropitious date set for the Medusa's departure, the avowed fallibility of his navigational aids, his lack of recent experience, and the political hostility of his officers and men, Chaumareys was, from the first, a captain under stress.

When Charlotte-Adelaide Picard, one of the eldest daughters in a family of nine colonists bound for Senegal, approached Rochefort at the end of May 1816, she found it bustling with activity. There was the clatter of the workmen in the shipyards and the clanking of the enormous chains that yoked convict dock laborers together as they dragged the heaviest loads along the wharves.[46] There were soldiers, stevedores, port officials, sailors, and officers like Chaumareys, strutting self-importantly about, attracting sneers and snide remarks from those condemned to drink away their enforced retirement in cafés, dreaming of glorious, old imperial days. There were blacks from Africa, mulattoes from the West Indies, and the buzz and hubbub of a recently revivified naval port.

Charlotte Picard had left Paris on the morning of May 23, and even the earliest stages of her journey had proved to be not without misadventure. On the first evening, the innkeeper almost burned down his establishment while preparing an omelette for the travelers. On the following night their driver got completely drunk, and between

Niort and Rochefort the road was so bad that they got stuck in the mud. These incidents must have given her pause; if such misfortunes could happen on home ground, then what lay in store for her in a wild and distant land? The spirited young lady, wondering if she would ever see her own country again, gazed with deep affection at the lush, fertile green of France's beloved Loire valley as her coach sped on toward her port of embarkation.[47]

Arriving in Poitiers on June 1 near the end of his journey to Rochefort, Charles-Marie Brédif, a mining engineer who kept the only surviving notes of the *Medusa*'s voyage written during the journey, checked to see if the Fortin barometer that he had entrusted to his friend Dechatelus was intact after the bumpy journey. To his great chagrin, he found it broken, and registering a rare note of pessimism he remarked that "our voyage has really begun badly." To his further dismay, he found his chronometer was not working and hoped to be able to have both instruments repaired at Rochefort, where he arrived on June 4, the same day as Colonel Julien Schmaltz, the future governor of Senegal. Brédif lodged, like Schmaltz, his wife, and his daughter, at the Coquille d'Or and found Rochefort, which stood near the mouth of the Charente River, attractive and astir. Brédif and Dechatelus set about having their instruments repaired and had the pleasure to meet up with several old friends from their student days at their respected engineering college.[48]

Alexandre Corréard, in his second determined attempt to escape from France, along with the other colonists supported by the Philanthropic Society, were arriving in Rochefort, eager to depart, all seeking the fresh air of a new start. The climate in Senegal may have been oppressive, but the chance to get away from the stifling constraints of restoration France filled them with optimism.

On a showery and windy June 9, Brédif boarded a boat to carry him downriver to the *Medusa,* which was in the roads, a sheltered area offshore where ships could safely anchor. After a while, the rain became steady and the passengers were forced to take refuge in the sailors' quarters or in the hold. Despite a high tide, the incompetent pilot managed to beach them near some chalky rocks ominously known as the House of the Devil. It took an hour to free the boat, by which time the tide had gone out and they touched bottom again. This second time, the crew were unable to dislodge the boat from the mud and so the passengers spent the night stranded on board.

Enduring a dirty bunk and devoured by fleas, it was with some relish that Brédif, a stranger to the sea who was having second thoughts about voyaging into a dangerous unknown, lovingly recorded the details of the meals that he took when they disembarked the following day at Verjou, only half a league from Rochefort. Lunch consisted of a milk soup, an omelette, and a soft cheese, his supper of "peas and excellent little fresh fried sardines."

At Verjou they took on more passengers bound for Senegal, including the Picard family, and then went sailing out of the Charente in a good wind that sped them along toward the ships at safe anchorage off the Ile d'Aix. Among these, they discerned the newly repainted black and white hull of the flagship *Medusa*. By nine a.m., Brédif and the Picards had boarded the frigate where they found everything in complete disorder. Bad weather had prevented the ship from being notified as to their arrival and matters were further complicated by the recent embarkation of 161 unruly soldiers from the Africa Battalion.[49]

Three days later, on June 13, everything was shipshape and the officers, in full dress uniform, welcomed Governor Schmaltz, his wife, Reine, his daughter Eliza, and their maids on board. Reine was of a nervous disposition and a patient of the celebrated and revolutionary mental specialist Dr. Esquirol. She was immediately alarmed to find out that one of her great doctor's disciples, Falret, who was to have sailed on the *Medusa,* had canceled his passage at the last minute.[50]

It was a motley collection of vessels assembled for the voyage out. There was the corvette *Echo,* detailed for a hydrographic and reconnaissance mission along the Senegalese coast. There was the supply vessel *Loire*, a flute built in India and, according to the director of construction in Rochefort, too slow and unwieldy to participate in such an expedition. There was the brig *Argus*, the former HMS *Plumper*, which had been captured from the English. The *Argus* was a type of ship normally employed for short coastal trading voyages, a function she was intended to fulfill upon arrival in Senegal. The *Echo* was weatherly and fast, but both the *Loire* and the *Argus* would soon find it impossible to keep up with the convoy's flagship. Originally, another ship, the *Elephant*, had been designated to lead the expedition, but instead she was appointed to other duties, a fate that did not allow her to escape from the incompetent appointments of the vicomte DuBouchage.

After delays caused by strong headwinds on the fifteenth and sixteenth, as the convoy finally got under way Brédif noted that the *Medusa* did not hoist all of her sails so as not to leave the *Argus* and the *Loire* behind. By three o'clock on that first afternoon, the *Loire* sent signals that she was drifting badly and Chaumareys gave the order to drop anchor. It was hardly a promising start for a convoy urged by the minister to make all possible haste for Saint-Louis in Senegal. The colony was to be repossessed as rapidly as possible as there was this year's valuable gum harvest at stake.[51]

Toward the end of the eighteenth century, West Africa had been considered simply a loading stage for the slaves captured, largely by Moors, from the interior; the continent was seen as little other than "a mine of men to exploit." Restoration France, trailing behind England in its abolitionist thinking and suspicious that the moral stance of its recent enemy masked commercial intentions, vacillated over the legality and acceptability of the trade. Nonetheless, the avowed intention of Louis's government was to reestablish a legitimate colony in Senegal and the crown thus offered grants of African land to the colonists who were going—or escaping—to start a new life. There were projects for the growing of cotton, cocoa, and sugarcane and plans to profit from the lucrative gum trade. With its laxative and antihemorrhaging properties, gum was valuable in medical applications. It was also an ingredient in the manufacture of inks and dyes and a substance much used by confectioners.[52]

The commanders and crew of the various vessels were as heterogeneous as the ships themselves. A man of identical rank and sharing Chaumareys's loyalty to the crown was the captain of the *Echo,* François-Marie Cornette de Vénancourt, who, descended from American plantation colonists, had been born in Martinique in 1778. A monarchist like Chaumareys, during the Hundred Days his crew on board the *Actéon* mutinied in favor of Napoleon while anchored in the roads of Fort Royale, Martinique. Vénancourt was wounded trying to restore order and became a prisoner on board his own ship. Nevertheless, he dissuaded the sailors from hoisting the Napoleonic tricolor, which would have put them at risk from the English ships patrolling those waters. When they eventually sighted an English brig, the mutineers pressed their prisoner to take command of an attack. Pretending to acquiesce, Vénancourt merely signaled his difficulty to the English, who promptly escorted the *Actéon* to Martinique. Safely arrived, Vénancourt began a campaign to rid the island of Napoleonic supporters and further the royalist cause in the West Indies. If sympathetic to Commander Chaumareys's politics, Vénancourt clearly resented the superior appointment held by an inferior mariner.[53] Not only was Vénancourt a more experienced sailor but he had been recently and demonstrably brave in his loyalty to the crown.

Gicquel des Touches, captain of the unwieldy *Loire,* was of the opposite political persuasion. He had also revealed an exemplary courage unknown to Chaumareys. Aged ten, he had been on board a ship sailing for Guadeloupe when she was given chase by the English. The captain beached the ship in order to give the enemy the slip, but the young boy was denied a place in the lifeboats. Left on board the wreck with a handful of unruly sailors who started to drink themselves to death, the young Gicquel discharged a cannon in the direction of the enemy, which achieved the desired effect. The English approached and boarded the French wreck and took the plucky young Gicquel and his mates prisoner. He was, at length, transported back to England in the stifling 'tween decks of an old frigate, in conditions resembling those of the slave ships where air was in short supply, the odor rank, and the insects legion. After a year in prison in England, he returned to France to fight for the republican cause. Gicquel des Touches served at Trafalgar, after which, once again, he was taken to an English prison. Having persistently revealed his audacity and his presence of mind, and with two of his brothers dead in the service of the republic, it is hardly surprising that des Touches took exception to the airs put on by an undeserving monarchist such as Chaumareys.[54]

The captain of the *Argus,* Léon Henry de Parnajon, was, like Vénancourt, of colonial origin and, like des Touches, had fought at Trafalgar. Later captured by the enemy, he had languished in an English prison from April 1809 until August 1811. Apart from that brief interruption he had been sailing since 1799, so he too was more seasoned than the expedition's commander.[55]

On board the *Medusa* herself, the official second in command was the republican Lieutenant Joseph Reynaud. His career against the English had been lively. In 1804 he had been shipwrecked on the French coast after an engagement with two enemy frigates. During a mission to Santa Cruz in 1805–6, he had captured the HMS *Calcutta* after a two-hour battle. Latterly, however, his duties had involved protecting coastal shipping, and so in his present rank of lieutenant he had little experience of long voyages. What is more, his politics made relations with his captain awkward.

The second lieutenant on board the *Medusa,* the "very knowledgeable and zealous" Jean-Baptiste Espiaux, had been wounded twice in the wars with England and was captured by the English in the Bay of Cádiz in June 1808. He had escaped while being transported to England, courageously diving off an English ship and returning to the siege of Cádiz. Later, aboard the *Medusa,* participating in Napoleon's escape bid to America, Espiaux witnessed the humiliation of his emperor's ultimate surrender to the English.[56] Such an officer can have had but a slight regard for his obsolete, out-of-touch captain, a man sustained by the discredited idea that he was capable simply because he was of noble birth.

Ensigns Chaudière, Lapeyrère, and Maudet had all fought against Britain and all spent long periods in English prisons. They made no secret of their contempt for their captain, a disdain generously reciprocated as these officers had all sprung from the bourgeoisie.

Only the most forceful and knowledgeable commander would have been able to harness officers and men so dangerously at odds with him. The clamor of contradictory voices on board the *Medusa* echoed the discord that resounded throughout France, where divisiveness, selfishness, and suspicion were the upshot of thirty years of ideological struggle. If passions ran high at home, emotions intensified in the creaking confines of an overloaded frigate, only 154 feet long from prow to stern, 39 in its beam, and sailing into the tropical heat at the height of summer.[57]

A Captain No Longer in Command

At seven p.m. on June 17, the convoy weighed anchor once again, cleared the Straits of Antioche, and finally set sail. But only hours after this second start, the wind dropped and the *Medusa* became ungovernable and lay stranded in the lull before the storm. Slowly, the sky darkened, the sea swelled, and strong gusts of wind squalled about the ship. Suddenly and quite violently, the frigate tacked in order to avoid drifting onto a reef, an accident that would have ensured her destruction.

For those on board who were aware of what had happened, such a brush with calamity can hardly have added to what little faith they had in their dubious captain.[58]

The departure roll call on board the *Medusa* listed 166 officers and crew, 61 passengers, 10 members of the frigate's artillery, 161 soldiers in two cosmopolitan and volatile companies of the Africa Battalion, and the wives of a couple of these soldiers—a neat total of four hundred souls. The passengers on board the *Medusa* included explorers and geographical engineers, such as Corréard and Dechatelus, the naturalists Lachenault and Kummer, the mining engineer Brédif, and clerks, administrators, and settlers such as Picard with his prodigious family. There were the professionals and tradesmen needed to build and maintain a colony: pilots, gardeners, scouts, schoolteachers, bakers, hospital directors, and surgeons. There were twenty-three colonists sailing under the auspices of the Philanthropic Society: carpenters, cabinet makers, locksmiths, and two women with three young children.[59] Among the passengers, there was also Gaspar Mollien, a man who later made a name for himself as an outstanding geographer and who, usefully, prefaced an account of his travels into the interior of Africa with a narrative of his eventful voyage to Senegal. Besides Mollien, there were several people on board who, for a variety of motives, would provide records of their adventures. Brédif kept his diary regularly. Charlotte Picard published, under her married name Dard, a narrative of the voyage and its aftermath. The most exhaustive version of events was the result of a collaboration between the ship's second surgeon, Henri Savigny, and Alexandre Corréard. Their observations were subsequently challenged in print by Lieutenant Anglas de Praviel of the Africa Battalion. The cargo on board the frigate included munitions, supplies, state papers, statute books, travel writings about Africa, a bust of Louis XVIII intended to preside over the governor's residence, and, in the hold, three casks containing 90,000 francs in coin.

During the following days, passengers who had never been to sea such as Corréard, Brédif, and Charlotte Picard variously adapted to the pitching and rolling and heaving and groaning. They marveled at the optimism and thunderous splendor of sails unfurling. They found the sharp, salt sea breezes bracing, the speed and the spin drift exhilarating. They were awed by the lateral tilting of their tall ship in a squall. They learned the hard way that they had to stoop, supporting themselves against unexpected jolts as they moved around the dimly lit and encumbered spaces between decks. They adjusted to the smells of those confined spaces as the frigate moved south. They became attuned to the creaking of her joints, to the noise and flurry of the changes of the watch when sailors scurried up and down vertiginous ratlines as if they were doing it in their sleep. When the winds changed, they observed a great buzz of activity. Charlotte Picard noted that "the crew was busy everywhere, climbing the rigging, perching on the extremities of the yards, climbing the highest masts, bellowing as they rhythmically and forcefully pulled on certain ropes, swearing and whistling" as "the yards were turned on their pivots, the sails were stretched and the ropes fastened." The sailors seemed to be in control of what appeared to be giant bundles of laundry fastened by myriad stays strung about every which way from deck to mast and mast to mast in seeming confusion. The passengers experienced in the abrupt reports—"Sail ahoy" and "Two points off the starboard bow"—and the sudden order—"Lower away on the main"—strange and novel incantations that promised, in their mystery, that this vessel would indeed deliver them safely to their exotic destination.

When the wind dropped on June 18 Brédif, struck by the fact that he could see nothing but water encircling him as far as the great disc of the horizon, recorded that the sea was "extremely calm and of an indigo blue." But by one o'clock the weather was changing and that evening, when he dined with the commander at a table meticulously laid and amply provided, he wasn't sure that he would be able to hold his meal down: "The movement of the boat is more pronounced in his quarters and it made me feel unstable. After dinner, the walk which we took with the ladies on the quarter-deck made me feel better and I went to bed feeling fine."[60]

Many passengers were, indeed, seasick and Charlotte Picard was, at times, terrified by the new sensations surrounding her. During the night she went up onto the quarterdeck and "watched with horror as the frigate flew across the water." There were "sounds of cracking from every corner as this large mass of wood seemed ready to smash under each wave that thwacked us in the side."

The commander's indecisiveness was made dramatically apparent in his slowness to react when, at sunset on June 23, a fifteen-year-old sailor slipped off the breechblock of a cannon and through a forward porthole. When the cry "Man overboard!" was heard, many of the crew and passengers were on the poop and at the bulwarks, entertained by the antics of a school of porpoises. A bosun's mate managed to grab the boy by the neck of his jacket but had to let him go lest he too be pulled into the sea. Buffeted in the waves, the boy grabbed at a dangling rope, but the rapid motion of the frigate ripped it from his hands. Sailors attached themselves to ropes and plunged into the sea— but in vain. When an attempt was made to signal the *Echo* it proved to be too far off, and so it was decided to fire a cannon as a substitute but none of the fourteen on board was loaded.

At length, a life buoy was thrown, the frigate hove to, her sails were shortened and trimmed, and a skiff was let into the water from which three sailors began to search the heavy sea. They pulled toward the life buoy, disappearing under billows, reappearing on the crests of each wave until they were forced to give up. Brédif remarked on the considerable "disorder in the manoeuvre," with excited passengers impeding the efforts of the sailors. In the narrative of the voyage to Senegal that Corréard and Savigny felt compelled to bring before an astonished public, they commented that the "manoeuvre was long" and that "we should have come to the wind as soon as they cried 'man overboard.'" The failing light, which slowly obliterated all hope of rescue, darkened the spirits of the helpless onlookers as the youth who should—and perhaps could—have been rescued was left to drown.[61]

Already the expedition was beginning to fall apart. The recently modified *Echo* was a match for the *Medusa,* but the *Argus* and the *Loire* were starting to lag behind. Chaumareys was torn between his duty to keep a convoy together and the wishes of DuBouchage and Governor Schmaltz to reach Senegal as swiftly as possible. By the time the captain of the *Loire* lost sight of the command ship, des Touches had received no indication regarding the route. Maintaining his course for several hours in the hope of sighting the *Medusa,* des Touches then decided to set his own. Vénancourt, the captain of the *Echo,* who kept close enough to Chaumareys to receive communications, noted a discrepancy between the prescribed course and the actual navigation of the *Medusa.* He thought it wise, at that stage, to follow what Chaumareys did rather than what he signaled. When, on June 24, Vénancourt and Chaumareys compared their respective estimates of their position, they were out by eight minutes of longitude, or nearly six nautical miles, and forty-six minutes of latitude, a measurement equivalent to the identical number of nautical miles.[62]

The disorderly manner in which the captain had reacted to the fatal accident set passengers and officers whispering. The rougher soldiers and humbler sailors began to mutter their superstitions and Chaumareys would find small groups falling silent as he approached. Increasingly, he found himself isolated and excluded. The pull between innate and excessive arrogance and his desire to hide his inadequacy from those whom he had been appointed to lead meant that the commander was acting erratically from the start.[63] Among the passengers at his table, however, was a member of the Philanthropic Society, a man by the name of Antoine Richefort. An ex-mariner and a braggart with a clouded history, Richefort claimed great knowledge of the

West Coast of Africa. Finding himself an outsider on his own ship, Chaumareys turned increasingly to this man, ignoring the advice of his unsympathetic officers. With seeming relief, Chaumareys placed his unqualified trust in this blusterer.

Once the gloom over the lost sailor boy had begun to lift, the usually optimistic Brédif records many agreeable moments of life on board: how he delighted in climbing onto the bowsprit while the *Medusa* was plowing through the foaming sea at ten knots, white spray showering about him; how the crew and passengers took great pleasure in catching tuna with fishing lines that the sailors dangled from various parts of the ship; how there was great excitement as a stowaway was found on board, Marie-Antoine Rabaroust, an infantry surgeon's junior assistant who had resigned after the Hundred Days and who wished to escape France to start afresh in Senegal; and how, once discovered, he was swiftly assimilated into the governor's retinue as a domestic.[64] People marveled, as they sailed south, at the stars that hung above them, stars of a different world, another hemisphere. A splendid adventure, the chance of a lifetime.

Chaumareys had predicted that they would sight Madeira by the morning of June 26. As it was not until sunset that land was eventually spotted, his margin of navigational error had increased; his calculations—or perhaps those of his sidekick Richefort—were now off by a whole degree, or sixty nautical miles.[65] That night the *Medusa* tacked so as not to draw in too close to the islands, and on the following morning she sailed along the southern coast, past Ponta do Sol toward Funchal. Disparaging the advice of his officers with whom he was politically at loggerheads and placing his complete trust in the boastful Richefort, Chaumareys allowed the *Medusa* to be directed too close to the coast. In lee of the land, there was a sudden calm and the frigate was at risk of being swept ashore by the strong current.[66] After a lively exchange of views, Lieutenants Espiaux and Reynaud prevailed and the *Medusa* made for open sea and a fresh wind. As a result of such a perilous, inept, and time-wasting maneuver in the bay of Funchal, Chaumareys decided against sending a boat ashore for provisions. The crew and passengers were left with a passing impression of an island whose fertile slopes were covered with vineyards, orange and lemon groves, and fields bordered with banyan trees. The fiery color of the volcanic earth and the fragrance of citrus fruits blowing out to sea made a powerful appeal to those inexperienced voyagers who hankered for land and who had never before glimpsed such extravagant vegetation.[67]

By the evening of June 28, the highest point on Tenerife came into view, the peak aflame with sunset. As they approached the island the following morning, the fiery crown had given way to a misty veil through which the *Medusa* sailed into the bay of Santa Cruz. At seven a.m. a boat was lowered, and a party, including Lieutenant Reynaud, Ensign Lapeyrère, and midshipman Sander Rang, was chosen to go ashore. They suffered as they sat in their boat awaiting the completion of landing formalities; loud, incessant bells tolled for the Feast of St. Peter, and, as the morning mists cleared, a fierce sun beat down upon them. At length, the French sailors were allowed to disembark and were introduced to the governor, don Pedro de Rodriguez, a Francophile and royalist who was curious about the political situation in Europe. After this meeting, the shore party set about making purchases and were aided in this by some French inhabitants. The Spanish wife of one of these urged the sailors to stay and make some amorous conquests on the promenade that evening. They were tempted but they declined. Their captain and Governor Schmaltz were eager to make haste for Senegal and so they were back on board the *Medusa* by late afternoon.[68]

Toward midday, while the party was ashore, the *Echo* rejoined the *Medusa* and Vénancourt came aboard. His log somewhat reproachfully makes it clear that he considered it injudicious to have put a boat ashore in such a strong breeze.[69] While on board the flagship, he was an appalled witness to the dangerous trust Chaumareys had placed in the loudmouthed Richefort. In what seemed to be a repeat of his vainglorious performance along the coast of Madeira, Richefort decided that it was unsafe to stay at anchorage off Santa Cruz and, again, Chaumareys took his advice. Charlotte Picard accused Richefort of changing route

> for no other reason than to show that he knew how to make the necessary manoeuvres to tack. Every moment . . . we came, we went, we came back again, we drew near to reefs in order to defy them. . . . All this went on so long that after a while the sailors refused to obey the scheming pilot, saying loudly that he was nothing but a vile impostor.

Indeed, several officers "complained to the Captain that it was shameful to place his confidence in someone unknown," adding that "they would not obey a man who didn't have the temperament to command." Chaumareys scorned this intimation of mutiny and, according to Charlotte Picard, "was, without doubt, relieved to have someone else doing his job." To that end, he ordered the crew and pilots to obey his self-appointed surrogate. Adrift, among officers more competent than himself, Chaumareys was now dangerously out of his depth.

Even before reaching Tenerife, Brédif had started complaining about the "insupportable sun"; now the weather had become heavy, giving him a headache and making him feel sick. Nonetheless, he claimed to be in good health generally, possessed of a hearty appetite, and, despite the continual creaking and straining and heaving of the boat, he slept well.[70] The heaviness and the headaches were signs that the *Medusa* was sailing into the tropics at the very hottest time of the year. Charlotte Picard recalled how, as they neared the Tropic of Cancer, the sun seemed suspended directly above their heads and "the burning wind blowing off the Sahara" offered its parched welcome to a strange land.[71]

From the maintop a ringing was heard, and a raucous hunting horn broke in, followed by a shower of pulses and dried peas, which hailed down onto the deck. These announced the "Lord of the Tropic" who would preside over the ritual festivities that accompanied the crossing of the Tropic of Cancer. When the hard rain halted, a booted courier, whip in hand, arrived on the quarterdeck and delivered a dispatch to Captain Chaumareys, who seemed mildly flattered to be the center of such attention. At last, a sailor disguised as the despotic lord, covered in skins like a Lapp yet shivering in the sweltering heat, arrived, interrogated the captain, and said that he would visit him at ten the following morning. At this point Chaumareys, happy to have any release from the disquieting concerns of navigation, granted a day of festivities on the morrow.[72]

Waking at 2 a.m. on July 1, Brédif was astonished by the thousands of points of reflected light that surrounded him. Slowly he understood that his little cabin was covered in two inches of water, which, he later discovered, had flooded from the gutters of the ship. Going up on deck, he marveled at the lucent wake and the brilliance of the sails, seeming as if they had been lit by torches from beneath. Moonlight on the foam and billows had ignited the sea into a thousand flames, and with myriad stars milking the sky it seemed the most sublime privilege to be aboard that ship that night.[73]

By morning the baptismal vat was ready. Into it would be plunged any passenger refusing to pay tribute to the lord while crossing his tropic for the first time. Sailors dressed as priests heralded the ancient lord in his twelve sheepskins and hempen wig, accompanied by a sailor disguised as his wife with scandalous protuberances and scaly hands. The couple was dragged on an old gun carriage by two sailors disguised as bears. At each side, to the front and back of their chariot, processed sailors representing the four corners of the world: Europe with plumed hat and epaulettes, Asia, Africa, and America variously blacked or bronzed by a mixture of soot and tar. Sailors who were crossing the line for the first time were embraced by both their majesties, after which the passengers were rushed through a friendly baptism. But just as they thought they had escaped the worst, a signal sounded and thirty bucketloads of water held in reserve on high rained down on the quarterdeck. Everybody was soaked—passengers, sailors, officers. The four corners of the world were blanched as water splashed and gushed in every direction. In this uproar, the defrocking of the Lord of the Tropic began. His beard, his diadem, his scepter were all torn from him; even the excessive breasts of his travesty of a wife were ripped from her body and tossed about from sailor to sailor.

While Chaumareys played his part as the captain of a ship participating in a time-honored ritual, Richefort was strutting on the forward deck, casting his untutored eye on a treacherous coast not half a cannon shot off the port side. This charlatan was pumping himself up with his own rhetoric, bragging that he had already saved the *Medusa* from certain shipwreck, boasting of his experience of this coast, and vaunting his knowledge of the perilous Arguin Bank.

Within the previous twenty-five years, at least thirty ships of differing nations had been wrecked on the stretch of the African coast between Cap Bojador and Cap Blanc, along which the *Medusa* was now sailing. Not eleven months earlier, the American brig *Commerce* had been wrecked near Cap Blanc and the crew taken into captivity by hostile Moors.[74] While Chaumareys was so enjoying his carnivalesque diversion, a humble echo of the court burlesques of the ancien régime, a maritime disaster that would shake the fledgling restoration was in the making. Given the conflicts on board, the mutterings of discontent, it seems most appropriate that the shadow-play subversion of the masque should act as a prologue to tragedy.

The officer of the watch, Lapeyrère, knowing that the *Medusa* was sailing too close to the coast and was much at risk from the strong onshore drift, put an end to the celebrations and changed course without consulting the captain. This unauthorized initiative resulted in a brisk exchange with Chaumareys but saved the frigate from running onto a reef that stretched half a league out to sea. The commander of the expedition, having mistakenly identified Cap Barbas earlier that morning when the *Medusa* was still to the north of that cape, had already set in motion the miscalculations that would result in the loss of his ship. Even a landlubber like Brédif correctly recognized the cape as they doubled it at midday.[75]

Throughout that afternoon the *Medusa* sailed at a safe distance from the coast as the *Echo* followed off the stern on the port side. Toward evening, the weather became hazy, and anxious passengers watched as the shore melted into the mist and darkness.

The *Echo* spent the early part of the night of July 1–2 signaling to the *Medusa*. Until eleven p.m. she remained off the port stern but then she overtook the frigate. Vénancourt, wanting to maintain contact in these dangerous waters, lit extra lights and sent up a flare. He also took soundings, finding a depth of forty fathoms at eleven p.m. and forty-five fathoms at midnight. Losing sight of the *Medusa* shortly afterward, he sent up a second flare but, getting no response, he continued, wisely, to steer west-southwest.

It was Ensign Chaudière's watch from eight to midnight. At ten, he took a sounding of thirty-five fathoms and at twelve he registered a depth of forty-five. Chaudière did not inform Captain Chaumareys when the *Echo* disappeared from sight. This was irregular but perhaps, by that time, Chaudière questioned the utility of communicating anything of importance to his captain. Henri Savigny was on deck when Reynaud took over the watch at midnight and was surprised that the lieutenant failed to reply when a signal from the *Echo* was, at last, sighted. The *Medusa* once again lost touch with the *Echo* at three a.m. and this fact, along with the information that the *Echo* had overtaken the *Medusa* and was now off the starboard, or offshore bow, was communicated neither to Espiaux, who relieved Reynaud, nor to Captain Chaumareys.[76]

By now mistrust was running so high that a group of officers attempted to dupe Chaumareys in order to secure a wider margin of safety. The accepted wisdom was that to reach Senegal, avoiding the dreaded Arguin Bank, which extends out into the ocean from the bay to the south of Cap Blanc, a ship simply sights that cape and continues sixty-six miles south-southwest before changing to a course south-southeast. Officers anxious about the competence of their commander could thus indemnify themselves against any errors that he might make simply by "moving" Cap Blanc farther south. Several of these conspirators went to rouse the captain at five a.m. on the morning of July 2 and persuaded him that a huge white cloud in the distance was, in fact, Cap Blanc itself. Although Chaumareys had already claimed to have identified it during the previous afternoon, a perfectly logical consequence of having "identified" Cap Barbas well in advance, they succeeded in their deception without the least difficulty. But they had not counted on the arrogance of Richefort, who thought it necessary to sail only thirty miles after sighting Cap Blanc before setting a southerly or southeasterly course. The cunning group had taken the trouble to dupe a captain who was no longer in command.

People's nerves were frayed; an officer who dared challenge the competence of Richefort was arrested. Ensigns Lapeyrère and Maudet calculated that they were heading straight for the dangerous shoal and when they challenged Richefort they received the blithe rebuff: "Never mind, we're in eighty fathoms." The colonist Picard, who had made two previous trips to Senegal, sought out the captain to alert him that the ship was making straight for the ill-defined sandbank. As with the protestations of the officers, Picard's opinion was ignored. Richefort patronizingly asserted, "We know our job, get on with yours and rest calm." Seeing that he would not prevail, and hopeful that providence would keep them from danger, Picard went down to his cabin and tried to bury his fears in sleep.[77] When, at half past seven, a sounding gave a depth of a hundred and twenty fathoms, a course was set south-southeast.

During the morning, even those passengers with no previous experience of the sea noticed a steady change in the color of the water. Corréard noticed that deep blue had given way to green. Shoals of fish flashed just beneath the surface. Then they detected sand scrolling in the little waves agitated by the gentle breeze blowing from the north. The sailors set about catching large numbers of fish, delighting in a sport that distracted them from the other telltale signs of shallow waters: the kelp, appearing in great quantities, floating on the surface; a sea becoming clear.

At midday Ensign Maudet and midshipman Rang took over the watch in little doubt that they were on the fringes of the Arguin Bank. Brédif had measured the temperature of the sea at eight o'clock that morning; taking a reading after lunch, he found that the temperature of the water had, alarmingly, risen by over four degrees centigrade in as many hours. A sounding was taken that gave only eighteen fathoms. Chaumareys was informed. He hastened up on deck and gave the order to steer a quarter to starboard. Everyone became silent. Another sounding was taken. Ten fathoms. Brédif watched as Rang turned pale. Two quarters to starboard. Six fathoms. The frigate's sails swelled with a sudden gust of wind. There was a shudder. A scrape. A jolt. A roar from the keel rasping against some undesired obstruction. The *Medusa* lurched to a halt. An absolute silence was broken only when a sudden panicked clamor resounded throughout the stranded vessel. On the quarterdeck officers were shouting orders. The captain alone was unable to speak.[78]

Politics and Passion

Whether Louis XVIII was a liberal at heart or merely appeared to be one because that is what the situation dictated is unclear; certainly, in 1815–16, he seemed happy to uphold sentences that condemned his subjects to the guillotine for political crimes. In July 1816, the month in which the *Medusa* came to grief, three men accused of participation in a Bonapartist conspiracy had their right hands severed prior to being guillotined before a huge crowd in front of the Hôtel de Ville in Paris. And still the ultra-dominated chamber criticized the government for not rooting out sedition.

Throughout the early stages of the second restoration, the person whom Louis XVIII increasingly came to treasure was Elie Decazes, the minister of police. To gain such favor, Decazes had played the part of devoted young man, eager to learn the ways of government from a master. The ruse worked and Louis began to consider Decazes a disciple, a spiritual son—even perhaps the offspring he never had. Decazes, a political animal who won favor by telling Louis what he wanted to hear, was also a clearheaded tactician who believed that he knew what was good for the crown and, hence, for the country.

Anxiety had been mounting among the liberal ministers that the reactionary policies of the ultras would lead to the downfall of the monarchy. During the cold and rainy summer of 1816, which gave rise to a serious famine in many parts of France, Decazes set out to turn the king against the hostile and reckless policies of the extreme right. A threat to the charter, to national security and sovereignty itself, the ultras, Decazes suggested, would push as far as civil war in order to realize their reactionary aims. Carefully selecting what he brought before the king and Richelieu, the leader of the government, Decazes presented the picture of a country suffering at the hands of a right-wing chamber. During the summer recess, with support from Pozzo di Borgo, the ambassador to Russia, and even from Czar Alexander I himself, Decazes persuaded Louis XVIII that the chamber must be dissolved to make way for autumn elections that could reduce the parliamentary influence of the ultras.[79]

Théodore Géricault's shift from dandy and man about town to serious and dedicated artist took place against this ministerial struggle for the safety of the realm. Géricault's political attitudes were beginning to mature and his decision to leave the Musketeers at the end of 1815 had been influenced by his realization that there was a good deal of arrogance and vanity in his devotion to the royal family.[80] He had settled in the rue des Martyrs, in that part of Paris that was too bourgeois to be called bohemian but was nonetheless a quarter occupied by the painters, writers, politicians, and wits who were agitating against the status quo. The young painter's change was also part and parcel of a pervasive shift in the attitude of middle-class youth that was beginning to occur in France. In the chamber of deputies, citing young men born between the early 1790s and the early 1800s, Benjamin Constant spoke of a generation "Less frivolous than that of the ancien régime, less passionate than that of the Revolution" and "distinguished by its thirst for knowledge . . . and its devotion to truth."[81] The young painter's decision to leave the king's service was prompted by his desire to do more serious work in preparation for the 1816 Prix de Rome while, at the same time, juggling the logistically difficult affair with his aunt.[82]

On March 18, 1816, along with twenty-nine painters and fourteen sculptors, Géricault sat for the first round of the competition. Along with seventeen others, he made it through to the next round but on March 30, Géricault was informed that he had failed to make the list of ten finalists and the contest was eventually won by an artist who, as is so often the case when it comes to these prizes, fell into obscurity.[83] Apart from the kudos of an award, the independently wealthy painter had no need of financial assistance in order to go to Italy and, as this was considered to be an important part of an artist's education, it is what Géricault decided to do.

An incident that took place not long before his departure testifies to Géricault's growing embarrassment with his image as a bright young thing. Théodore Lebrun, who was to have accompanied Géricault on the two-year Italian trip, came to see him and found Géricault making elaborate preparations for a ball, with his hair in paper curlers, intended to give it added bounce. When Lebrun was forced, for reasons beyond his control, to cancel his journey, Géricault assumed that he had done so merely to avoid traveling with so vain and frivolous a companion.[84]

The role of winsome man about town had, to a degree, become a mere facade for the intense affair that embroiled Théodore and his pretty aunt. Yet Géricault had become a divisive presence in Alexandrine's comfortable life and he was rattled, distracted, unable to fix and maintain a course of work. A substantial motivation for his Italian trip was the belief that he must distance himself, physically and emotionally, from the turmoil of his relationship.[85]

On August 15, 1816, the chief commissioner of police issued Géricault with a passport for Switzerland and Italy. The young painter obtained a highly laudatory letter of recommendation from his teacher Guérin, who claimed that he "is one of the pupils on whom must rest our greatest hopes."[86] And so Géricault was off to Italy in search of inspiration. He was fleeing the wreckage of his emotional life and leaving France at a time when the *Medusa* scandal was breaking. Obviously he had his mind on other things, but for Elie Decazes, eager to change the government and set a new course for France, the news of the shipwreck fell like manna from heaven.

3

THE WRECK

After the silence of the shock, after the shrieks of panic and the inaudible commands, came the volley of recriminations. Increasingly during the voyage, murmurs of discontent had escaped from the quarterdeck, down through the moaning confines of the *Medusa,* to where veteran sailors vouched that they, by guess or God, would have a better chance of steering the frigate to its destination than this toffee-nosed Hugues Duroy de Chaumareys. This shipful of grousing erupted into accusation and affront when the frigate ran onto the Arguin Bank. Ensign Lapeyrère darted up onto the bridge and confronted the captain's man Richefort: "You see, sir, where your pig-headedness has led us!"

Groups formed intent on convincing themselves that they were not in danger. Others speculated on the exact nature of their dilemma, while nearly everybody proposed extravagent theories about what should be done. Only Chaumareys, stunned into silence, seemed incapable of coming up with a plan. Loath, in any case, to pay much heed to their captain, the officers, all with differing ideas, issued a barrage of conflicting orders and a chaos of activity squandered the afternoon and evening of July 2. Certain necessary steps were, nonetheless, taken; midshipman Rang, who never doubted that they would refloat the *Medusa,* set about executing the orders that he had been given. Studding sails, set on the outer parts of the topgallant and topmast booms, were pulled in, the topgallants dismantled, and preparations made to lower the boats, an operation interrupted while the longboat, ignored in the rush to dispatch the expedition from Rochefort, was of necessity recaulked.

Lieutenant Espiaux went out in the skiff to take soundings. The *Medusa* drew five meters and, although it was high tide when she beached on the sandy bottom, skillful seamanship would be able to disengage and save her; it would take merely a modicum of informed humility to set matters right. A kedge anchor was dropped. This device, designed specifically to haul a ship into deeper water when she has run aground, did not produce, with this first attempt, the desired result. During the night, Sander Rang put out a boat to move the kedge farther from the ship, but at four a.m., when the tide was once again high, another attempt to pull off the bank resulted in the anchor, rather than the frigate, tearing free. The plan to drop the much heavier bower anchor was delayed as the only boat capable of transporting such a weight was the governor's barge, which was also discovered to be in a bad state of repair. Time was wasted while she was patched and sealed, and even then empty barrels had to be fastened to the barge to give her the extra buoyancy needed to bear the bower's great weight. When it was, at last, dropped into the sand, mud, and shells of the bank, the sea was so shallow that one fluke remained above the water while the purchase of the other fluke on the shifting bed proved so tenuous that this attempt also failed.[1]

Despite Brédif's impression that everything was being done in complete disorder, several worthwhile measures were in fact taken by the lieutenants and the ensigns in their attempt to refloat the frigate.

The hull was proving mercifully resistant to the shocks of the billows, although it was necessary to repair damage to the hold where water was entering. The dismantled topmasts were put overboard, but the lower yards were left in place to act as crutches should the ship list dramatically. To prevent this happening, barrels of powder were thrown into the sea and the cannon were moved to the port side to compensate the tilt of the frigate. Lightened by the jettisoning of the powder, the *Medusa* nearly floated on the high tide, and had they ditched the artillery there would have been a strong chance of success. Stubbornly, Chaumareys refused to sacrifice the cannon of the king, unable, it seems, to comprehend that the frigate herself was His Majesty's ship!

As chances for successful rescue now seemed slight, a council was convened.[2] With Richefort shamed and Chaumareys in disgrace, it was at this moment that Governor Schmaltz began to take control. If the captain proved unequal to his task Schmaltz, by contrast, seemed able to adapt himself to almost any situation. He was a survivor, his every action motivated by his overwhelming desire to succeed. While Chaumareys's incapacity starkly revealed itself, Schmaltz's maneuvers were more shadowy and his responsibility for the events that followed less easy to determine. In a fictionalized account of the wreck of the *Medusa* published in 1929, the author, Auguste Bailly, has Chaumareys sitting on the poop deck with Schmaltz when he hears a sailor singing "The Marseillaise," the fervent republican anthem that Napoleon so perceptively appreciated "would save many a cannon"; the royalist Chaumareys is furious and orders the man to be clapped in irons, at which point, the "debonair" Schmaltz has a discreet word in the captain's ear and the incident is forgotten.[3] Illustrative of the way Schmaltz could smooth things over, it also suggests that the governor, who was happy to blow with the prevailing wind, was a less zealous supporter of the Bourbon monarchy than he pretended. Dubbed "an amphibious reptile" by a contemporary satirist, his sudden ardor for the monarchy in 1814 simply smacked of opportunism.[4]

His father German and his mother half Gascon, half Irish, Julien Désiré Schmaltz grew up in the cosmopolitan world of Lorient, a thriving port in Brittany. In 1797, when he met and married Reine, "merchant" appeared as his profession on their marriage certificate.[5] A daughter, Eliza, was born the following year, but six days after giving birth, Reine suffered a severe postnatal depression that developed into manic rage during which she took an aversion to her husband and daughter.[6]

With this apparent liability in tow, Schmaltz departed for the Dutch East Indies where his advance was rapid and his life colorful. Despite a lack of military training, Governor-General Daendels promoted him to the rank of lieutenant colonel in May 1808. However, presumptuously sending the governor-general an essay on the defense of Java, he was suddenly retired in January 1809. Showing his ability for cunning readjustment, Schmaltz recalled that "I set myself up in manufacture and I trained several slaves that I owned, making of them good labourers. Both my wife and I worked with our hands and we succeeded." After several months of manufacturing notions, Schmaltz was happy to be recalled to strengthen the defenses of the port of Surabaya. When the English attacked the town in September 1811, Schmaltz was taken to Bengal as a prisoner of war. Madame Schmaltz, who had suffered a second breakdown in 1805, succumbed to a third as a result of a terrible sea voyage and the imprisonment of her husband. At the end of 1812 Schmaltz was taken to England from whence, a year later, he was repatriated; the *Picturesque Biography,* a contemporary satire, insinuated, rightly or wrongly, that he had traded privileged knowledge about the island of Java for his freedom.[7]

With the return of the Bourbons, Schmaltz enjoyed an incredibly swift rise. On July 8, 1814, he was confirmed in the grade of major and in August appointed lieutenant colonel. He was awarded the Légion d'honneur and assigned to Guadeloupe as commandant of Basse-Terre.

The destabilizing episode of the Hundred Days served Schmaltz well. While in Guadeloupe he let it be known that he harbored Jacobin sympathies, yet a daring bet on the failure of Napoleon's adventure gave him the appearance of a diehard royalist. During a period of vacillation among the administrators of the island, a schooner, the *Agile,* arrived from France persuading all except Schmaltz to back Napoleon. Schmaltz's refusal meant that he was arrested and sent for trial. But the *Agile* had arrived in Guadeloupe only three days before the Battle of Waterloo; by the time Schmaltz arrived in France Louis was back on the French throne and the commandant of Basse-Terre was in a position to cash in on his fidelity. He was thus confirmed in his appointment as commander for the king and administrator of Senegal on April 25, 1816, promoted to a colonel of the infantry, and on May 22 further decorated as a Chevalier de l'ordre royal et militaire de Saint-Louis.[8]

In November 1815, Reine Schmaltz suffered another attack of mania and it was then that she came under the care of Dr. Esquirol, whose treatment appears, in the short term, to have been reasonably effective. She was not only able to accompany her husband on the expedition to Senegal but, what is more, she appeared calm and even insensible to the danger in which the *Medusa* found herself in the first hours after running aground.[9]

In the council, plans were discussed for the evacuation of the frigate. Given the enormous number of shipwrecks during this period, it was incredible that the small craft carried were often unsuitable as lifeboats. Frequently in bad shape, they were intended for light duties in and around the ship such as the laying out of a kedge anchor; there was no dedicated navigational equipment, no food, no water ready to be loaded in case of disaster. Given such insufficiencies, one of the most intelligent ideas put forward at the council was to ferry the passengers and crew to the inhospitable shore in a series of round-trips. Reassembled into a troop, armed against the hostile Moors, and provisioned from the boats that would follow the castaways along the coast, they would thus march together on foot to Saint-Louis in Senegal. Another creditable idea was to lighten the frigate as much as possible and dispatch the most seaworthy of the boats posthaste to Senegal for help. Another idea, the construction of a raft capable of carrying a large number of men and all the supplies, was proposed by Governor Schmaltz. At mealtimes, the six boats, which would be carrying the rest of the passengers and crew, would approach the raft and collect their rations. This suggestion, seconded by Captain Chaumareys, was thus adopted and construction began at once for the sea was becoming rougher and the winds wilder, reminding all the frightened souls on board that the stormy season would soon be upon them.

During the evening of July 3, another attempt was made to position the anchor. The crew struggled with the capstan to pull the frigate free, efforts met with a sudden, universal shout of joy as those on board felt the first strains and stirrings of success. But the clamor of exultation suddenly collapsed into deadly silence as the sailors were ordered to stop. Night was falling, the sea had become heavy, and the attempt to free the *Medusa* would have to be postponed until the morning tide.[10] The frigate groaned, the sea pummeled the ship, pounding and punishing the hull as sailors vigorously pumped out the seepage and the carpenters made all possible haste to advance the construction of the raft.

The crying of the wind in the cordage, the yelping of badly disciplined men, the contradictory commands shouted and swallowed by the night terrified the already frightened passengers. Song—rarely heard under Chaumareys's command—echoed through the vessel as soldiers and sailors, oiled by drink, went on the rampage. They ransacked trunks and strongboxes in search of fine clothes and precious objects. They boasted of how they had broken into the captain's cabin, preferring his wines and liqueurs to his safe. Nobody mustered for meals; everyone grabbed what they could as life on the ship rapidly descended into anarchy.

There was another burst of optimism when, on the morning of July 4, a further attempt to float the frigate appeared as if it might succeed. A kedge anchor was dropped on the port side to pull against the bower anchor off the starboard and swing the *Medusa* around so that she could float back into deeper water. The operation began encouragingly. The ship began to turn and, with breath held, the hopeful passengers watched as she swung about completely, leaving only her stern on the bottom. Ensigns Lapeyrère and Maudet wanted to jettison every possible object to lighten the vessel but they were stopped from doing so. Schmaltz even forbade the dumping of barrels of flour, claiming that hunger was a huge concern in the European trading posts. The ultimate failure of the refloating operation underscored the fatal inadequacy of the leadership. As Savigny and Corréard commented, "only half measures were adopted, and in all the manoeuvres, great want of decision prevailed."[11]

The construction of the raft, which had been designed by Schmaltz, was put under the charge of that accomplished mariner Lieutenant Espiaux. The boom, masts, and yards from the *Medusa* were lashed together. A prow to aid navigation was fashioned from two topgallant yards and in the main body of the raft spars were placed at intervals onto which planks were fixed. Long pieces of wood were placed laterally and projected nine feet on either side to give the craft stability. A little raised deck was constructed with some spare planks and fixed with large nails and rope. The six-foot-long prow was not solid enough to support people and neither was a portion of similar length in the stern so, although the craft was a sizable sixty-five feet long by twenty-two wide and therefore nearly a quarter the size of the main deck of the *Medusa,* an eighth of its surface was all but useless. Barrels were placed in the corners and an ineffectual railing only fifteen inches high ran around the raft. The inadequacy of these defenses made it immediately clear that those who designed the craft were unlikely to assign themselves to its care.[12]

As soon as the makeshift platform was finished, Schmaltz and Chaumareys, standing before the white Bourbon flag, promised the assembled company that the five largest boats would tow the raft to the coast, and there, equipped with provisions and firearms, everybody would make for Senegal on foot. But these were a politician's promises. Anglas de Praviel, the infantry lieutenant, recalled that a secret order of disembarkation had been drawn up by those in command, who assigned themselves to the safest places in the boats. When the allocations were, at last, made public, the Picard family, already much distressed by the violent scenes of drunken plunder, found to their horror that they had been assigned to the raft along with a grab bag of rough, drunken soldiers and sailors, assorted Cap Vert colonists, and several officers who were out of favor with Chaumareys or Schmaltz. Picard was indignant and swore that if they were not given a place in one of the boats, his family would stay on board the frigate, which remained well provisioned and showed little sign of breaking up. Although, as Charlotte Picard reflected, he was probably considering only how posterity would judge him, Schmaltz at last relented and promised them a place in one of the boats.[13]

The evening of July 4 began so agreeably that Brédif decided to put his mattress up on the quarterdeck and lie there under the unfamiliar stars. This brief respite was soon interrupted by a freshening wind that, toward midnight, became very strong. Waves struck the hull with a new vigor until the frigate began to crumple amidships as the keel split in two. The sudden violence of these shocks and jolts and the hunch that they were about to be abandoned unnerved the fiery soldiers of the Africa Battalion. They ranked in battle formation and threatened to shoot anybody they caught trying secretly to escape. Schmaltz came up on the quarterdeck to calm them. When they seemed disinclined to heed his words, he mustered all the troops, crew, officers, and passengers and, once again, repeated his vow to abandon no one. Everybody, he insisted, would be transported to the shore.

Assembled as a caravan four hundred strong, they would all make their way on foot to Senegal.

Rather than these doubtful reassurances it was the raft breaking loose from its moorings and drifting out to sea that reestablished calm. Watching as their chance of rescue started to float away, the troops and crew, some constricted in their movements by the five or six stolen jackets they wore and were loath to surrender, united in an operation to recover the raft.[14]

All available pumps were working flat out when, at three a.m. on July 5, the master caulker informed the captain that the frigate had taken in a dangerous quantity of water. The increasing anxiety that the remaining masts would fall and crush people when the hull finally collapsed prompted the officers to finalize their evacuation plans amid the ruckus of a ship crazed with drink or fright. Sailors and soldiers continued to carouse as if all time were theirs, ignoring the captain who had, in any case, informally been relieved of his command. Pillagers were stumbling about carrying plates and candlesticks and other objects unlikely to aid their escape or survival, decked in finery that made it seem as if the whole misadventure were merely an extra episode in the tropical burlesque that had been in full swing such a short time ago.

Between five and six a.m. the water reached a sufficient height for Governor Schmaltz to order the evacuation. The list that had been drawn up on the previous day was little heeded, as those with rank or power sought the best manner of saving themselves. Provisions had been carefully prepared and placed in iron-hooped barrels, but such was the lack of leadership and panic in the face of disaster that many of these were left on deck or flung indiscriminately into the sea.[15]

The soldiers were the first to leave; Anglas de Praviel, supervising their descent onto the raft, took pains to ensure that any swag and, above all, their weapons were left on board the frigate. Another officer, observed by Charlotte Picard, "whose brain seemed severely affected, mounted on the bulwarks as if on a horse and, armed with two pistols, threatened to shoot anybody who hesitated to descend." Standing on the quarterdeck, Rabaroust, the stowaway, was assigned a place on the raft. Convinced that to accept would prove fatal, he refused to budge. When Chaumareys chivied him, he retaliated: "I prefer to die on the frigate. I'm at least allowed to chose my own manner of death."

By the time forty men had clambered aboard, the raft had sunk by up to two feet in certain places. Provisions that had been put on board the night before, barrels full of necessary supplies, were rolled off into the sea. Only six tubs of wine and two containers of water were left after this rash attempt to lighten a craft that would only sink further under the weight of the next hundred bodies. To supplement the few provisions left on board, a twenty-five-pound sack of biscuit was thrown from the frigate only to land in the sea. By the time it was retrieved the contents had become a soggy, salty paste that would, nonetheless, prove invaluable in the days ahead.

Praviel followed his men down onto the raft but was unable, through the glut of one hundred and fifty bodies, to reach the little deck that had been constructed in the center where other officers, along with the surgeon, Savigny, and Corréard, had formed an impregnable nucleus of command. Blocked in the sunken stern with water up to his waist and waves sweeping over his head, Praviel decided to jump into the sea and clamber back on board the frigate.

Unable to move and hence incapable of checking what had been left aboard the raft by way of provisions and instruments for navigation, Corréard hailed Lieutenant Reynaud:

"Have we got the necessary instruments and charts?"

"I've provided you with everything you need."

The exchange was difficult against the ocean's roar, but Corréard persisted.

"Is there an officer coming to take charge?"

"It'll be me. I'll be with you in a moment."

And then, having urged an unconscionable number of souls aboard the makeshift structure, Lieutenant Reynaud went off to take his place in one of the boats.[16]

Throughout the confused evacuation the frigate's ladder was insufficient, so men slithered down ropes or made a jump for it. Despite the sea swell, they made it to the raft or the boats and in all the undisciplined chaos it is remarkable that no one was seriously hurt. Apparently unruffled by the crisis—and wrapped in a large fitted coat, protecting her from the wind and the spray—Reine Schmaltz and then her daughter were, in turn, lowered into the governor's barge, a twenty-eight-foot, fourteen-oared boat whose command was entrusted to Lieutenant Reynaud, the very officer who had promised to captain the raft.[17] As for Governor Schmaltz, whom Charlotte Picard credits with "taking care of nothing but the wish to save himself," he was lowered in an armchair suspended from a hoist and deposited in the well-provisioned barge where he joined his wife, daughter, and dearest friends. When five or six sailors who had jumped into the sea approached this barge and pleaded, in the name of humanity, to be picked up, they were repelled by the thick, curved saber of Schmaltz's aide-de-camp. Settled comfortably among the other thirty-six passengers, who were well distributed in a barge capable of taking fifty, the governor's family viewed this incident with complete indifference. Fearing for their lives, the repulsed sailors scrambled to get back on board the frigate.[18]

The Picard family was still stranded on the deck of the *Medusa*. Charlotte hollered to the captains of the boats who appeared to be abandoning them, and when the governor's barge circled the frigate, as if to take on more passengers, Charlotte hoped against hope that the Schmaltz ladies, who had taken an interest in her family during the voyage, would make room for them in their boat. But as the barge pulled away again, Chaumareys opined disdainfully that they would not wish to burden themselves.

Picard hailed Lapeyrère, who had been ordered to take the family on board the pinnace, but his boat continued to distance itself from the ship. When the skiff came alongside, Picard beseeched the sailors to take them to Lapeyrère's boat, which was as sizable as the governor's barge and far from full. When they refused, he snatched a rifle and threatened to shoot whoever rebuffed him, adding that the skiff was the property of the king and that he and his family must profit from it as much as anybody else. The sailors capitulated and accepted the large complement of four small children, four women, and Picard himself. Precious papers, clothing, and two bottles of ratafia were seized from them and thrown into the sea by the sailors; they had been forced to leave all their other possessions on board the *Medusa*. As they drew close to the pinnace, they were greeted by a volley of excuses from an embarrassed Lapeyrère, who claimed that he had been ordered to pull away without them. Not necessarily believing such protestations, for the family constituted a large and obvious liability, the Picards were nonetheless relieved to be rescued.[19]

With the boats now beginning to move off for fear of becoming overloaded, Chaumareys decided, against all the laws and usages of the sea, that it was time for him to leave the frigate. Petit, a noncommissioned officer, confronted the captain with the utmost composure: "Since you are leaving us, at least give us the pleasure, if you reach France, of giving our families the news."

Chaumareys descended by a forward rope, escaping onto the captain's barge where midshipman Rang was already installed and in charge. Rang claims that the captain's intention was to put himself in a position from which he could rally and regroup the less laden boats. But from the deck of the *Medusa* it appeared otherwise. Anglas de Praviel, furious at the selfishness and cowardice of the leaders of the expedition, grabbed a rifle and threatened to open fire. Rang hollered from the captain's barge that the boats would return for them. Bucked by such comforting news, those on board the *Medusa* hoisted a white flag and started shouting "Long live the king" and "Long live the governor," cries that passed along the convoy that was forming in order to tow the overloaded, half-submerged raft. The captain's barge, with its mizzen hoisted, was at the head of the line, followed by the Senegal boat. This was commanded by Ensign Maudet and had its full complement of twenty-five on board. Next came the pinnace, under Ensign Lapeyrère, leaving the governor's barge, under Lieutenant Reynaud, closest to the raft.

Realizing that he and the other sixty-three men remaining on the *Medusa* had been abandoned, Praviel became delirious and threatened to take his own life. An infantryman raised his rifle to take aim at the cowardly Chaumareys, but Rabaroust, thinking the man crazed, tussled with him and spoiled his shot, much to the dismay of the incensed and stranded victims. Believing that there was space for everybody in the boats, Brédif had not hastened to leave the frigate and was left among this increasingly irate and drunken rabble.

Although the wind had dropped and the sun was breaking through the clouds, the tide and current were dragging the heavy raft, which, in turn, pulled the convoy of four boats, in a northwesterly direction, away from the shore to the east and Saint-Louis in Senegal to the south.

The skiff was too small to form any useful part of the convoy and Lieutenant Espiaux's longboat, though sizable, had not joined the towing operation. Alone among the officers, Espiaux decided to return to the ship. Conscientious and brave, he believed that his comrades in the longboat would rather die than abandon the helpless. Drawing close to the frigate with considerable difficulty, Espiaux was surprised to find that there were upwards of sixty soldiers and sailors remaining on the *Medusa*. His plan was to ferry everybody to the other, less laden boats, and he managed to embark, at his peril, all but seventeen.

Praviel and Brédif found themselves in the fragile and overladen longboat among nearly ninety people, the sea on the point of pouring over the sides and submerging them. Approaching the governor's barge, hoping to place nine of their number on board, Espiaux met with a blunt refusal; Schmaltz claimed that he had accepted too many already and that his barge was taking on water. Espiaux approached Lapeyrère in the pinnace but was also refused, a callous officer interjecting that as Espiaux had gone to rescue them he would have to look after them.

The derisive cry resounded from boat to boat that the longboat was going to sink them all. Indeed, Espiaux's encumbered and unwieldy craft appeared to be on the point of colliding with the Senegal boat, when its commander, Ensign Maudet, in order to avoid this accident, was obliged to release the towrope attaching him to the pinnace. This divided the line of towing boats into two. Maudet hailed Chaumareys: "Captain, take the towrope again."

The blithe reply came back: "Yes, my friend."

Now only the governor's barge and the pinnace were towing the raft and before the captain's boat and the Senegal boat were able to rejoin them the whole line was surprised by the cry: "The governor is abandoning the raft!"

From the sinking platform it was clear what was happening. The sudden confusion caused by the maneuvers to avert the collision gave Reynaud his chance. Standing up in the stern of the governor's barge, he raised his arm like an executioner. The hatchet in his hand came down in hard, repeated blows on the thick rope, hacking until he had severed their last threads of hope.

The captain's barge came within earshot of the governor's barge and Chaumareys called out, "What are you doing?"

The reply came back, "The towrope has broken."

"Get hold of it again."

"We're abandoning them."

"We didn't hear you."

"We're abandoning them."

Clanet, the paymaster of the frigate who was on board the governor's barge, repeatedly protested against the chopping of the towrope but to no avail. Lieutenant Reynaud had cut it on the order of Governor Schmaltz. Several men in Espiaux's longboat, understanding what was happening, took aim at the culprits in readiness to open fire, but Espiaux prevented them.

As several of his friends were aboard the longboat and facing an uncertain fate, Picard renewed his appeal to Ensign Lapeyrère to take them on board their boat, which could easily accommodate a few more souls. Indeed, Picard was already enthusiastically holding out his arms, in order to help them, when suddenly Lapeyrère released the rope that tied them to the governor's barge and rowed away toward the east. At that instant, all the boats imitated this maneuver in order to distance themselves from the foundering longboat. As Gaspar Mollien put it, surveying the scene from Maudet's boat, "Egotism and cowardice triumphed," and in their scramble to distance themselves the raft was forgotten.

Cries erupted on the frightened platform: "The towrope's broken! The towrope's broken!"

Hollow, desperate screams of "Long live the king" and "Long live France" reached the ears of Charlotte Picard as the pinnace rapidly pulled away from all immediate responsibility. The leaders and commanders in the other boats took up this cry, which, ironically, seemed to vitalize them. Chaumareys, obviously exhilarated to be rid of his unhappy command, was gaily waving his braid-trimmed hat.[20]

After a few moments, the cries from the raft died down as the silence of apprehension settled on its ill-fated occupants. The half-submerged structure, void of sails, oars, ropes, anchors, instruments, and charts, was abandoned, ungovernable, in the middle of the sea.[21] It was eleven a.m. by the time the boats pulled away from the raft; the chaotic and cowardly evacuation had taken upwards of five hours and those stranded on the platform were stunned by the realization that the twice-sworn solemn promises made so recently on the deck of the *Medusa* had been broken.

Brédif, crammed aboard Espiaux's longboat, had managed to save his diary from the general jettisoning that ineffectively attempted to lighten the craft. He recorded the cutting of the ropes and the distancing, under full sail, of the less-hampered boats, adding with sarcastic stoicism, "Whew! My friends, since that's the way it is, leave us to our fate" as he looked out on the increasingly empty and desolate ocean.[22]

4

On a Scorching Shore

Storms and Breakers

As the overloaded longboat was unable to aid the raft, let alone rescue those on board, she too pulled away to the east. Within four hours land was sighted. At three p.m. on July 5, as he made his diary entry, Brédif recorded that "all is well, the weather is good and there's hope of saving our lives." With nearly ninety people straining the frail craft well beyond its capacity, this observation exhibited a laudable optimism that was soon put to the test. In the early evening the longboat struck bottom. The night came down, closing in with thick mist, and it was not until nine p.m. that the sailors disengaged their craft. Off the shoal, all on board received a small quantity of water and a biscuit, their third distribution of rations since leaving the *Medusa* that morning.

Steadily the wind had been strengthening, blowing off the mist and whipping up a storm. Crouched down in the cramped longboat, his earlier confidence undermined, Brédif described it as a "night of distress and fear" as wave after wave threatened to engulf and drown them. But they survived the turbulent night. As day broke under a fresh wind on a heavy sea, they struggled eastward using their drenched bodies as a shield against the overwhelming waves.

With the coastline once again visible, the majority of those aboard decided to take their chances on the dry, inhospitable land rather than risk uncertain navigation in a sinking longboat. Lieutenant Espiaux thus put ashore fifty-seven people at Cap Mirick on the southern point of the Arguin Bank. Lieutenant de Praviel was among those who went ashore to contend with the blistering heat on a desert march of over two hundred miles south to Saint-Louis in Senegal.

Lieutenant Espiaux, along with Brédif and the twenty-six others left on board, put out to sea.[1] About an hour later they sighted some of the other boats from the *Medusa*. Espiaux, always thinking of how best to manage things, hailed them, offering to take people on board in return for water. Incredibly, he was refused. Nobody on the other boats believed his story about the landing. How would men be so crazy as to elect to march through the desert to a likely death from dehydration, or into captivity and enslavement by the Moors? Suspicious, the occupants of the other boats believed Espiaux's band to be concealed under the seats, ready to surprise them and steal their rations. While such distrust was undermining all sensible attempts to coordinate the rescue, the small skiff was beginning to break up and fifteen passengers, including Rabaroust, were taken on board by Espiaux.

Toward evening the weather deteriorated once again and Brédif, facing another stormy night, impassively awaited his fate. Hanging his head over the side of the longboat he succumbed to a much needed sleep. The roar and splatter of the waves smacking against the hull provoked a dream about a pure alpine torrent to which the parched victim was running in order to plunge his head under its freshwater spray and quench his thirst. In the manner of such dreams he never achieved his goal, but rather woke to find his lips stuck together by a crust of salt, his tongue glued to the roof of his mouth, and his soul possessed by the most terrible desire to end his nightmare by throwing himself into the sea.

By midday on July 7 the temperature was unbearable. Brédif wanted to dangle his feet in the sea to cool them, but as sharks had been sighted he did not dare. Portions of the coast they followed were, from time to time obscured by thick red sandstorms, which blew out over the sea, dusting them and leaving a boatload of terra-cotta bodies immobile in the oven-hot afternoon. Drinkable liquid was already scarce as some unruly sailors had already downed the several bottles of Madeira that were on board, so everybody sucked on little balls of lead to keep their saliva circulating.

That afternoon they sighted the Senegal boat. After the breakup of the convoy, this craft, under the command of Ensign Maudet, soon lost sight of the others. During the first stormy night she was tossed about wildly, up onto the crests of immense waves and then, stomach scoopingly, plunged into chasms over which giant arcs of water reached to engulf her.

When on the afternoon of July 7 those in Maudet's Senegal boat were scared by the sight of what they took to be Moorish pirates, they were relieved to discover that it was, in fact, the *Medusa*'s longboat. Their only rations, a small cask of wine, had been lost overboard by a sailor scared out of his wits by the high waves. They were thus deeply grateful to Lieutenant Espiaux when he handed them two bottles of brandy.

About six o'clock they discerned a group of Moors on the beach, mending their fishing nets. Frightened by the sight of two strange boats, the fishermen went off on their camels. At this, two brave—or desperate—men decided to take their chances with the breakers and swim ashore to see what food they could scavenge. Successful, they feasted on the dried fish and fresh water left behind by the Moors and then struggled back to the boats.

The following morning, Maudet's Senegal boat was carried toward the coast where she was swept into the breakers that threw her up on the beach. People scrambled onto the sand and scattered to search for fresh water. Observing this, the sailors aboard the longboat angrily pressed Espiaux to go ashore. A sail was hoisted and the longboat likewise sped into the breakers and crested up onto the sand, where she beached, plunging people overboard into the waves. Brédif found his diary notes miraculously intact, and returned to the longboat, several times, to stuff his pockets with sodden, saltwatery biscuits. Back on the hot sand he found a group of sailors broaching the only remaining barrel of water. Fighting through the desperate group, he wrestled to get his mouth on the bunghole, managing only a couple of gulps before it was torn away—two swigs worth two gallons to a body that, for three days, had taken in dangerously little liquid.[2]

Staggering from a phantom pitch and roll, the legacy of three weeks at sea, the castaways from Espiaux's longboat joined the crew and passengers of Maudet's Senegal boat. Some drenched, others already covered with sand and without shoes, they could hardly recognize one another, standing in the odd scraps of clothing they had managed to snatch from the frigate before or during the evacuation. This sorry, ragtag band began to move south along the coast and had walked for only about half an hour when they saw the pinnace speeding toward shore.

Under Ensign Lapeyrère, the pinnace had kept in convoy with the captain's and governor's barges as they descended the coast. Both Schmaltz and Chaumareys had insisted that they sail straight for Senegal, and there had followed a lively exchange in which the dearth of supplies on board the pinnace, the need to make for land, and their obligation to return to save those on the raft and still on board the *Medusa* proved useless arguments against the egotism of the governor and the commander. If the plan to proceed to Senegal by sea was to be respected, the pinnace, needed to take on some of the excess of supplies provisioning the barges. Chaumareys, between great gulps of wine, which he swigged from a huge demijohn, nonchalantly informed Lapeyrère that they didn't have sufficient supplies for themselves. At length, the leaders of the expedition forbade the pinnace from making a landing, reiterating their wish to make for Senegal by sea, and to that end they dropped anchor for the night.

By six a.m. on July 6, when the convoy once again got under way, several sailors demanded to be put ashore. Entreaties flared into threats and it was only the firmness of Ensign Lapeyrère that quelled a mutiny on board the pinnace.

By midday they were blinded by the hot particles of sand blown out to sea by infernal desert winds, coloring the sun a hellish red and coating the insides of their mouths with the grit-filled air. In the late afternoon a northwesterly breeze cleared this storm and with a second meal—a little glass of water and a soggy biscuit—spirits rose. But the breeze freshened to a wind and throughout the night, waves threatened to submerge them, washing overboard one of their sails and those few effects that several people had managed to sneak on board. A large hole opened in the stern through which water was pouring into the boat. Trousers, sleeves of shirts, strips of dresses, shawls, hats—everything available was used to plug it. As the sea rose with its white foam tracing deep black chasms, Picard broke down and started to cry with fear for the safety of his family. Wanting to suckle her baby, his wife found that her milk had dried for want of nourishment.

The compass broke during the night and the boat meandered first to port and then to starboard until the first streaks of morning light gave them their bearings. Land was sighted and the sailors, once again, agitated to be put ashore. This time, with the craft deteriorating rapidly, Lapeyrère agreed to navigate the pinnace toward the beach, at which point, whoever wanted to could plunge into the

waves and swim ashore. In the attempt, faced by the size of the breakers, the eleven men who had insisted thought the better of it. Pull-
ing away from the shore, they received their third distribution of
food since leaving the *Medusa*. With only four pints of water and a
dozen sodden biscuits left on board, the question of putting ashore
in search of sustenance was being seriously debated when the sight
of a caravan of Moors dissuaded them. Lapeyrère now thought it
best to continue by sea, reckoning that they would reach Senegal
the following day.

The sun set the air ablaze and people, in desperation, capitulated
to the dangerous urge to drink seawater. To alleviate desiccation, some
started to consume their urine, cooling it first in the sea. The youngest Picards cried incessantly and little Laure, aged six, lay on the verge
of death at her mother's feet. Devastated by this sight, Picard pulled
out his knife. Staring at his daughter, he brought the blade down
purposefully onto his arm. He was on the point of slitting a vein so
that his blood might serve to assuage the thirst of his child when he
was stopped.[3]

The freshness of the evening offered some respite and the pinnace anchored a little distance offshore while people slept. Ravenous
as dawn broke on July 8, stranded without even a whisper of wind on
a dead sea, they tried to row in the direction of Senegal but were too
weak to make any headway. A fourth and final distribution of food
was a mockery; six waterlogged biscuits and four pints of water were
eked out among the forty-two people on board. Again, Moors appeared on the shore and the boat distanced itself a little until someone
noticed a small troop of men standing on a hillock, gesticulating wildly.
Recognizing them as castaways from the *Medusa,* they hoisted a white
handkerchief by way of acknowledgment and decided to make every
effort to reach the shore.

Rolled and tossed by the surf, the pinnace sped toward the coast.
When the helmsman misjudged the crest of a wave the boat was all

but capsized. So an older, more experienced pilot took over and ordered the mast and sails to be thrown into the sea. Having successfully navigated the boat through the storm, he took charge in order to get the frightened passengers safely ashore. A towering wave remained between them and the beach. As the boat angled to ride the crest, she lurched, plunged into the wave, which swallowed and rolled her over, splintering oars and ramming the vortex of debris up onto the sand, where it was battered by successive breakers. Sailors tried to hook the grapple anchor in order to secure their landfall as others threw themselves into the surf to rescue the children. Engineer Brédif pelted down the beach and into the waves to help save the Picard ladies and, after a few moments of hectic effort and confusion, Charlotte Picard found herself standing on the firm sand beside her mother-in-law and her half-dead brothers and sisters.[4]

The Tattered Band

The castaways found themselves on a scorching shore under a lacerating July sun without water, without food, and with many of the exhausted and famished party nearly naked. The immense expanse of undulating sand that stretched before them appeared every bit as daunting as the heaving sea.[5] All the warnings given in published accounts about the dangers of sailing the African coast had not saved them from shipwreck, and all the stories of the menacing desert could only have raised their apprehensions about a region where the Moors viewed all ships and boats thrown up on their coasts as gifts to them from the heavens.[6] Whatever practical difficulties the castaways faced, their perceptions, molded by ignorance, prejudice, and limited experience, prepared them for the worst; over and above their desperate physical situation, they anticipated the perils of enslavement and, worse still, cannibalism.

History provided examples of expedient cannibalism and cautionary tales made use of it as a symbolic punishment, but only since the days of the great European explorers had cannibalism appeared as a real threat.[7] The subject of cannibalism had thus come to fascinate and terrorize the so-called civilized world. Published in London by Henry Colburn, who was to produce the English edition of Savigny and Corréard's best-selling account of the *Medusa* saga, a book by the German doctor and explorer George Heinrich von Langsdorff provided a kind of traveler's "good food guide" to the human species.

> Incredible as it may appear, there have been, and are still, particularly in South America, and in the interior of Africa, as well as upon its western coasts, people who feed upon human flesh merely on account of its delicacy, and as the height of gourmandise. These nations not only eat the prisoners they take in war, but their own wives and children; they even buy and sell human flesh publicly. To them we are indebted for the information that white men are finer flavoured than Negroes, and that Englishmen are preferable to Frenchmen. Farther, the flesh of young girls and women, particularly of new-born children, far exceeds in delicacy that of the finest youths or grown men. Finally they tell us that the inside of the hand and the sole of the foot are the nicest parts of the human body.[8]

Charles Cochelet, shipwrecked on the West African coast in 1819, described some indigenous figures as barely human, writing that "I should have looked upon them as apes of the most frightful species, had not their bodies, which no clothing concealed, possessed the human form."[9] So widespread were such reactions and their attendant fantasies of cannibalism that Joseph de Grandpré had, in 1801, set out to dispel "the disgusting absurdity" that "the Congo is governed by a King who feeds on human flesh. "Grandpré claimed that Africans were not cannibals and that it was, ironically, on board European slave ships, chained and clapped in irons and watching the sailors drinking bloodred wine and dark, dried meat, that the fear of cannibalism gripped the minds of the captured Africans being so inhumanely transported. They agonized that they would soon be served to their rapacious captors.[10]

Whatever hardships the castaways from the *Medusa* confronted, they would encounter no cannibals among the indigenous people they met during their arduous march to Saint-Louis. However, the far more real fear of captivity was ever present to the almost defenseless and severely weakened troop of eighty-six people that came ashore near the deserted trading post at Portendick, about halfway between where the *Medusa* ran aground and their destination in Senegal. There were many stories about the savage treatment of shipwreck survivors at the hands of Moorish slavers. In 1814, Geoffroy de Villeneuve had documented a particularly ferocious tribe, the Azounas, who wandered between Cap Bojador and the Senegal River, plundering whatever they could find either from shipwrecked boats or, farther south, from black villages along the river. They were armed, hated, and enslaved their captives.[11]

As the clothes of the castaways were in tatters, and fearing that the women may be at greater risk, several gallant officers proposed their uniforms to the Picard ladies. Charlotte inexplicably declined, keeping her torn dress, which, she would soon discover, afforded her legs little protection against the prickly shrubs that punctured the desert sands.

They were, at once, forced to abandon a man whose legs had been smashed coming ashore; they laid him out on the sand to almost certain lengthy and painful death and set off into the desert to look for fresh water. Their saliva sticky and tongues furred, they eventually found clumps of foul-smelling and thorny vegetation and they started to dig, crazily pawing and scraping at the sand like dogs. Down they dug into the claylike earth to a depth of two or three feet until they discovered a whitish, stinking liquid, which Brédif dared to sample. Finding it to be saltless, he called out that they were saved. Several other holes were dug at once and the parched survivors gorged themselves on more of the stomach-turning water.

After slaking their thirst, some people set about gathering bunches of purslane, an herb that had been known in the Middle Ages as an antiaphrodisiac. Although reputed to "mitigate great heat in all the inward parts of man," it was unlikely to have afforded protection against the blistering swelter of the desert sun. However, it did help to keep the famished troops alive. The drenched ship's biscuit had by now dried hard as stone; they tried to eat it but it stayed solidified in their mouths until they spat it out.[12]

The group rested for another hour before setting off in a southerly direction with the women and children in the front of the party and Brédif carrying one of the youngest on his shoulders in the hope of inspiring the sailors to do the same. For those still shod, the fine, burning sand poured into their shoes and boots as their feet sank inches deep, making each step impossibly hot and heavy.

With the arid, sand-filled air caking their eyelids and firing their throats, they were happy once again to cross the dunes that gave way to the sea's edge. The wet sand soothed them as they stopped to rest. They drank a little of the sulfurous water that they had carried with them from their first stop, and as the sun fell the temperature cooled. It was obviously less arduous to travel after sundown, in the early morning, or at night, but it was then that they felt more vulnerable, easy prey for the fierce tribes and wild animals that haunted the coast.

On the first night ashore, after their rest with sentries posted to guard against marauders, the bedraggled band began their journey again at three a.m. Those without shoes were stabbed and cut by the shells strewn along the beach. They halted every half hour at Picard's behest; his intense anxiety for the weaker members of his family made his attitude somewhat imperious and, in his wearied state, he lacked sufficient reserves to manifest his gratitude for these rests. Two officers, believing that only drive and determination would get them to their goal, grumbled that the family was dangerously slowing their progress. Picard immediately sprang to the defense of his kin who were, unfortunately, at that moment straggling at the rear. With nerves frayed by fatigue, bodies tested by the extremes of climate, and with the question of their survival at stake, the argument grew fierce and swords were drawn. The older members of the family, shocked once more by the selfishness that had spread through the ill-fated expedition like an epidemic, pleaded with their father to stay with them in the desert rather than travel on with people they judged more barbarous than the dreaded Moors. Captain Baignères, a leader of one of the companies of the Africa Battalion, intervened, shaming those who wished to abandon the family with notions of honor and duty and discourses on what it meant to be French, a quality that had been aired and tested and rolled uncertainly around in the minds of many of the *Medusa* victims.

As the day declared itself, burning off the dawn chill, they searched behind the nearest dunes for more edible plants. A green creeper strung across the sand was found to be bitter. Other plants were identified as poisonous. So further quantities of purslane were gathered and devoured ravenously. One plant, milkweed, with its silky white plumes, played havoc with perception. Waving in the distance, it looked to several people like clumps of Moorish tents. Determined to find fresh water even at the cost of enslavement, they started to stagger off in that direction only to realize that it was a mirage. Others saw distant pools or wide, rapid-flowing rivers and hastened to reach what their stricken minds were swiftly forced to accept as a trick of the dazzling sun rebounding off the white, burning sand.

The naturalist Kummer, one of the delegates of the Philanthropic Society, recklessly decided to leave the group and strike off into the burning interior of the Sahara in search of Moors who might feed him. Two days later, his friend Rogery, also a delegate of the company and an ex-infantry officer, would suddenly and secretly leave the band in order to trace a parallel path deep into the desert.

Again wells were dug, yielding the now familiar fetid liquid with which the castaways refreshed their sand-choked mouths and moistened their cracking lips. At first, this strange and arid environment had seemed a sea of silence after the ocean's incessant roar, but slowly the group adjusted to the desert's sounds: the grating of the fine crystals against their bodies and their clothes, the whispering as the wind chivvied the sand into little rills, the moaning and the growling of a storm.

After their rest, they set off back over the blazing dunes to the succor of a fresher, harder surface that had been cooled and compacted by the action of the waves. Such zigzagging was adding distance to their journey but it was necessary and they gratefully lay down in the water and caught some large crabs, which gave them sustenance as well as moisture as they sucked on the claws.

On the night of July 9, when the weary group halted between dunes, they heard the sounds of what they thought were leopards and they decided to spend a good part of the threatening night bunched in the safety of a tight group. When someone thought he spotted a lion, people roused themselves to take a look. After staring intently into the desert for some time, they realized that the lion swayed but didn't move and that it was nothing but the moonlight playing tricks with the ruffled milkweed.

Despite the risk of wild animals, they moved off long before dawn. At about six a.m., they had their first encounter with human predators, a small bunch of pillagers who seemed content to rob some of the stragglers and then ride off. Several men had been hatching a plot to kill the officers in order to seize the gold they vainly imagined them to be carrying; others fantasized about robbing everybody and running off to become marauders. Slowly the sun's disabling heat burned off these thoughts, as parched and swollen-footed, these would-be renegades stumbled along with the rest of the tattered band. At length, they sighted and approached a humble camp of shabby tents. Gaspar Mollien observed that the Moorish women inhabiting the camp, with their stick legs, sunken torsos, and withered breasts, were hardly less alarming in appearance than the wizened castaways themselves. This second meeting with the feared Moors proved a little expensive but not dangerous. The black servant of one of the officers acted as an interpreter and the women sold them goat's milk, fresh water, and millet. Picard purchased two kids from them to feed the group, but unable to wait for the animals to be cooked the sailors tore off half-raw morsels, which they devoured, leaving hardly any meat for the officers.

While Picard was busily seeking contributions toward the cost of the animals—being denied only by Richefort—suddenly, out of nowhere, a small band of blacks and Moors charged the group. Grabbing their rifles, several soldiers ranked in formation as if to defend the castaways from the sudden assault. When the assailants abruptly halted without attack, two officers and the interpreter, covered by several soldiers, went to speak to them. What had appeared as menace proved to be nothing more than commercial enthusiasm as the would-be attackers offered their services as guides to Senegal, suggesting that they set off at once.[13]

As they traversed the spiky shrub-covered dunes, Charlotte Picard's feet and legs were scratched till they bled and her dress was snagged and torn. She struggled to keep up as the guides led them to their camp. When at last they arrived, exhausted, they were not welcomed but viciously taunted by a horde of women and children who swarmed around them, showering the sorry visitors with sand. Dogs snapped at their raw and blistered shins. The women pinched them, tugging at their hair to inspect it, ripping all the shiny buttons and braid from the uniforms, and spitting with delight into the faces of the frightened Europeans. After what seemed like an interminable barrage of abuse, the guides shooed off the vicious gang so that water could be distributed, and dried or rotten fish and bitter milk sold to the castaways.

"Hey, Picard, don't you recognize me? It's Ahmet."

The sound of French tumbling from the mouth of a large young figure swathed in Arab costume startled the hungry band and Picard turned to find himself greeted by a goldsmith whom he had employed on one of his previous trips to Senegal. Apalled by their wretched state, Ahmet arranged for more milk and water to be distributed without charge. As the weather was turning, he also set about constructing a tent of skins to shield the Picards; forbidden by his religion to lodge Christians in his own house, he was anxious that the family of his old employer should be protected against the ravages of a desert storm. Lighting large fires to comfort the frightened Europeans, Ahmet and his fellow tribesmen bid good night, assuring them that the Christian God is also that of the Muslims.

By midnight the weather had improved, so they decided to set off with the Picard women and children balanced precariously on donkeys. They now rested every quarter of an hour, fueling resentment against the Picards as such frequent stops were thought to risk the safety of the group at large.

Brédif began to experience extreme fatigue in the early hours and felt so comatose that he nearly slept as he walked. Happy to hear the command "Halt," he collapsed onto the sand, dreading the moment that came after all too short a time when they were urged up and on their way. During one such interlude, Brédif fell into a particularly profound sleep and failed to hear the command to move on.

Consigned to captivity or certain death, he lay asleep, unobserved as his compatriots moved off. Only by chance was he spotted by a man at the back of the caravan, who returned to revive him.

On their strange, snaking journey, the frayed group reached the coast once again at dawn. The donkeys, after their labors in the shifting sands, became so excited to set their hooves on the firm wet shore that they galloped, out of control, into the surf, and the one Charlotte Picard was riding almost crushed her as it rolled over in the foam. In this spree, one of her young brothers was nearly carried off on the backwash, but she scrambled up in time to save him.

Shortly after this revivifying frolic, another uplifting event, the sighting of a sail, raised the spirits of every member of the shattered band. As she pulled closer, those on shore identified her as a French brig. The vessel had set about lowering her sails and had put a boat in the water. The brig was recognized as the *Argus,* last seen by these people an eternity of only three weeks earlier, in the Bay of Biscay, before the convoy had broken up so shortly after setting sail from France. A white handkerchief was hastily fastened to the bayonet end of a musket that a soldier stretched to wave on high. The ship acknowledged the signal, and Lieutenant Espiaux scribbled a message that was stuffed in a bottle and hung around the neck of one of the five Moorish guides who courageously rushed into the dangerous waves. About half an hour later, the Moors who had reached the longboat that was fighting unsuccessfully with the current reappeared floating three little barrels in front of them and carrying a reply stoppered in a bottle from Captain Parnajon to Lieutenant Espiaux. The *Argus,* having arrived safely and without incident in Senegal, had been dispatched to search the coast and to find the lost *Medusa.*[14]

The barrels appeared to the castaways like a gift from the heavens: wine, Dutch cheese, brandy, and biscuits. They set upon the cheese, which was beading with sweat in the vibrant late morning, and cupped the wine in little shells they found along the beach. Despite the tropical heat, the women, with the exception of Charlotte Picard, eagerly downed the brandy. Preferring liquid in quantity to a liquor capable of softening pain, Charlotte swapped her ration for more wine. There was great relief, a feeling that their luck had turned. Although the breakers prohibited the weary band from attempting to reach the *Argus,* at least they had been sighted. Their whereabouts were known, they had fed on familiar food, and help would surely soon be on its way. They signaled all the elation that their wasted bodies could muster and a new sense of hope rekindled a spark of purpose and possibility. People who, on the punishing sand and in the intolerable heat, had somehow found the energy to scrap with one another became, at a stroke, more tolerant. Smiles painfully broke the cracked lips of the children for the first time in days.

The appearance of the ship had also drawn the attention of a large group of Moors, who now approached the castaways, curious about these half naked, burned, and blistered remains of human beings who seemed, despite their state, so deliriously happy. Among the Moors were women keen to sell milk and butter, offering, at high prices, further sustenance to these deprived bodies who had fortunately escaped from the *Medusa* with a little cash. The cost of camel's milk was variously recorded by Charlotte Picard and Charles-Marie Brédif at three and ten francs a glass. Perhaps the women took pity on a young girl in tatters, judged Brédif to be better off, or simply sensed his irritated assumption that he was certain to be fleeced.[15]

Having provisioned the tattered band, the *Argus* sailed off on its mission to find the *Medusa*. As the march recommenced, the morning's unexpected bounty and delight gave way to the realities that stood between the castaways and their destination. Whenever the wind blew from the east, the horizon became like a white-hot furnace, and, as they marched along, the relentless sun burned their blistered skin. Brédif was filthy; his trousers, without braces, kept slipping and he was covered from head to toe with a thick coating of sand. His ragged clothes, a knife and fork—hardly useful here where the diet was purslane and rank water—a watch, and his small diary were all that he possessed in the world.[16] Commenting on the behavior of the sailors whom he found so unruly as to be of danger to the rest of the group, Brédif wrote that if he were a naval officer, he "would like to shoot more than ten of the scoundrels," for they were "real animals, beasts that should be driven with a cane or led with a rope. They are a thousand times unworthy of the kindness or the care of their officers whom they do not respect."[17]

The dawns evaporated into mornings, mornings burned into afternoons, which melted into dusk and darkness. The castaways were beginning to lose all track of time. Picard was showing signs of complete exhaustion and Charlotte and her mother-in-law stayed with him while the other members of the family went on with the donkeys. Resting beside him, watching their kin disappear, they gave in to fatigue and fell asleep. Waking up to find the sun gone down, Picard realized that, despite all their efforts since leaving the *Medusa,* despite the promising start to the day, his ultimate weakness in submitting to a fatigue that he had fought with such determination had finally brought them to their end. There could be no rescue for those who had been reckless enough to break ranks and fall behind. Disturbed by his agitation, the two ladies awoke, started to get up, but fell back in a faint, traumatized by the sight of several large, bearded Moors towering above them on camels. Their shock, however, was momentary as one of these fearsome men began to speak in a broguish and tolerable French:

"Madame, reassure yourself, beneath this Arab costume is an Irishman come here to help you."

He told the astonished Picards that the rest of the tattered band was waiting for them some five miles down the coast. His name was

Kearney and, as he lived among the peoples of the region and knew the lay of the land, had been dispatched to search for the castaways by Colonel Brereton, the English commander in Senegal. They were told that a camel, loaded with supplies, had already been sent north in the direction of Portendick to look for other groups that might be struggling down the coast.

Finding themselves in a landscape in which the dunes were lower, their surroundings greener, and where there was fresh water, the main body of the group planned to rest until the small hours. Under Kearney's guidance, the straggling Picards soon joined them.

The castaways began to sense that the end of their troubles was at hand. Not wishing to risk any threat from the wild animals they had heard on the previous evenings, they asked the soldiers to gather bracken and start a fire to keep danger at bay. Bloody-minded and wasted, the soldiers refused. Kearney gently calmed everybody's nerves by assuring them that experienced Arab guides would be on guard while they rested.[18]

Journeying through the second half of the night, by early morning on July 12 they had passed from Moorish territory into that of the peaceful black tribes who inhabited the region of the Senegal River. The donkeys suddenly started to act up again. Standing rooted to the ground they hee-hawed, bucked their riders into the spiky bushes, and ran off. The heat now grew so intense that the frazzled group was, once again, obliged to cross the dunes in search of shelter. Without a donkey and barefoot, Charlotte Picard likened the temperature of the sand to that of an oven at the moment when a baker opens it to withdraw his bread.

Their speech had become slurred and although they were exhausted, there were scraps, scuffles, all kinds of combustible moments between half-crazed people seared by the heat. Perhaps they imagined that if Chaumareys and Schmaltz could do it, others too might try to put one over on them. The blistering trek was drawing on their last reserves of strength but they pushed on, not, Charlotte Picard adds, "without cursing the person who was the first cause of our sufferings."

The worn out band was forced to stop and shelter from the savage heat under some acacia trees and wait while the tide, which blocked their progress down the coast, receded. The furnace-hot air refused to refresh them. Charlotte feared that, after overcoming so much hardship, she was at last going to surrender to death. A blacksmith named Borner handed her a little of the muddy water that he had conserved in a small barrel and she readily accepted it, taking great gulps of the nauseating solution. The ever attentive Captain Baignères, guessing at the repulsive aftertaste, offered Charlotte some crumbs of precious biscuit that he had conserved in his pocket. She chewed the mix of bread, dust, and tobacco but, unable to swallow it, gave it all mushed up to one of her famished younger brothers.

While Kearney went in search of supplies, black women arrived with water and some excellent cow's milk, for sale. All drank their fill but few had the energy to eat when Kearney rejoined them, not with the promised ox but with rice and dried fish. Despite the high heat of the afternoon, when the tide had receded they went down to the shore, where they found their obdurate donkeys and where they cooled themselves in the waves that streaked up onto the beach. When Charlotte and her sister, after bathing in the sea for a good half hour, went to rest in the shade, one of the Moorish guides who accompanied Kearney, thinking them asleep and fascinated by the braid and buttons on the uniform worn by the sister, crept up close in the hope of detaching one or two of these trappings. Realizing that the ladies were just resting, and that he had been detected and recognized, he seemed content merely to inspect at close quarters.

As they took up the march again, they sighted several groups of Moorish raiders, notorious slavers who operated along the frontier of the Senegal River. Poorly armed and completely exhausted, some of the soldiers brandished their swords in the air to make the marauders think that they were fighting fit and well equipped, gestures that successfully sent the tribesmen on their way.

The breeze picked up, covering the sky with clouds. Thunder roared and a storm threatened. Again the marchers decided to stumble over the dunes in search of shelter. The sighting of an English schooner detained them on the shore as three blacks were sent out in a canoe to meet the ship, which had indeed been dispatched by the English governor in Saint-Louis to search for castaways. Returning from the schooner, the canoe was overturned, and though the blacks made it back to dry land, the supplies did not. Happily, however, Kearney had by then returned with the promised ox, and the troop trudged behind the hills to set up camp in a little clump of gum trees beside several freshwater wells. The ox was slaughtered, skinned, divided, and grilled over a fire and these raw remnants of people, sand-blasted by endless swirls of grit, sat like ghouls in the flickering flames of the campfire, chomping on dripping morsels of meat.

Some stretched out and tried to sleep, only to be plagued by a new menace, mosquitoes. Charlotte Picard had fallen into a kind of delirium. She imagined her companions depicted on canvas as cannibals. She trembled at the distant roars of wild beasts and, only after much tossing and turning, fell asleep.

The group set off in the early hours in order to make Saint-Louis as soon as possible. About seven a.m., Charlotte found herself toward the back of the caravan when she saw several aggressive Moors approaching, armed with lances. A ship's apprentice of ten or twelve years old who walked a few paces away from her turned and, in a frightened voice, murmured, "My God, they've come to capture us."

Encircling them, one of the Moors reined in Charlotte's donkey and yelled into her face with violent gestures. The ship's apprentice had scampered off and Charlotte started to cry as the Moor showed no signs of relinquishing his grip. By his gesticulations she guessed that he was asking where she was headed and so she shouted, at the top of her weakened lungs, "Ndar!"—Saint-Louis—the only word of his language she knew. At this, the angry marauder dropped the bridle and rejoined his friends, who all burst out laughing. Charlotte, mercifully, was free to rejoin the castaways.

The Senegal River was now only about five miles away. They were moving through a greener, lusher terrain in which parrots and promerops perched in the sheltering trees. Hummingbirds buzzed in the morning air. Where they had seen only white-hot sand, sky, and sea, now a roof of green relieved their sore and dazzled eyes. The softness of the vegetation and signs of sympathetic life provoked the most intense relief and stinging tears tumbled down over their red-raw cheeks.

In the final descent to the river's edge, Charlotte's donkey stumbled, throwing her into a spiky bush, tearing at her already tortured skin. While Kearney, accompanied by two officers, went ahead to alert the authorities in Saint-Louis that one contingent of about eighty survivors had made it to their destination, the castaways rested in the shade and, despite the crocodiles, eased their weary limbs and festering wounds in the fresh water of the river.

In the early afternoon they watched as a little boat rowed furiously toward them against the strong current. When it arrived, two Europeans leaped ashore, greeted the group, and asked for Picard, saying that they were here on the orders of his old friends Artigue and Labouré. They had a large basket for his family, containing fresh bread, cheese, Madeira, and filtered water as well as dresses for the ladies and clothes for Picard. The delighted family eagerly shared these provisions with those who had shown them kindness during the march.

By four p.m. on July 13, after more than three days in their lifeboats and a five-day desert march, the troop climbed aboard the boats sent by the English governor and started to sail toward Saint-Louis. When they arrived at six p.m., it seemed that the entire colony, with the exception of Colonel Schmaltz and Captain Chaumareys, had turned out to greet the euphoric survivors.[19]

Under Oath

"Respect, above all, the rights of man; so that no one can say of us: 'The French have drunk the blood of their brothers, stuffed themselves with their flesh; the French were cannibals.'"

The group of fifty-seven people, the first to have been put ashore by Lieutenant Espiaux on July 6, found themselves stranded near Cap Mirick without supplies or water, listening to this admonitory declaration by their leader, Lieutenant Anglas de Praviel.

From the little hillock that Adjutant Petit climbed in order to take stock of their situation, he saw only an endless sweep of dunes, hypnotic like the sea, void of landmarks and dwellings, and offering no respite from the inhospitable and baking desert. Not only forbidding, it was fickle. When the desert wind whipped up, the battering, suffocating sand would dry up springs, efface paths, and change every contour so that what was there one day might disappear the next. Even the short, hot slog up to the vantage point made clear to the adjutant that any attempt to walk on this shifting terrain would plunge one's feet deep into the burning ground. Fortunately, the safest route south to their destination was along the coast where the sand was firm. It may not be the shortest way to reach Saint-Louis, but it certainly seemed to be the best.[20]

In a heat that made Praviel's head feel as if it were full of bubbling boiling liquid, they proceeded with greater military organization than was possible with Espiaux's assorted band. They posted four armed men under a sergent-major as an advance guard, four armed men under a corporal in the rear, two corporals on their left flank, and used the sea to protect them on their right.

By the evening of July 6, without having eaten or drunk anything all day, and having slogged over the Mottes d'Angel, the high hills to the south of Cap Mirick, they found some deserted cabins, which, from the heads and feet of locusts scattered on the floor, they took to have been recently occupied by Moors. Sheltering from the wind that had been swirling up the sand and making the going tough, they rested there until, in the coolest part of the night, they set off again, hoping to find edible roots or plants and some sign of water. Unsuccessful, they fell back on seawater as a last resort, but were checked by sudden outbreaks of vomiting and diarrhea, reactions that doubtlessly saved some lives. Although seawater temporarily slakes the thirst, great quantities have a dehydrating effect: the kidneys are unable to cope with such large amounts of salt, and delirium and death follow in a matter of hours. As a safer alternative, several members of the troop chose to drink their own urine, but this, naturally enough, was hardly plentiful. In any case, those who tried it were revolted and soon gave up.

By July 8, hollowed by hunger, their skin cracked, their lips chapped, their tongues black and pasted to the roofs of their mouths, the castaways were more than half wishing to be rounded up and taken as slaves by the Moors; at least then they would be given water.[21] On the following day, July 9, their fourth day of deprivation, a corporal's wife fell exhausted onto the sand and died. The only witness to the fatality was her husband, who had stayed behind with her when she had collapsed; several people suspected him of having run her through with his saber to put her out of her misery. Alarmed by the woman's death—most probably caused by the murderous climate and lack of water—fear spread among the exhausted troop as they staggered to a saltwater pond, where they spent the first part of that night. At about three a.m., when it would have been wise for them to move off, half the group was unable to summon the requisite strength. Praviel, paralyzed with exhaustion, beseeched a sailor to shoot him through the head, but his entreaty was flatly refused.

Portendick was where Espiaux had put ashore and was, for Anglas de Praviel and his troop, more than a third of the distance between Cap Mirick and Saint-Louis. The trading post had been in the possession of the English since 1808, so both groups of castaways hoped to find some sympathetic signs of European life. Instead they found the settlement, or what was left of it, deserted. The sight of the sand-covered remains of the longboat, the pinnace, and the Senegal boat with scattered traces of clothing or abandoned objects close by led Praviel and his frightened group to suspect the worst—that their comrades had been taken into captivity by hostile tribesmen.

During the next day, these wasted men looked on as one of their number started to dig into the sand. Thinking he was searching for water, they gathered around, only to watch him climb into the hole that he had hollowed out for his own grave. Glancing from person to person, he implored his comrades to take his life. Refusing his desperate, half-crazed pleas, they began to move on. Hanging back, one sailor, who had previously lent the man a jacket, climbed down into the grave and, believing the man to be dead, started to ransack his corpse, looking for anything of value. The victim, still alive, started to cry out in terror, summoning another straggler to his aid.

Their senses numbed, their tongues unable to articulate, and their minds increasingly succumbing to distraught fantasies, they struggled desperately to respect the oath they had taken as five or six of their number died, providing them with a possible source of sustenance. Now desperate for fluids, several men blocked the circulation in the end of a finger, pricked the skin, and sucked the oozing blood. Even the liquid from their numerous blisters offered some relief.

In the coolest part of the night, Adjutant Petit took three soldiers to explore some huts. Perhaps taken for raiders, or simply tired fools drawn into an obvious trap, they were surprised by a band of thirty Moors brandishing swords. Eventually encircling the entire troop, these Moors grabbed the shirts and uniforms hanging in tatters from the backs of the castaways. Then they led them off to a stagnant, moss-covered pool from which the troop gulped great quantities of stinking water, only to vomit seconds later. Conducted to the Moors camp, women and children, delighted in taunting the weary band while the two officers, Praviel and Petit, were summoned to meet with the chief who, in broken English, put several questions.

"What country?"

"France."

"Where from?"

"France.

"Here how?"

"A storm wrecked our ship."

"Where?"

"A day's journey would take you there."

"What carry?"[22]

Praviel tried to communicate the purpose of their voyage and expressed their urgent desire to reach Saint-Louis as soon as possible, offering the chief rewards of tobacco, guns, and powder if he would guide them. Pleased by the proposition, the Moor ordered a small portion of dried fish to be distributed, the first real food the castaways had eaten in six days. He then arranged for goatskins to be filled with water, and prepared everybody for immediate departure. They marched all day on the eleventh until, in the late evening, they arrived at some huts inhabited by Moors belonging to the same tribe as their guides and were subjected to the same cruel and insulting behavior that had greeted them in the middle of the previous night. Exhausted, they were allowed to rest for only two hours before resuming their march.

They had not traveled far when out of nowhere sprang a large band of bellowing Moors. They pulled up a little distance from the troop and told the castaways, in English, not to be afraid, that their argument was with the Moors who were guiding them. The bigger, better-armed troop that had charged as if in attack clearly fancied themselves the rightful proprietors of the unfortunates and wanted to take the troop as their prize, perhaps to guide them, perhaps to enslave them, perhaps to trade them. The dispute swung in the favor of the new arrivals who, before dispatching the outnumbered guides, cut off the vanquished chief's beard as a sign of contempt.

"You belong to me," declared the imperious Hammet, leader of the new band. The castaways were rounded up and led to a camp where they were left for two days. The Moorish women, every bit as cruel as those in the first camps, exacerbated the sufferings of the Europeans, taunting them sadistically and flinging fistfuls of sand at their running sores. As they slept, the blisters covering their sunburnt bodies rubbed against the ground and burst. To clean their wounds, they went down to the sea's edge and attempted, against fierce, stinging pain, to wash them in saltwater.

On the fourth day of their captivity, they sighted the *Argus* tacking offshore, but as the castaways frantically signaled to the brig, it distanced itself, obviously mistaking them for Moors. During the next two days, they found no water but their captors gave them milk mixed with camel's urine. This common source of nourishment for the nomadic desert tribes who spend up to a week without solid food was, at least, preferable to the putrid water they had been obliged to drink.[23]

On their sixth day with the Moors, they encountered the camel loaded with supplies that had been sent in the direction of Portendick by the Irishman Kearney. They were considerably sustained by these supplies and, three days later, the swarthy figure of Kearney himself, in magnificent Arab robes and mounted on a large camel, came into view, carrying a letter.

> My dear Anglas, the person who brings you this letter is an English officer whose large and generous soul exposes him to all the dangers and inconveniences of a trip towards the place where you disembarked. . . . He knows the country, its language and customs perfectly . . . follow his advice

carefully . . . The rest of us aboard the longboat and those from the other boats arrived here yesterday; we found a most generous welcome. Our ills are already eased, and we wait for the complete happiness that our reunion with you and those with you will bring. . . . Your friend, Espiaux.

Kearney distributed portions of rice, which some impatient sailors, to their subsequent discomfort, ate raw. Despite their terrible indigestion, the lesson appeared lost on them as they proceeded to devour the tough, raw meat of a bullock they had killed, suffering immediate diarrhea and vomiting. The less desperate or impetuous cooked their ox, following the Moorish example of making a hollow in the ground and starting a fire. The skinned and gutted animal was thrown into this heated pit and covered with sand over which another fire was lit.

Still about sixty miles from Saint-Louis, the castaways sighted the *Argus* once more and Kearney fired several shots to attract its attention. This time, the brig put out a boat, but the breakers proved too strong for it to reach the shore. Risking their necks, Hammet, his brother, and the Irishman plunged into the waves, managing to scramble aboard the boat. They rowed out to the ship and braved the pounding waves to return with biscuits and bottles of brandy. Though food and water was no longer a problem, conditions remained grim. Shoes that had been toughened in the intense heat cracked and disintegrated into the burning sand so that fired, blistered feet were further scorched and torn. The blinding reflection of the sun off the desert provoked pounding headaches and seared eyes. Mouths were parched white as frost. Tongues cleaved to hard palates as the baked air resisted their attempts to breathe. Yet after a further march, when the palm trees of Saint-Louis at last came into view, the troop became delirious.

It was seven p.m. on July 22, sixteen days after the castaways had been put ashore in the desert, when Praviel arrived in the tiny village of Guet N'Dar on the banks of the Senegal. A hideous sight in the underpants given to him by Kearney, his legs swollen from sunburn and insect bites, his body scarred and emaciated, his skin broiled, he looked like someone about to be ferried over the Styx as he climbed into a canoe to cross the river to Saint-Louis.[24]

5

The Raft

At eleven a.m. on July 5, as the boats pulled away from the half-submerged raft, there were 147 people on board. Among the officers and leaders who huddled self-protectively in the center were the surgeon Henri Savigny, the geographical engineer Alexandre Corréard, and Jean Griffon du Bellay, secretary to Governor Schmaltz. The most senior naval man on board, midshipman Coudein, lay with his wounded left leg perched on a barrel in an attempt to keep it as much out of the saltwater as possible. Even though precious flour had been jettisoned to lessen the weight of the makeshift platform, many people clinging to the structure were submerged to their waists, and everybody was swamped by the repeated batterings from waves and spray. As the boats disappeared into the distance, the belief that they had been heartlessly sacrificed, coldbloodedly abandoned, numbed every soul on board. Slowly, dismay gave way to anger, fueling threats of vengeance hurled into the void.

Unable to obtain the governor's permission to assign his twelve workmen places alongside him in a boat, Corréard realized that duty compelled him to stay with his men and so he had joined them on the raft. Looking out on the desolate expanse of ocean, this young man who had behaved honorably reflected on the cutting of the ropes attaching the makeshift structure to the towing boats. That arm, hacking like an executioner, performed an act of the most extreme cowardice. If that was the kind of leadership that the Bourbon restoration gave the French then it was clearly in the interests of France and, indeed, of humanity itself to overthrow this regime. Looking out at the friendless sea and lowering sky, Corréard determined to stay alive in order to record and accuse. In a perfectly human way, he may have regretted his decision to take a place on this impossible platform, and perhaps he now questioned his decision to flee to Senegal instead of staying at home where an important political struggle was simmering.

The leaders immediately set about searching for the compass, charts, and anchor that Lieutenant Reynaud had promised were on board. None was found. The lack of a compass was a particularly serious want, but Corréard remembered seeing one in the hands of the workshop foreman who was on board. Happily, the man did have one but, as he handed over the tiny instrument to Coudein, it slipped, fell between the wooden supports, and was lost in the sea.

The 146 men and one woman crammed onto the raft could hardly have been a more diverse group. The navy had indeed been favored in the evacuation of the frigate as there were only about twenty sailors on board. Otherwise there was a butcher, a baker from Rochefort, an armorer, an artillery sergeant and captain, a master cannoneer, a barrel maker, a helmsman, domestics of the staff officers on the *Medusa,* members of the Philanthropic Society, and, among the soldiers from the Africa Battalion, men from Italy, Arabia, Guadeloupe, San Domingo, India, Asia, America, Poland, and Ireland—an explosive grab bag of mercenaries, captives, and ex-convicts, all furious with the French leadership.

Midshipman Coudein's father, the captain of a man-of-war who had witnessed Napoleon's capitulation to the Bellerophon, had recently been retired to make way for men like Chaumareys. Coudein's scorn for the captain of the *Medusa* was clearly shared by most of the leaders on the raft but was at odds with the secretary to the governor, Griffon du Bellay, who displayed a surprising loyalty to the commanders of the expedition. One of the first to crack, Bellay threw himself overboard during the first day. Saved by Savigny, he attempted suicide again but found it impossible to release his frightened grip on the raft.

Several days before their departure from France, Coudein had suffered a severe bruising to his left leg that had not healed and the effect of seawater washing over the painful abrasion almost made him faint with pain. His condition made him unable to move and the "strong and courageous" Savigny took the initiative, becoming the de facto leader. Born in the bloody year of 1793, Jean-Baptiste-Henri Savigny passed his medical exams in Rochefort at nineteen and went to sea for the first time in October 1812. For the following three and a half years he served on four different ships before being assigned to the *Medusa* as a surgeon, second class. When he sailed for Senegal, his sweetheart in La Rochelle had given him a belt ribbon as a love token and talisman. This he intertwined with republican colors, thus declaring his political sympathy with the likes of Alexandre Corréard.

As a gentle breeze was blowing, Savigny supervised the erection of a small mast and sail. While this enabled the raft to move, without a compass to guide them and a rudder to steer them they remained at the mercy of the winds and currents. The fact that this mast was erected under the supervision of a surgeon while there were engineers and carpenters on board suggests the degree to which Savigny had taken charge. He proposed their first meal of sodden biscuit, made somewhat palatable by a soaking in a little wine. Having distributed and consumed this uninviting mixture, the biscuits were gone and the raft was left without food. The human body can survive for up to fifty days without solids so this was not, in itself, alarming, but in the sweltering heat it would be necessary to satisfy the need for liquid and the remaining water and wine would not last long, shared among the 147 people on board. All through the rest of that first day, this combustible bunch fed off their need for revenge. Having someone to blame, someone to attack, made them eager for survival and provoked lively exchanges about how best to achieve it.[1]

As night fell the wind freshened, the sea rose, and clouds and darkness obscured the horizon. Savigny, along with some other resolute individuals, began lashing ropes to the raft with which people might attach themselves for extra safety. As the sea smashed over the platform, everyone struggled to secure themselves. They were bucked back and forth by the agitated ocean and bodies fastened to the ropes were flung overboard and buffeted, banging back against the raft. Through the pitch black, broken only by the whitecapped waves, the desperate leaders thought they glimpsed a distant light. They signaled by igniting some gunpowder and firing shots from a pistol they had hung up, out of harm's way, near the top of the mast. There was no response, and as the light disappeared they were left to conclude that it could only have been some distant breaker catching a streak of moonlight as it pierced the rumbling cloud.[2]

The first sight that breaking day afforded was that of squealing people who had been trapped and mangled between the masts and spars that had been laid and lashed together to form the deck of the raft. The saltwater that swamped the deck at each scoop and pitch of the craft drenched their lacerations, causing them excruciating pain. Slowly, their shrieks and moans diminished as they lost consciousness and died of their wounds or slipped off the platform and perished in the sea. The deck was still too crowded to permit a clear view of what had happened and so, before the next distribution of drink, a roll call was taken. Although the number was approximate, for in such a throng anyone could easily call out twice in order to secure a double portion, the total revealed that about a dozen people had already been lost.

With day's calm came the heat and a thirst hardly alleviated by the meager ration. A baker and two apprentices could bear the situation no longer and committed suicide by hurling themselves into the sea. A tightly packed mass on a vulnerable structure under a suffocating expanse of sky sparked flash points of panic, charging the heavy atmosphere till it became as electric as the breaking of a tropical storm. By nightfall, people began to hallucinate and bawl out as fear overpowered them. The wind whipped the sea into a frenzy more furious than that of the night before and again people clutched at the raft while struggling to protect their limbs from being crushed between the heaving spars of its deck. Mountainous waves arced above the platform in a manner that reminded Corréard of his native town of Serres, overhung on its steep mountainside by a threatening arc of rock. In the misadventure of his attempt to flee from a country overwhelmed by calamitous circumstances, that giant wave of rock, now so far away, might never be seen again.

The raft was now running before the wind, easing the force and frequency of the waves drenching those on board. This meant, however, that the vulnerable stern was taking the full force of the gale, sending men surging forward. As the prow was likewise fragile, the overcrowding in the middle of the raft resulted in the crushing or trampling to death of several people in the stampede from port to starboard as the mass attempted to counterbalance the lateral pitch of the craft. When the sea calmed, a group of terrified soldiers, thinking their end was upon them, decided to drown their last moments in drink. They broke open the wine cask lashed near the center of the raft and gorged themselves on a liquid swiftly mixing with the saltwater that sloshed in through the hole they had gouged. Soon oblivious to the increasing undesirability of the mix, these famished men became easily intoxicated. Already crazed by the onslaughts of the angry sea, they became hell-bent on slaughtering everybody and smashing the raft in an orgy of destruction.

An enormous Asian made for the edge and began to hack at the cords holding the raft together. Raising his hatchet and swiping viciously at an officer who made haste to stop him, he was run through with a saber and pushed into the sea. Immediately, the drunken band elbowed toward the leaders who had placed themselves, in relative security, around the base of the mast. A soldier lifted his saber to attack an officer but was cut down with repeated blows. Such a firm response repulsed the attack and the rioters, still wildly swinging their swords and bayonets, regrouped in the stern where one of them, pretending to rest, slyly set about cutting the fastenings of the raft in order to sink the structure and kill everybody on board. A leader, getting wind of what was going on, rushed at him. Another soldier pulled his knife to intervene and slashed at the officer's coat in his attempt to cut him down. The leader swirled round, grabbing both men, and hurled them into the sea. This clash triggered a riot in which the drunken soldiers started to chop the shrouds and stays, toppling the mast across the thigh of Captain Dupont, of the Africa Battalion, who tumbled, senseless, to the deck. The drunks fell on him and heaved him into the sea from which he was rescued by the other leaders who then laid him across a barrel. From that perch he was dragged by the rioters, who, according to Savigny and Corréard, were intent on settling some score by gouging out his eyes. Such relentless and murderous frenzy forced the leaders to counterattack, slashing or clubbing the drunken mob into submission.

Corréard had slumped in a kind of trance when the noise of this brawl roused him and he assembled with his workmen in the bow. Far from protected in their rear, they were attacked by both the mob on board and by those who, having fallen off into the sea, tried to scramble onto the raft again. A traitor among Corréard's workforce, a carpenter named Dominque, had sided with the mutineers. Nevertheless, finding that this renegade had been thrown into the waves, Corréard plunged in to save him. When they were back on board, the traitor's wounds were treated, after which he once again sided with the rebels, a choice that cost him his life.

Seeing the only woman on the raft thrown overboard with her husband, Corréard and the foreman, Touche-Lavillette, roped themselves together and plunged into the sea to save them. Back on deck, husband and wife collapsed into each other's arms as, once again, the tanked-up mutineers attacked and the leaders counterattacked till the raft was strewn with dead and bludgeoned bodies.

Corréard heard the woman he had saved calling out to Our Lady of Laux. Like the mountainous waves that peaked above them, this invocation took him back to his native region where a church dedicated to Our Lady of Laux was a place of pilgrimage where the lame and paralyzed sought miraculous cures. He was particularly pleased to have saved a woman from his part of the country, which, it transpired, she had left twenty-four years before. A sutler, she had since traveled with the Grand Army through many campaigns and battles.

After a short period of relative calm during which many of the soldiers fell on their knees and asked to be pardoned, a furious band of drunkards, brandishing knives and sabers, attacked the raft's leaders. Rioters without weapons went at their victims with their teeth and several people were savagely bitten, among them Savigny, who was also hit by a sword in his right arm, depriving him of the use of two fingers for a time. One of Corréard's workmen was seized by a frenzied soldier who chomped at his Achilles tendon while three others slashed at him with their knives and smashed him with the butt of a rifle. Lavillette saved the man from certain death. Other leaders rescued Lieutenant Lozach, whose assailants in their stupor had mistaken for Lieutenant Anglas de Praviel, an officer, they claimed, who had been harsh with them prior to the departure of the expedition and whom they had become obsessed with killing. Throughout the conflict, amid the dark tangle of wet, bloodied bodies, Coudein remained incapacitated on his barrel, protectively nursing a young sailor only twelve years old. Suddenly, the midshipman was seized and flung, along with the barrel and the boy, into the waves. Despite his wounded leg and the heavy swell, Coudein struggled to save them both, dragging himself and the boy back onto the raft.

The riot quelled; Savigny fell into a profound torpor. He was hardly aware of his saber wounds but his ratcheting stomach pains were insupportable, his vision was blurred, his legs would hardly support him, and he was dimly aware that he was finding it difficult to think. He heard people around him crying desperately for a leg of chicken or some bread. Some, thinking themselves still aboard the *Medusa,* asked to be allowed to sleep in their hammocks. Several cried out to imaginary boats to save them. Some assumed they were moored in pretty harbors with well-provisioned towns embracing them. Corréard was rambling on the Italian hills when Griffon du Bellay interrupted his reverie.

"I remember, we were abandoned by the boats, but don't worry, I'm writing to the governor and within a few hours we'll be saved."

To which the drifting Corréard replied, "Have you a pigeon to carry your request swiftly?"

Horror, half dreams, and hallucinations were merging the real with the imaginary so that existence on the raft became an impossible kaleidoscope of fact and fiction. In the grip of such delirium the day had no need to accept what the night sanctioned.[3]

The naturalist Gaulthier had led an expedition to explore the Senegal River in 1795. Moored in the delta in the terrible heat, the men on board his ship succumbed to a kind of delirium, threw themselves overboard, and perished. Although some contemporary doctors thought that this behavior, accompanying a condition known as calenture, was caused by sunstroke, others, pointing out its appearance at night, argued that such derangement was the result of the continual buildup of hot air trapped inside the hull of a ship. Oppressed by the excessive temperatures of the stifled spaces between decks, sailors in the tropics became dangerously overheated, hallucinated fantastic objects on the surface of the water, and fell victim to fever and frenzied delirium in the hours of darkness. They awoke babbling, with flashing eyes and menacing gestures; fantasizing the fields and forests of homes a world away, they would throw themselves overboard into the sea. Although there were no confined spaces on the raft, there was certainly congestion. During windless afternoons when the platform lay baking in the searing July sun, the air became sufficiently incandescent to provoke tropical fever.[4]

As dawn broke on the third day, those left alive were jolted by the scene of utter desolation. The raft was a butcher's block. Strewn out, heaped up, sixty people had somehow been murdered or killed or had committed suicide during the night's fighting. The remaining two barrels of water and two barrels of wine had been slung into the waves, leaving only one last cask of wine on board. Into another day of drifting, the survivors were in a wretched state, their clothes slashed and ripped and their bodies smeared with the blood of battle and blistered red by the sun. Summoning up unguessed-at resources of determination, the leaders repaired and reerected their mast, trying to position the sail so that onshore breezes would, despite the contrary currents, speed them to the coast. But they made little headway and merely zigzagged across the longitude on which they had been wrecked, steadily, but not swiftly, moving south.

A small ration of wine was distributed over the carnage of the second night's battle. Hunger was champing at them so, using sharp or pointed decorations from their uniforms, they made hooks with which to fish. They even bent bayonets to make hooks large enough to catch sharks but, despite the attractive trail of blood pooling from the raft, they were unable to hook one. Indeed, the entire venture failed as the current swirled the improvised fishing lines beneath the raft where they snagged.

Without a successful catch, and with no food left on board, the men became desperate. Some took to eating the leather harnesses and scabbards of their sabers or their ammunition pouches. Others ate fabric or portions of their hats that were covered with grease or scum. In other shipwrecks, or in similar situations of deprivation, such resources had often been consumed. The crew of the *Fattysalam* had, in 1761, eaten the buttons or leather from belts and cartridge cases. Captain Bligh and the few faithful from the *Bounty* had resorted to raw seabirds. On board the raft, one sailor, pining for food, steeled himself to eat excrement but, lifting it to his mouth, found he was unable to persist.

Those still just about alive studied the heaps of dead human bodies strewn across the deck. There was a resource, a heap of nutriment lying at their feet, carcasses of meat that certain writers had likened to veal or pork. One such authority had asked what difference it made to a "lump of clay, whether it be devoured by worms, by animals, or by its fellow creatures." Taking the precaution of counseling his readers against the dangers of developing a taste for human meat, which had once happened after a famine in India, the German explorer von Langsdorff asserted that when survival was at stake, such as in famines, sieges, and shipwrecks, the gravity of the situation sanctioned the breaking of any taboo. In the Old Testament, the Israelites under siege were told that they would eat the fruit of their own bodies, "the flesh of thy sons and daughters." Von Langsdorff reminds his readers that in the Third Book of Herodotus, when the Persian army under King Cambyses was crossing the desert to Ethiopia and they ran out of food, the king ordered the killing of every tenth man in order to feed the rest. While such extermination was the act of a ruler who held human life cheap, there had been sufficient examples of expedient cannibalism for it to become, for shipwrecked men, a custom of the sea. In 1710, when the ship's carpenter of the wrecked *Nottingham Galley* died and "his Skin, Head, Hands, Feet and Bowels" had been buried in the sea, his body was quartered and eaten. In 1727, a similar fate awaited those who perished on board the stricken *Luxborough Galley*. On some occasions, the desperation of starving men had even driven them to murder. In 1759, the crew of the *Dolphin* had cast lots and an unlucky passenger was shot through the brain. Decapitated, his head was flung overboard, while the rest of his body kept the crew alive.

In 1766, after the wreck of the *Tiger,* a slave was killed and smoked. When the American sloop *Peggy* was stricken in a storm during her return from the Azores and supplies dwindled, two pigeons and the ship's cat were killed, cooked, and served. The captain received the cat's head and "devoured it with greater relish than he had ever enjoyed from tasting food." In the days that followed, the survivors consumed candles and oil, tobacco and leather, until those supplies ran out. In a complete reversal of European suppositions about cannibalism being a habit of the African tribes, the sailors pulled a black man from steerage, shot him through the head, and began to cut him up. They were about to fry up his bowels for supper when "one of the foremast men . . . was so ravenously impatient that, tearing the Negro's liver from the body, he devoured it raw." Having pickled all but the head and fingers, the rest of the body kept these men alive for the following nine days, at which time lots were drawn for a fresh execution. The unlucky straw fell to one David Flat, who remained brave and chose the same executioner who had killed the black man. Mercifully, rescue arrived before he was shot.

Although in their narrative Savigny and Corréard approach the moment with great dollops of remorse, at sea, in times of extreme peril, cannibalism appears to have been considered a legitimate and accepted means of survival. Thus on the third day of drifting helplessly, some of those left alive on board the raft set upon the dead bodies strewn about and started hacking off limbs and eagerly chomping on raw human flesh. They incised and pulled away the skin from a shoulder or stomach or thigh and ate off the body, slicing or scooping out the brownish purple flesh.

During the third night the sea was calmer and it was possible for the survivors to get some fitful rest. The water washing over the raft swelled up to their knees and it was necessary to doze standing up, crushed against one another for protection. When dawn broke on the fourth day, they found ten or twelve more dead bodies scattered about the raft. It was an unsettling awakening for the survivors, who realized that they too must soon meet the same fate. Slowly, they consigned the bodies to the deep, saving only one, who, as Savigny and Corréard put it, would "nourish those who, only a short while before, had clasped his hands in friendship."[5]

Pangs of hunger plagued those who had not yet succumbed to the ready supply of human flesh and, toward evening on the fourth day, when a shoal of tiny flying fish landed on the raft, those with sufficient energy trapped a huge quantity, which they gutted and placed in an empty barrel. Somewhat bucked by their sudden good fortune, they managed to rig up a makeshift oven and cook the catch, which they immediately devoured. The fish were tiny and ultimately unsatisfying, so some took advantage of the fire to grill human flesh, rendering it less odious. It was at this point on the fourth day that Savigny and Corréard and the other leaders first tasted one of their late companions. From then on, they were forced to continue their cannibal diet but it was never again possible to cook the flesh because there was nothing left on board the raft with which to start a fire. Instead, they decided to cut the flesh into slices and hang them up on the stays to dry, making its eventual consumption a less nauseating prospect.

Satisfied by their meal and exhausted, everyone attempted to fall asleep, gingerly trying not to rub or pummel their ulcerated wounds. Hardly had their immense fatigue overcome their chafing pain than another riot broke out. According to Savigny and Corréard, some Spanish, black, and Italian soldiers attacked the leaders in an attempt to finish them off, rabid for Lieutenant Anglas de Praviel, whom they could not believe was not on board. They started to scale the mast, intent on capturing some money that had been hung on high to keep it safe for when the raft was washed ashore. Again there was butchery. Again the battle-worn sutler was flung overboard and again she was recovered. At last, the troublemakers were overthrown, stabbed to death, and discarded, leaving, out of the original 147 souls that had been crushed aboard the raft, a group of only thirty survivors.

There was a belief that frequent submersion could rehydrate the body by virtue of the absorbent nature of the skin; the efficacy of wearing clothes drenched in seawater, an idea handed down from James Lind, the man wrongly credited with finding the cure for scurvy, was widely upheld. The problem on the raft, however, was that too frequent submergence combined with the drying vigor of the tropical sun created serious problems. Frequent dousing in seawater refreshed the body to a certain extent, but it also removed the grease from the skin and, as the seawater evaporated, salt crystals acted as irritants, provoking boils, excoriations, and ulcers. Their bodies, covered with pustules, became so sore that each movement proved agonizing and, by the fifth day, the seawater had scoured the sun-blistered skin from the feet and legs of those left alive.[6]

The survivors, in their increasingly deplorable state, calculated that they had enough wine left for four days, after which, without liquid and at the end of their tether, death would swiftly follow. Such calculations were made futile when, on their seventh shadowless day afloat, two soldiers snuck behind the remaining wine cask, drilled a hole, and started drinking. This crime was judged, by common consent, to be capital and the sentence was executed at once.

The twelve-year-old cabin boy Léon, whom Coudein had already rescued from death by drowning, perished in the midshipman's arms. This left only twenty-seven souls alive, fifteen of whom, from all appearances, were likely to be lost in the following hours.

Gravely wounded or critically ill, those left alive had lost their sense of time and much of their reason. A council of the inner circle of leaders was held at which they discussed the state of their supplies and at which they considered putting those closest to death on half rations. With a sinister logic, they perceived that this would condemn the weakest to a slow but certain end and, at the same time, still consume the raft's dwindling resources. Working under such a rationale, they agreed on a tougher and more desperate solution. Amid intense despair at the horror of what they agreed to do, they decided to throw the weakest overboard and thus secure, for those remaining, at least six more days of precious wine. Certain that they would all perish unless such hardhearted measures were adopted, their instincts for self-preservation made them resolve to eliminate those too weak to resist. But who among them was willing to be the callous executioner? Who would be able to carry out such an inhuman act? Savigny and Corréard record that three sailors and a soldier "took upon themselves this cruel killing." There was no command recorded, no drawing of lots. Perhaps there was a question of rank, but by that stage, after the innumerable sufferings, the violence, the degradations and indignities that had so deformed their sensibilities, any one of those who remained might have been capable of such an act.

Among the victims was the lone woman, whose thigh had been broken between the masts and spars of the raft's deck. Also murdered was her husband, who had been severely wounded in the head. Using the pathos of this sutler's story, Savigny and Corréard, aware that they were recording a new depth of abasement, interjected an appeal into their narrative, "Readers, who shudder at the cry of outraged humanity, recollect, at least, that it was other men, fellow countrymen and comrades, who had placed us in this abominable situation."[7]

The fifteen survivors of this cull next agreed to throw their sidearms into the sea so as to avoid the crazed quarrels likely to erupt between such crippled spirits. They kept one saber and a few tools, and were soon diverted by an unexpected visitor. A familiar sight in a meadow on a summer's day in France, a common white butterfly flittered above this shambles before settling on the mast. It signaled the proximity of land and the overjoyed but broken men scrambled to scour the horizon. Then more butterflies arrived, sending the men's spirits soaring and fluttering with hope. Soon afterward, a gull was sighted, as if to confirm that land must be close; and so they prayed for a new storm that would carry them in and dash them onto the nearby shore. When other gulls arrived the famished men attempted to snare one, without success. Such gentle evidence of a world beyond the bloodstained frontiers of their raft brought them up sharp. But despite their self-disgust, they were so cheered by these sightings that they set about constructing a new raised platform near the mast. On this they would make a shelter.

Their efforts considerably improved their living conditions and alleviated some pain. Hunger had diminished since the first few days though their heads still ached from the dazzle of the sun and their thirst was brutal, their tongues were swollen, their lips cracked. Some wet their mouths with urine cooled in small tin containers. Griffon du Bellay downed ten or twelve cupfuls in succession but another man found he could not touch the stuff. It was a widespread but mistaken belief that urine is poisonous and that its consumption could do permanent damage. In fact, with its high proportion of water, it is a valuable source of ingestible liquid. Those left on the raft, heartened by the promise of nearing land, diverted themselves with comparative tastings. Savigny observed that certain people produced decidedly tasty urine, whereas the output of others was bitter and unpalatable.[8]

When a lemon was miraculously found along with a few cloves of garlic, the disputes over rights of apportionment became savage and almost ended in further killing. Two vials of teeth-cleaning liquid were also found and drops containing cinnamon and cloves eased parched tongues and slaked chronic thirst if only for a few seconds. Some tried putting pewter in their mouths, which gave a sensation of coolness and kept the saliva moving. Sipping their meager wine ration through a quill had a more restorative effect than drinking it outright, which only intoxicated these broken men and made them feisty.

By the tenth day, when it seemed that the slightest upset might make any one among them snap and a general testiness was building toward a full-scale brawl, several sharks, each about thirty feet long and perhaps only somewhat sated by the bodies thrown from the raft, surrounded the platform. Watching the sleek backs moving in so close, the men half wished the sharks would do their worst and finish them off. Some even defied them by lying on the submerged part of the raft in a painful attempt to refresh themselves. But though the sharks, surprisingly, did not attack, these men were stung all over by medusae or Portuguese men-of-war, giant jellyfish whose stinging filaments can reach up to fifty feet long. The agony of their sting lasted only a few hours but induced vomiting, fever, and fearful stomach cramps.

By July 16, their eleventh day on board the raft, the survivors knew themselves to be close to death. Branded by the white-hot heat, skin blistered into huge ulcers, these wild-eyed, bearded specters nonetheless summoned up their last reserves of strength to build a smaller raft out of the slats and supports from the edges of their platform. Oars were made from barrel staves and the plan was that eight of them would try to row for shore. A sailor went aboard to test the structure, which sank immediately, and so they resigned themselves to their raft and to inevitable death. Prostrated by the heat, chafed and inflamed by the salt water, blinded by the screaming light, emaciated, hallucinating, and wasted, they passed the night of July 16 in a state self-recrimination and terror. They mumbled, in their delirium, about the sad state of France. Lavillette observed that, in the good old days, he had been afraid only in the heat of battle, whereas now he was surrounded by Frenchmen who threatened him all the time. Others craved the chance to take on the Bourbon enemies of liberty. Still others longed for a death that would deliver them from the oppressions of the new regime. Savigny suggested that, with one of the tools left on board, they carve their names and some indication of their misadventure on a piece of wood and fix it to the mast, in the hope that after their deaths it would be found and the contents communicated to their families and friends at home.[9]

In the early morning of July 17, while they were consuming their small ration of wine, a sail was sighted. Thrilled out of their delirium, the men struggled to attract its attention. It was so distant that they could make out only the tops of the masts of what they slowly recognized to be a brig. They fastened different-colored handkerchiefs to some straightened hoops from a cask and a man was helped up onto the mast to signal. For half an hour their stomachs were tight with an agony of expectation. Some imagined the ship was moving closer, others that it was sailing away until, at last, it did indeed disappear from sight. Their excitement collapsed into a most fathomless despair. It had been, like the fastening of the towropes to the raft all that hell ago, a false hope, and now there was nothing left but to resign themselves to death.

Two hours later the master gunner, wanting to go forward to take some air, poked his head out of their shelter. Flying French colors and sailing straight toward them was the *Argus*. Tears erupted and rolled down burned and blistered cheeks. Dessicated bodies throbbed with unbelieving exultation. The brig hove to and put out a boat to investigate. For those on the raft, the sight of a well-kempt and kitted crew clustered on the bulwarks, waving their hats and handkerchiefs, was like the most fantastic mirage. When the boat lay to beside the raft, the officer, zealous and tender, lifted the most badly burnt and ulcerated of the survivors on board, placing Alexandre Corréard, who was in the most urgent need, beside him. As they were gently carried aboard the *Argus,* these skeletal figures presented a most pitiable and frightening sight. Hardly able to move, their eyes were sunken, their beards had matted, and their flesh had shrunk against their skulls as if in readiness for death.

They were given a good hot broth and their wounds were dressed attentively. The surgeon, during the two days that the survivors remained on board, put them on a strict diet to gradually re-adapt their bodies to normal fare. But delirium persisted. One army officer who wanted to throw himself overboard in search of his lost wallet had to be restrained. Those who managed to sneak behind the doctor's back to gorge themselves were rewarded with excruciating cramps.

The *Argus* had given up her search for the *Medusa* and was heading back to Saint-Louis when first detected by the survivors on the raft. After the brig disappeared from their sight, a change of wind made Captain Parnajon resolve to continue his search for the wreck, a decision that led to the discovery of the raft, which had drifted south to a point about ninety nautical miles from the wreck and thirty-two nautical miles off Portendick.

Under a favorable breeze they sailed for Saint-Louis, where they dropped anchor at three o'clock on the afternoon of July 19. In his report to Governor Schmaltz, written in the roads of Saint-Louis, Parnajon noted that

> I found on this raft fifteen people. . . . These unfortunates had been obliged to fight and kill a large number of their comrades who had revolted in order to seize the provisions. . . .

Others had been taken by the sea, or died of hunger or madness. Those that I rescued had fed themselves on human flesh for several days, and, at the moment when I found them, the ropes which held the mast were covered with morsels of this flesh which they had hung up to dry. The raft was also covered with scraps which further attested to the food which these men were obliged to consume; they had been sustained by a little wine which they handled as carefully as possible; they still had several bottles when I found them.

Of the 147 people abandoned on the raft two weeks earlier, fifteen were left alive: Dupont, the infantry captain; l'Heureux, a lieutenant in the infantry; Lozach and Clairet, second lieutenants; Griffon du Bellay; midshipman Coudein; Sergeant-Major Charlot; Courtade, a master gunner; Lavillette, the workshop foreman; Coste, a sailor; Thomas, a helmsman; François, a male nurse; Jean-Charles, a black soldier; Corréard, the engineer; and Savigny, the surgeon. Of these fifteen, who had the exceptional stamina and indomitable will to survive, five would be dead within the next few months.[10]

6

Tea and Pastries in Senegal

After cutting loose from the raft, the governor's and captain's barges managed to stay close to each other. Governor Schmaltz had stashed on board fifty pounds of biscuits, eighteen bottles of wine, two bottles of brandy, and sixty bottles of water. Captain Chaumareys was less lavishly provisioned: for the twenty-eight people in his barge, there were only eighteen bottles of water, a dozen bottles of Madeira, a sack of biscuits, and some overripe pears.

As they pulled away from the raft, freed of immediate and crippling responsibility, they profited from a north-northwesterly breeze that sped them in the direction of Portendick and Saint-Louis. They sailed briskly through the day, in the knowledge that if they made good time the provisions would last until they reached Senegal.

By July 8, as the tropical sun burned down upon them and the ocean's glare dazzled their eyes, midshipman Sander Rang was on the point of putting into shore when he calculated that as they could be only about thirty-five nautical miles from Saint-Louis, they would do best to continue by sea. At ten o'clock that evening, a French brig and a French corvette were sighted. The barges hoisted their mainsails, sent up flares, cried, "Long live the king," and "Long live France," and with all possible speed made in the direction of the lights on board the ships. They were hailed from the deck of the *Echo* and astonished the watch by replying that they were boats from the *Medusa*. The surprised officer demanded the whereabouts of the frigate and Rang replied that Captain Chaumareys would explain anon.

The twenty-eight people from the captain's barge were already aboard the *Echo* when the governor's barge drew alongside. Desiring nothing but rest and sleep, everyone was given a good supper before settling down for the night, thankful to be aboard a ship from their convoy at safe anchorage off Saint-Louis in Senegal.[1]

The French connection with this part of West Africa dated from the end of the fourteenth century when merchants from Dieppe were active along the coast. During the first third of the fifteenth century, Portuguese explorers profited from the imperialist ambitions of the papacy. Under obligation to convert the heathen population, whose goods they were authorized to steal, they were also granted permanent rights of possession over the territories they discovered and were busy charting the mouth of the Senegal River. By the end of the century the Spanish, likewise benefiting from papal endorsement, were exploiting the region. The Dutch came later to barter and plunder, eventually losing their foothold to the French who, in the seventeenth century, came to dominate trade in the area. They eventually attempted to secure the delta of the Senegal River by building a giant, ill-designed, and vulnerable mud fort on the island of Saint-Louis. In 1758, during the Seven Years' War, the English obtained control of Senegal and kept it until 1783, after which the colony reverted to France with England continuing to enjoy commercial rights. Along the coast a series of trading posts had been established on Arguin Island, at Portendick, Saint-Louis, Galam, and on the island of Gorée. At all of these posts, gum was traded and, at Saint-Louis and Gorée, there was a thriving traffic in human beings.[2]

In 1800, with the capture of Gorée, the English demonstrated their considerable commercial interest in the area. Benefiting from Napoleon's indifference to French colonial holdings, they took Saint-Louis in July 1809 without a struggle. So when, on July 9, 1816, Governor-designate Schmaltz went ashore, he came under the jurisdiction of the English governor, Thomas Brereton, until such time as the British government, in accordance with the recent Treaties of Paris in March 1814 and November 1815, sanctioned the handing back of the settlements of Senegal and Gorée to the French.

Though they were to appear dilatory in giving up the colony, the English were quick to react to the hardships endured by the French colonists. British officer Major John Peddie, whose compassion for the shipwreck victims was considerable, noted that "every attention within the means of this Garrison was immediately afforded."[3] Governor Brereton wrote to Schmaltz on July 9: "A most ready and prompt compliance shall be given to your wishes in affording every bit of assistance in my power and I have ordered two craft . . . best suited to the purpose. They will be dispatched without delay."[4] Representatives of both governments sent men and ships to search for survivors, although Schmaltz's initiatives seemed, in comparison with those of the English, bafflingly sluggish.

The first group of castaways, including Brédif and the Picards, arrived in Saint-Louis on July 13 and were greeted by the English governor on horseback, accompanied by Kearney and several officers. Dismounting, Colonel Brereton, in marked contrast to his French counterpart, seemed most affected by their sufferings, and those in the worst condition were at once admitted to the English hospital.

Although many French merchants and all the French administrators had been forced to leave Saint-Louis in 1809, there were still some tradesmen in the colony and the successive waves of survivors were welcomed by these compatriots, as well as by a host of deeply sympathetic English families. Most of Picard's children lodged with

Artigue, his old friend from his previous stays in the colony. Charlotte and her sister, Caroline, however, were billeted with a kindly
English couple, the Kingsleys, who occupied one of the fifty European-
style bungalows in the center of the island of Saint-Louis. These dwellings had meager gardens and terraced roofs and housed the five hundred
resident merchants and administrators. There were also two thousand
free blacks and mulattoes along with seventy-five hundred slaves on
the island, which was just over two miles long and, at its maximum,
half a mile wide. The French fort stood in the middle of the island,
flanked by large, unpaved roads that proved unpleasant thoroughfares
when the wind blew, carrying sand off the Sahara. At the northern
end of the island, inland from the mangroves, there was a hospital, a
church, and a store for gunpowder. In the southern part, amid the
palm trees and baobabs, stood the natives' badly constructed straw huts,
largely blackened by smoke.[5]

Upon arrival, the sisters were taken to be washed and treated with
ointment by two of the Kingsleys' servants. They were given clothes
and linen of a smoothness and whiteness that were shocking against
their frazzled skins. Throughout their recent ordeal, Charlotte had been
kept alive by her exceptional fortitude, but once saved and finding
herself in the luxury of European-style surroundings she feared for a
complete breakdown. Having gone beyond the limits of all she had
ever known or could imagine, the sheer comfort of white linen seemed
oddly terrifying. When her hostess invited her to join the family in
the drawing room, Charlotte struggled to summon up hidden reserves
of strength in order to negotiate this difficult return to civilization.
The young lady, who only days before had drunk muddy, putrid water
from a soldier's greasy cap, was taking tea and pastries in the company
of late enemies who were offering her, in conspicuous contrast to her
own leaders, the most gentle welcome.

Picard's understandable outburst over the cowardice of the commanders of the expedition had been reported to Schmaltz and was most

probably the cause of the governor-designate's neglect of the family. When Picard asked for supplies, Schmaltz refused. Unable to obtain anything from his leader or from Durécu, the prosperous merchant who was currently financing and supplying the French expedition, Picard was eventually obliged to borrow money to rent a small apartment in which to lodge his entire family, all of whom had, miraculously, survived the desert trek. If he had made enemies among the nastiest and most powerful of the survivors from the *Medusa,* Picard luckily still possessed a group of old friends from his previous visits. Furthermore, natives from the surrounding countryside came to offer help, carrying donations from their simple harvest. Thus, living cheaply on native dishes, the Picards were discovered by the kindly Major Peddie, who immediately instructed the mayor of Saint-Louis to grant the family the rations expected by English officers.[6]

Although the various accounts do not agree on the details and the extent to which the English were of assistance, neither are they unanimous concerning the actions of the French merchants. Brédif, who praised the English officers for their kindness and attention, also writes that he was received with "tender hospitality" by Durécu and his nephews, noting that "it was with great simplicity and without ostentation" that Durécu helped the victims of the shipwreck. Charlotte Picard, on the other hand, suggests that Durécu was an opportunist who, it was rumored, was taking a hundred percent profit on all the loans he made. Yet because he was Schmaltz's chum, he was awarded the Légion d'Honneur. This portrait of Durécu as a calculating profiteer is upheld by Savigny and Corréard, who suggest that the governor had entered into a kind of business pact with him, a pact that would lead to some very sinister dealings.

Whereas Major Peddie's actions and attitude are universally praised, the conduct of Colonel Brereton is frequently questioned. Savigny and Corréard are incensed by his apparent procrastination in handing over the colony. As the gum harvest was imminent, a holdup in the transfer would guarantee the English merchants this year's profit from the lucrative trade.[7] Gaspar Mollien and Savigny and Corréard record that any kindness shown by Brereton was short-lived. As early as July 17, before the raft had even been found or all the desert castaways accounted for, many French soldiers, sailors, and officers were obliged to embark for their settlement at Cap Vert. Schmaltz would follow, while those too sick to travel would remain in Saint-Louis until they regained their health. However guilty the French governor-designate was of sluggishness or hardheartedness, the situation in which he found himself was obviously uncomfortable and logistically problematic.

Describing Cap Vert, Geoffroy de Villeneuve wrote of its "perpetual greenness," of the "singular vigour of its productions," which "proclaims an earth fertilized by several centuries of vegetal decay, and by the two volcanoes of which we see traces everywhere." Cotton and indigo were cultivated; there was game in the forests and fish in the sea. Cornette de Vénancourt, in his survey of the area, noted "papaya, guava, citrus fruits, manioc, sugar cane and cows." Clearly, it was a potentially rich peninsula for the proposed agricultural establishments sponsored by the Philanthropic Society. Despite the breathless heat of early August, the explorer Mollien set about, with the help of the sometime stowaway Rabaroust, planting seeds of lettuce, carrots, celeriac, and melons.

Dakar was the largest of the six villages on the peninsula, and a provisional camp for the army and navy was established there by Vénancourt. Dysentery was endemic and excessive drinking reduced many to a stupor. People were dying daily. Chaumareys attempted to manage the growing disorder between the soldiers and sailors, but it was Schmaltz, arriving on July 26, who solved the problem. He separated the feuding members of the different services by containing the sailors on board the *Argus* and the *Echo*.[8] Meanwhile, Schmaltz installed himself comfortably on the nearby Ile de Gorée, which lies in the lee of the cape. It was an island where Europeans who became sick while living in Senegal went to regain their health.[9]

When, with the permission of the English governor, the raft survivors were disembarked at St. Louis on July 9, Lieutenant Reynaud, whom Savigny and Corréard accused as the person who had cut them adrift, was on the quay to shake their wretched hands. The crazed survivors were terrified that they would be put to death for murder and cannibalism. In the most wretched condition, Alexandre Corréard begged to be thrown into the sea. With their coming ashore, Brédif writes that those already arrived in the colony became aware of "the terrible butchery" that had occurred, how large numbers of men had been carried off by the breakers and how the survivors had been found with "pieces of human flesh hanging above them and urine bottled"—their only food and drink. "What horror," he observes, "caused by the incompetence of a single man." The government had appointed Captain Chaumareys in scandalous disregard of sound judgement.[10]

To those who had never been pushed to such extremes, the men who had been on board the raft were frightening beings who had transgressed all civilized standards in order to survive. They had lived beyond what was deemed acceptable and now appeared as strangers among friends. Their notions of what may or may not be permissable were blurred and, while dining with a merchant one evening, one of the survivors blithely commented that the liver of the pig they were eating was not half as tasty as the liver he had torn from a man on the raft. When he embraced Savigny and Coudein at Governor Schmaltz's, Sander Rang records that they seemed like figures risen from the tomb; indeed, he notes that letters had already been dispatched to France reporting their certain loss.[11]

Several were lodged with the merchants Durécu, Valentin, and Lasalle and the others were taken to the English hospital. It was there that those who had survived the ordeal of the raft, second lieutenants Lozach and Clairet, Sergeant-Major Charlot, the black soldier, Jean-Charles, and Courtade, the master gunner, would soon die.

Toward midnight on July 19, the same day on which the *Argus* had arrived, Lieutenant Anglas de Praviel reached the colony in "a state of utter destitution." The weakness of his voice making him difficult to understand, Praviel announced the arrival of the second group of castaways.[12] On the very next day, July 20, Kummer and Rogery, the two men who had been washed ashore at Portendick in the same group as Brédif and Charlotte Picard and who had wandered separately off into the desert and been given up for lost, were led into Saint-Louis by some Moors.

Soon after leaving his party early in their march, Kummer had found the camp of Prince Muhammed, the son of King Zaide of the Trazas tribe of Moors. He had boldly stridden into the midst of their encampment, and, in the few words of Arabic that he knew, passed himself off as the son of a Muslim woman. The Moors seemed overjoyed to welcome him, quizzed him about recent events in France, inquired as to why the trading posts on Arguin Island and Portendick had fallen into disuse, and asked him to lead them to the place where his boat had come ashore.

While they were resting by a pond, another group from the same tribe arrived with Rogery, who declared that he had not been treated well. The women and, above all, the children had pestered him and robbed him of almost everything he carried or wore. After a short rest, the Frenchmen were conducted to the camp of King Zaide. They negotiated a fee for their safe conduct to Saint-Louis and were able to observe the customs and pursuits of their hosts—the polygamy of the king, the fair treatment and education of black slaves, and the trade in salt, furs, feathers, and skins.

The king put a stop to the tormenting of Rogery, who, without the pretended traces of Muslim blood, had been made to feel less welcome than his friend. Zaide exhibited considerable knowledge about recent European events and pressed them for information about the Hundred Days. He treated the two Frenchmen with much kindness and sent them off on their journey to rejoin their countrymen.[13]

The victims from the raft were, according to Brédif, being badly cared for in the English hospital. Praviel visited them on July 23 and found Corréard still in the most desperate state. He also noted that the raft survivors were given preference over his own troop from the desert who had arrived during the previous days. The least healthy among the desert marchers were packed in a single room and given a ration of biscuit and bacon while those from the raft were given the English soldier's ration of white bread, meat, rice, sugar, coffee, Madeira, and rum. Despite this generosity, the survivors from the raft protested that such a ration was unsuited to the restoration of their health, and though the English surgeon and Governor Brereton proved deaf to their complaints, Major Peddie and some other English officers showed them considerable kindness, inviting the four officers in the healthiest condition to dine with them daily, even offering them a good champagne.[14]

Corréard, who remained in hospital the longest, was left on what he described as a hard bed with dirty sheets. He was in excruciating pain from the sores, the sickness, and the bayonet and knife wounds he had sustained on board the raft, and he passed endless days and often sleepless nights brooding on his misfortunes.

> Nothing relieves me; on the contrary, the length of the nights, the continuation of my sufferings, the sight of those of my companions in misfortune, the disgusting filth by which I am surrounded, the inattention of the army nurse who is always drunk or negligent, the insupportable hardness of a wretched bed, scarcely sheltered from the inclement air, all bode an inevitable death.

Having received no news from the French at Cap Vert, Corréard was becoming anxious to join them, but Major Peddie dissuaded him from going to a camp where dysentery was rampant. The major had come bearing gifts and had shed tears at the sight of Corréard's sufferings. He professed himself honor-bound to reciprocate a little of the kindness that he and his comrades had received at the hands of their late enemies during the Napoleonic wars. It was to Peddie and the three other English officers who exhibited much kindness toward him that Corréard claimed he owed his life. Not once, during all this period of suffering, did Madame or Mademoiselle Schmaltz care to visit the hospital.[15]

The *Argus* had returned with the survivors of the raft on board but without sighting the *Medusa,* so another salvage expedition was dispatched on July 26. This attempt was made by a far from seaworthy schooner owned by Durécu. There were other ships available that were more suited to the task but Schmaltz liked to deal exclusively with Durécu, whose ill-equipped vessel was forced to return after encountering adverse weather. Setting off once again, she was again forced to put back to port after her sails were all but destroyed in a gale. The third time she set sail she found the *Medusa,* fifty-two days after the frigate had been abandoned.

The ghostly hull was broken and she had slumped on her port side. On board, like some weird, Gothic vision from a contemporary poem, were three cagey, skeletal figures crouched in different parts of the deck among the scattered debris. They had only brandy left to drink and days, if not hours, later would have been dead. Indeed, a fourth had died only a short while before the arrival of the schooner and had been committed to the sea. Of the other thirteen who had been left on board on July 5, the crew of the schooner learned that for forty-two days they had survived with an ample supply of biscuit, bacon, prunes, wine, and brandy, but that when these had begun to dwindle, twelve of them had constructed a raft and set sail. This rudderless craft was eventually found washed up on the shore by some of King Zaide's men, without trace of survivors. One of the five other men tried to make for the shore on a chicken coop but sank a short distance from the frigate. The four remaining men preferred to stay safely on board rather than offer themselves to the "sea-monsters which are found in great numbers on the coasts of Africa." These four fed themselves on salt pork, tallow, and the remaining brandy until all but the liquor ran out and one of them died. At the time of their eventual rescue, despite their weakened state, the three remaining appeared ferocious, brandishing knives at one another and charily guarding their self-apportioned and broken domains.[16] When the schooner had salvaged what it could from the *Medusa,* these wild survivors were taken on to Saint-Louis.

The first day that Corréard was able to get up from bed and take a short walk in the town, he called on the family of the French governor. He was appalled to discover their attitude toward the schooner's expedition. Their only concern seemed to be the recovery of valuables and provisions from the wreck, no one caring a fig for the possible survival of the men on board. Already disgusted by their indifference, Corréard became irate when he learned that he would not be able to recover any of his own engineering instruments on which his livelihood depended. Later, when the schooner arrived in Saint-Louis, it was declared that what it had recovered from the wreck was a "prize." Lieutenant Reynaud was among these "pillagers" and carried off several trunks as Saint-Louis was turned into a weeklong market fair. Everything was up for sale, including the French flag that had been transformed into tablecloths and napkins. Blacks bought signal flags to make aprons and cloaks. Even vases belonging to Chaumareys were on offer and the captain himself later noticed them gracing the house of the governor. There was furniture, tackle, and instruments on offer—even clothes belonging to people who were still alive. Thereafter, the various other merchants in Saint-Louis were authorized to plunder the wreck in a fifty-fifty split with Schmaltz.[17]

But even before the finding of the wreck, the first moves in the discovery and exposure of the scandal of the *Medusa* began. On July 29, the *Echo* set sail for France. She carried a letter from Schmaltz to the minister of the navy, vicomte DuBouchage, stating that he was left with only half the complement of his garrison. On board were fifty-five survivors of the tragedy, among them the valorous Lieutenant Espiaux, Ensign Lapeyrère, midshipman Coudein, and Henri Savigny.

In complete contrast to the disorder that had endangered his outward voyage, Savigny recorded that in all his time in the navy he had never beheld such a well-kept and soundly run ship. Cornette de Vénancourt was in command, a man of skill and rigor; his navigation to Senegal had been exemplary and Governor Schmaltz praised his "zeal after the loss of the *Medusa*." In a report of the Philanthropic Society written at the end of July, Vénancourt was likewise singled out for his aid in exploring Cap Vert after the delegates from the *Medusa* had lost all their instruments in the wreck.[18]

Vénancourt was also an ambitious man. He took obvious satisfaction in tactful criticism of Chaumareys's handling of the convoy. Considering their respective careers in the navy, while Chaumareys had spent the last twenty years resting on the laurels of his fictitious heroism during the Quiberon campaign and steadily forgetting his maritime skills, Vénancourt had been sailing. Appointed captain of a frigate in 1815, after nine years as a lieutenant and twenty-five years at sea, Vénancourt had demonstrated the flair and courage needed to bring a ship full of mutineers to heel during the Hundred Days. Clearly, with such a long and distinguished career, superior qualities of seamanship, and royalist sympathies, it dismayed him to think that the bungling Chaumareys had been allowed to steer a large number of people to dereliction and death. During the thirty-four-day voyage home, when he found out about the manuscript that Savigny was writing as a kind of therapeutic rite of passage back to civilization, Vénancourt realized that the misjudgments and resulting horrors catalogued by the account could do nothing but demonstrate to the government that it had plainly appointed the wrong leader.[19]

Toward the end of the day on September 2, 1816, a telegraph arrived at the Ministry of the Navy in Paris from Vice Admiral Saint-Haouen in Brest, alerting the authorities that the *Echo* had arrived in his port carrying news of the wreck of the *Medusa*. Two days later, Saint-Haouen telegraphed the ministry to say that he had asked for reports from those officers from the *Medusa* who had arrived on board the *Echo* and would dispatch them forthwith.

The captain of the *Echo* also presented a neutral and nonaccusatory verbal report to Saint-Haouen. Furthermore, on his own initiative, Vénancourt sent the *Echo*'s log direct to Minister of the Navy DuBouchage. He also asked Savigny for a copy of the narrative that the surgeon had written during the voyage. At that stage, without the input of the politically agitated Corréard, the text was mildly accusatory, but not insistently antiroyalist. It was not therefore offensive to Vénancourt, nor would it be anything but an embarrassment to his minister. It would, moreover, prove useful in Vénancourt's desire to make clear the innate superiority of his seamanship, a fact that, once established, might serve him well both in regard to future appointments and in his solicitation for the Légion d'Honneur.

By the time Savigny set out for Paris on September 11 to deliver his narrative to the ministry, Vénancourt had already dispatched a copy to a friend who passed it on to Councillor Forestier, who was supposed, in turn, to hand it over to vicomte DuBouchage. Realizing the volatility of the document and presumably for reasons of political inclination, Forestier gave it not to his royalist minister, as was intended, but to the man who, over the previous months, had desperately been trying to save the restoration from hardening into a dangerous and unacceptable resurrection of the ancien régime: the minister of police and the king's favorite, Elie Decazes.[20]

7

Sex and the Street

Just as the news of the wreck of the *Medusa* was beginning to break, Théodore Géricault fled France for Italy. If, in the emotional turmoil of flight, he was much aware of the shocking news item it is, like the exact date of his departure, unrecorded. But as the laudatory letter of recommendation from his teacher Pierre-Narcisse Guérin to an unknown Florentine is dated September 20, it is safe to say that the news of the shipwreck and the horrors of the raft that was shocking France could not have altogether escaped the attention of a smart young man. Certainly Géricault was not yet ready to register the metaphorical potential of the catastrophe; for the artist to understand the personal and political resonances of the wreck, he would first need to experience both the feeling and the fact of loss. The former would result from his determination to try to put an impossible liaison behind him. The latter would shake his premature return to France.[1]

It is certainly possible that his aunt Alexandrine, a married woman with two children, a position in society to maintain, and much to lose, might have found the strain of a quasi-incestuous affair too great.

Whoever initiated the separation, Géricault's aesthetic education provided an excellent pretext. The year that Géricault spent in Italy is significant for the understanding of his emotional dilemma as well as his awakening engagement with a new kind of subject matter.

Neoclassicism had been popular for over thirty years and, though it had served the ideals of the revolution, the reality of what was happening in France could best be perceived in the streets rather than in the detached idealism on show at the Salon. In Italy, it was not in the museums and among the classical ruins that Géricault was to find his revolutionary voice, but on the street corner, in the piazza; it was there that he began to become a painter of modern life who treated scenes and events that revealed truths about his world.

The close friends who had planned to accompany Géricault on the journey were, for one reason or another, delayed and unable to join him. He traveled part of the way with a fabulously wealthy Polish nobleman who had served in the imperial army. It is perhaps through this connection that Géricault came to be invited to the opera in Florence, where he was accorded a place of honor next to the Duchesse de Narbonne-Pelet, wife of the French minister to the king of Naples. Such dazzling evenings did not belie the fact that Géricault was feeling very much alone. In a letter to the painter Dedreux-Dorcy of October 18, he urged his close friend to make haste to join him, rounding up as many good companions as he could muster, for "you can't have too many old friends around when you're abroad." This need for friendship and distraction was not only a question of homesickness, but also a reflection of his sorrow in having left Alexandrine. Restlessly moving on to Rome in mid-November after a short, unhappy stay in Florence, Géricault hoped to divert himself with some friendly faces but, once again, he found himself to be "far from consolation." Despite his exhilaration at the sight of the Sistine Chapel, he wrote that, generally, "things appear in their ugliest light." Wherever he went, whatever he saw, the melancholy within tarnished his vision. Dejection dominated his voyage, and, as he candidly confessed in a letter of November 27, "My heart is never easy for it is too full of memories."[2]

Rome was, along with Naples, cardinal to the artist's study of antiquity. However, early on in his Roman stay Géricault wondered if one year was not a sufficient period of study rather than the five-year span accorded to the residents of the French Academy. His observation registers an inkling of the declining importance of the study of the classical for a painter who was searching to take issue with modern life.[3]

The painter rented a studio in the Ludovisi quarter, near the Piazza Barberini. He visited that master of clarity and order Jean-Auguste-Dominique Ingres, the Provençale painter François Granet, and met the English architect Charles Cockerell, who would prove to be a good friend to him during his later visits to England. He saw, in fact, quite a number of old friends and yet remained, to all intents and purposes, depressed. His watercolor sketches of modern Italian life were vivid and accurate, but the poses of his Italian peasants remained academic.

There were, however, two events that seem to have provoked Géricault's increasing feeling for the scent of the street. The first was an execution that he witnessed, of which he produced a series of pencil and pen-and-ink sketches. Some of these demonstrate Géricault's continuing attachment to classical models. Others capture the spontaneous clumsiness of a sinister event, such as the moment in which menacingly hooded executioners, wishing to preserve their privileged anonymity, conduct their victim to a terrible end. It is a theme that would recur in Géricault's work in numerous guises: in the following year, in the abduction of the magistrate Fualdès; then at the hanging of the Cato Street conspirators in London; and, finally, in the violent seizure of innocent human beings in his drawings for a large projected canvas inspired by events in Senegal, *The Slave Trade*.

The other spectacle that seized Géricault's attention during his stay in Rome was the climax to the Roman carnival, the race of the riderless horses down the Via del Corso from the Piazza del Popolo. In Géricault's masterly small painting, a study for an urealized larger canvas, the horses strain with unbridled energy against the classical confines of the ordered public space. Dramatically backlit and symptomatic of the release of anarchic and subversive energy during carnival, the horses rear against the restraining stable boys while the shadowy rabble behind, a looming political force, can be seen to dimly echo their desire for freedom. The small painting captures more than a spectacle, or a contest; it hints at a barbarous eruption in a civilized space.

In addition to that important painting, the most robust and vital that Géricault produced during these unhappy months, was a series of drawings thrashing out themes of tortured eroticism. Prior to his departure he had, in fact, begun to sketch these sometimes personal, sometimes mythological explorations of violent or delighted sex. There are numerous extant drawings in this vein and there were, most probably, many more. In the mid-1850s, the painter Paul Huet discovered that some Norman relatives of Géricault possessed, among other works, a stash of several hundred drawings that they would not permit visitors to see. Huet assumed that as these were most probably of an erotic nature, they would eventually be destroyed. If Huet's estimate of the number is accurate, such a bulk of material argues the persistence and strength of Géricault's sexual dilemma.[4]

Some of the erotic drawings that the artist made in 1816–17 explore fantasies of violence and cruelty, perhaps reflecting his feelings of guilt and conflict about his ill-starred affair. A man of twenty-five, at the height of his sexual powers and recoiling from a passionate and forbidden relationship, was perhaps somewhat terrified of the extreme intensity of the drives that seemed to saturate his being; a dialogue with these urges, using the stock, sexually charged figures of mythology such as satyrs and centaurs, would help him to thrash out and objectify his lust.[5] Among the sketches that have survived, there is also evidence of erotic delight and physical exuberance. Embraces are often ecstatic, clearly the work of a man who knows the intensity of physical passion and who is reliving his rapture in a time of deprivation.

Géricault managed to conceal much of his soul-searching beneath the refinements of a young man of his class. During a reasonably happy interlude in Naples during April and May of 1817, the elegant young artist was praised for his "very pleasing ways" and "most considerate manners."[6] He made sketches and watercolors of the classical ruins at Herculaneum and Paestum and then returned to Rome for the rest of the summer, being held up by brigands on the way.

Despite his urge to get back to Paris after "a year of sadness," Géricault did manage a few days of sketching in the Uffizzi in Florence on his way home. Then he pressed on to Paris, arriving in early November 1817. Charles Clément, Géricault's biographer, characterized the Italian episode as "a real exile" and Géricault's contemporary Louis Batissier speaks of the period as one of "heartaches." It is more than likely that he prematurely terminated his Italian trip expressly to return to the arms of Alexandrine.[7]

If Géricault had left France as the story of the wreck of the *Medusa* was breaking, he returned just as the full complexity of the drama was unfolding, with the publication of Savigny and Corréard's immediately best-selling book *The Shipwreck of the Frigate, the Medusa*. In France, it had been a year of political upset and intrigue, marked by a struggle for justice and the beginnings of a serious and far-reaching investigation into the ill-fated expedition to Senegal. Once again, just over a year after the scandal broke, the wreck was very much on everybody's mind.

Géricault, however, was distracted by urgent personal matters. He had tried to make a break with Alexandrine. It had proved impossible. He had begun to sever himself from an impersonal, obsolete, and anodyne classicism. That seemed possible. Although they didn't meet, Stendhal had been in Naples when Géricault was there; a few years later, in his book *Racine et Shakespeare,* Stendhal was to discuss the classical, which he categorized as outmoded, and the romantic, which he dubbed modern and fascinating. Summarizing Stendhal's argument, Isaiah Berlin noted that romanticism "is a matter of under-standing the forces which move in your own life";[8] during Géricault's time in Italy, sex and the scope of the street had been tugging at his soul.

8

Breaking News
and Stifling Scandal

When Elie Decazes, minister of police and favorite of Louis XVIII, witnessed the dangerous abuses of the measures that had been introduced to stabilize France—when he perceived that the ultras would press on as far as civil war in order to destroy the constitutional charter, reclaim their old possessions, and return the balance of power to that of the ancien régime—he realized that the present government, the so-called *chambre introuvable* with its ultra-royalist majority, must be dissolved.[1] Ruthless in his attempts to discredit the ultras, Decazes formed a close alliance with the king with whom he shared the findings of his police spies. But the problem remained that if the right was significantly diminished, it would be difficult to check the resurgence of the left. Decazes was walking a tightrope and, by early 1816, his course of action had become apparent: he needed to "royalize the nation and nationalize the Royalists."[2]

Throughout the cold, dull, and agriculturally unproductive summer of 1816, Decazes was tireless in placing before the king persuasive justifications for the dissolution of the *chambre introuvable*. He demonstrated the divisive contempt that the ultras entertained for the soldiers of France.[3] He emphasized the ardor of ultra-royalism in the south, arguing that such passion was a tinderbox to insurrection. Backed by the Russian ambassador and supported by other allies, who feared that an ultra triumph would result in France reneging on her war debts, Decazes argued that it was essential to dissolve the chamber in order to demonstrate stability and regain the confidence of the country's recent enemies. Richelieu, the head of the government, detested meddlesome foreigners and Decazes cleverly persuaded him that the follies of the *chambre introuvable* were delaying the liberation of France from its Allied occupiers.[4]

Decazes shrewdly realized that the "policy of the king must have two grand objectives: firstly, the liberation of French territory and the reestablishment of order and royal authority; and secondly, the consolidation of a constitutional monarchy by the alliance of the throne with the notion of liberty."[5] By mid-August Louis was, at last, in agreement about the need to dissolve the chamber. It was a dangerous moment, particularly for the king: the minister of police may have engineered the Ordinance of Dissolution but the king had to sign it. In so doing, Louis was taking a daring initiative against members of his own family and particularly against his ultra brother, the duc d'Artois. He was, in fact, putting himself in opposition to the court and the first royalist assembly elected since the revolution.[6]

Throughout July and August, while these political deliberations were taking place, the king, government, and people of France remained in blissful ignorance of the fact that the expedition to repossess and colonize Senegal had gone disastrously wrong. It was not until three days before the king issued the ordinance of September 5 dissolving the *chambre introuvable* that DuBouchage at the Ministry of the Navy received a telegraph informing the government of the wreck of the *Medusa*.

At Brest, Vice Admiral Saint-Haouen began to put together a dossier of reports. It included two letters written by captain

Chaumareys, both dated July 29, the day of the *Echo*'s departure from Saint-Louis. In the first of these letters, Chaumareys blamed the wreck on unsatisfactory maps and noted that the strong currents off the West African coast made for a treacherously shifting, sandy seabed. In the second letter, in which he neglected to mention the castaways in the desert, Chaumareys spoke of the finding of the raft, although he chose not to mention the number of casualties involved.[7]

However, a collective report by those officers of the *Medusa* who had returned on board the *Echo,* including Lieutenant Espiaux and Ensigns Maudet and Lapeyrère, revealed some alarming facts: first, that Chaumareys had failed to take a sounding an hour before the disaster; second, that, at that time, the *Medusa* had been sailing south-south-east; third, that the raft had been abandoned because it was judged that the efforts of the boats towing the platform were proving ineffective; and fourth, that as a number of men had refused to leave the frigate, Chaumareys, its captain, could not have been the last to leave his ship. The dossier also contained a report by midshipman Coudein, the most senior member of the navy on board the raft. Although this report was objective and even nonaccusatory, it did hang huge question marks over what had been the motives prompting certain decisions.

Cornette de Vénancourt, in his testimony before Saint-Haouen, merely supported the assertion that the maps of the area were poor; his decision to supplement this bland verbal account, by sending the *Echo*'s log and Savigny's narrative to DuBouchage, was calculated to embarrass the minister who had entrusted the safety of French people and a great French enterprise to a moth-eaten monarchist who should have been put out to pasture long ago. While Vénancourt's intention had not been to provoke a scandal, within days the country would have its first indications of some alarming facts surrounding this avoidable catastrophe.[8]

That the news of the *Medusa,* particularly embarrassing to the ultras, should surface at a time when the king had, at last, signed the ordinance dissolving the *chambre introuvable* was, for Decazes, impeccable timing. If neoconservatives were a dangerous element in the delicate equation of constitutional monarchy, then the scandal of the wreck of the *Medusa,* captained by an unsympathetic and sycophantic royalist, provided a devastating instance of the danger of entrusting the affairs of state to such fossils. To confront the nation with proof of the fatal ineptitude of the likes of Hugues Duroy de Chaumareys afforded Decazes an unprecedented public relations opportunity.

The first announcement of the loss of the *Medusa* was a brief mention in the right-wing *La Quotidienne* on Friday, September 6, four days after the arrival of the *Echo* at Brest. There was, at that stage, no hint of any scandal; *La Quotidienne* was simply a right-wing journal full of society gossip, and at the time shipwrecks were commonplace. But on September 5, the day the king signed the ordinance, a telegraph had been received at the Ministry of the Navy declaring that "of the 150 men, soldiers and sailors who were put on the raft, 135 perished," and that news appeared in the *Journal des débats* on Sunday, September 8, the day on which the text of the ordinance was published.[9]

That night, Richelieu was at the opera and the crowd in the stalls cheered the president of the council; this was just the first of many signs of enthusiasm that greeted the ordinance, an act seen as a deliverance and understood as a strategy to consolidate the throne. In the king's statement, Louis had reasserted his commitment to the charter, and the stock exchange reacted favorably, with government shares immediately increasing in value. Abroad, the news was hailed as a step toward an era of peace and prosperity. At home, the left was thrilled; Royer-Collard, the liberal deputy, wanted to erect a statue to the great Decazes.

There were, of course, large portions of the population who were mortified by the act. On the subject of the dissolution of the *chambre introuvable* the vicomte Chateaubriand was acid: "This ministerial measure, they say, will save the legitimate monarchy. Dissolving the only assembly since 1789 that has shown purely royalist sentiments is, to my mind, a strange manner of saving the monarchy." But whatever the eventual consequences of Decazes's "coup d'état," in the short term the measure was greeted by a majority of the population with relief and enthusiasm.[10]

By contrast, the news of the raft published in the *Journal des débats* on September 8 provoked immediate anxiety and the Ministry of the Navy was besieged with anxious demands for further details. By September 11, however, some more alarming aspects of the drama began to come to light; *La Quotidienne* gave brief details of the wreck, commenting that the circumstances of the disaster "were unheard of in the history of the French navy" and that only fifteen people had been rescued from the raft. These would, had they not been saved, "have finished by devouring each other as their unfortunate companions had done."[11] The revelation of cannibalism added a new and sinister note to the tragedy.

It was on that same day that Henri Savigny, still suffering from his wounds and with his arm still in a sling, arrived in Paris to deliver his report to the Ministry of the Navy. But the copy that Vénancourt had requested had already found its way to Councillor Forestier, an adept courtier who wanted to further himself. Forestier slipped the unofficial report to his good friend Decazes, the architect of the downfall of the right, a man who was effectively altering the course of French history and who was powerful enough perhaps to oversee Forestier's possible appointment as nothing less than minister of the navy.

Thus Decazes found himself in possession of political dynamite. Although the papers were merely carrying the brief facts of the shipwreck, Decazes had in his hands a scoop, an eyewitness account that would horrify the nation. To leak the full story of the atrocity to the press in all its unmitigated horror would provide devastating proof of the wisdom of everything that he had been arguing. The ensuing outrage would inevitably galvanize the country into understanding the dangers and risks of allowing the extreme right to remain in control. Something as compelling as the *Medusa* scandal would prove more tangible, would impinge more acutely on the public's imagination, than the mere political act of dissolving a chamber. It would provide the living and dying proof of misguided leadership. It would give a popular and immediately comprehensible justification for a politically necessary action. As with the ultra violence in the south, the horrors of abandoning compatriots, of armed revolt on the raft, of cannibalism would affirm what Decazes had been abstractly propounding. France, it would be seen, would fare better in the hands of men such as Espiaux or Vénancourt, men who had profited from the time between 1789 and the present, than under the incompetent old guard. The realization that an ardent monarchist, appointed as commander of the Senegal expedition, was responsible for substantial loss of life, for the most horrific of crimes, for the loss of His Majesty's property and money, and for endangering His Majesty's colonial enterprise at a time when France was in search of international respect could prove enormously damaging to the right.

Decazes, wishing to leave nothing to chance in the wake of his constitutional coup, and perhaps fearful of a right-wing backlash, understood that some devastatingly anti-right propaganda had come into his hands. He leaked Savigny's report to the secretary-general at his Ministry, who just happened to be one of the codirectors of the *Journal des débats* and who, in turn, published it in his newspaper on Friday, September 13.[12]

Newspapers at that time were not sold on the streets but rather by subscription, and the sales figures were not therefore large. However, the *Journal des débats,* a moderately royalist publication with faith in the charter, attempted to appeal to a broad base of the population and had, along with the liberal *Constitutionnel,* the largest print run. Although sales were small, readership was, in fact, much greater, as many people devoured these publications in reading rooms and cafés where a single copy of a paper would be passed from person to person.

Papers tended to deliver the news straight, publishing editorial articles only once or twice a week, and so an eyewitness account that reported events that DuBouchage would obviously be keen to keep under wraps was guaranteed to provoke a stir.[13] What is more, Savigny's report was lengthy, occupying four and a half columns, more than half of the September 13 issue. The article was prefaced by a brief editorial statement vouching for the reliability of the eyewitness source and describing the event as being as "sinister as it is inexplicable."

Savigny records the promise, made by the officers, to tow the raft. He judiciously claims that he is far from accusing these men of not having acted honorably, but rather states that a string of circumstances doubtlessly forced them to abandon their plan, adding that nonetheless, the incident merits "scrupulous examination." What is more, Savigny provides a focus for that examination when he fixes on the actions of Lieutenant Reynaud, second in command of the *Medusa* and captain of the governor's barge: "seeing that his efforts had become futile, having towed us alone for a moment, he cut the cable attached to the raft." Savigny goes on to give a brief but thorough account of the appalling events that resulted from this action. Writing of the cramped conditions of the victims on board the raft, he speaks of limbs being trapped in the gaps between support struts, of subsequent death, of the mutinies, of the deteriorating health of the victims, of cannibalism, and of the awful decision to execute the weak in order to prolong the life of those whose chances for survival seemed less unlikely. The report was signed, "On board the corvette *Echo,* 22 August 1816. Savigny, Surgeon," and it appeared, with that

Théodore Géricault,
possible likeness of
Alexandrine-Modeste Caruel

Alexandre Colin,
Portrait of Géricault in 1816

Théodore Géricault,
Le Chasseur de la Garde

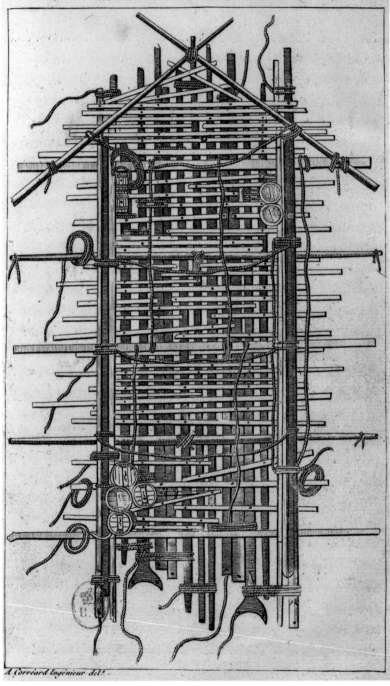

Alexandre Corréard, *Plan of the Raft of the Medusa*

Anon., *The frigate,
the Medusa*

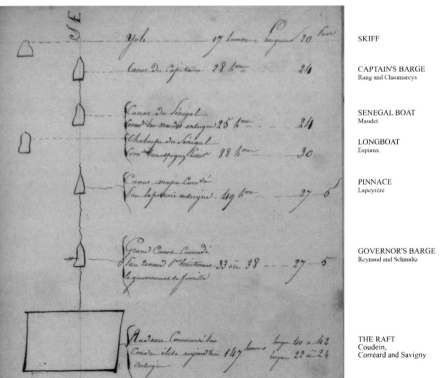

Yole .... 17 hommes Longueur 20 pieds	**SKIFF**
Canot du Capitaine 28 hommes 24	**CAPTAIN'S BARGE** Rang and Chaumareys
Canot du Sénégal Com.dt au maudet enseigne 25 h 24	**SENEGAL BOAT** Maudet
Chaloupe du Sénégal Com maudpigny lieut 88 h 30	**LONGBOAT** Espiaux
Canot major Com.dé Par lapeyrere enseigne 49 h 27	**PINNACE** Lapeyrère
Grand Canot Com.dé Par reynaud 8.e lieutenant 33 ou 38 27	**GOVERNOR'S BARGE** Reynaud and Schmaltz
Radeau Commandé au Condui élite aujourd'hui 147 hommes long 40 a 42 brigun larges 22 a 24	**THE RAFT** Coudein, Corréard and Savigny

Anon., Sketch on ms. report showing order of the boats towing the raft

Anon., *Shipwreck of the frigate, the Medusa*

Léon Antoine Morel-Fatio, *The Abandoning of the Raft of the Medusa*

Anon., *The Finding of the Raft by the Argus*

Anon., *Saint Louis in Senegal*

Théodore Géricault, *An Execution at Rome*

Théodore Géricault, *The Race of the Riderless Horses*

Sébastian Cœuré, *Fualdès being dragged and shoved into the Maison Bancal*

Théodore Géricault, *Fualdès being dragged and shoved into the Maison Bancal*

Théodore Géricault, *Studies of a Dancing Couple and a Centaur Abducting a Nymph*

Théodore Géricault, *The Embrace*

Théodore Géricault, *The Kiss*

Théodore Géricault, *Lovers Reclining*

Théodore Géricault, *Anatomical Fragments*

Théodore Géricault, *The Severed Heads*

Théodore Géricault, *Study for Cannibalism*

Théodore Géricault, *Drawing for the Mutiny on the Raft*

Théodore Géricault, *The Raft of the Medusa*

Théodore Géricault, *Study for the figure of Corréard*

C. Motte, *Valade
the Police
Commissioner
Confronting
Corréard in Prison*

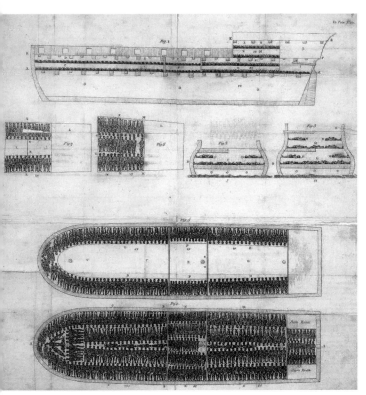

Anon., *The Shape and Dimension of the Places for the Slaves
in the English Slave-Ship, Brookes*

Alexandre Corréard,
Posthumous study of Géricault

Théodore Géricault,
Study for the Slave Trade

Théodore Géricault, *The Shipwreck*

ubiquitous lack of newspaperly decorum, above the results of the latest draws of the royal lottery, the healthy stock exchange rates, and the list of plays currently presented in the capital.[14]

This bolt from the blue redounded heavily on Savigny, who was at once summoned to the Ministry of the Navy where he was asked to prove that he was innocent of offering for publication the report that was scandalizing the country. Savigny went immediately to the editor of the *Journal des débats,* asking him to confirm that he had not obtained the report from Savigny's own hands. DuBouchage remained unsatisfied by the disclaimer offered by the paper and asked for further proof. A second, signed statement was duly provided, declaring, more explicitly, that it was not from the hand of Henri Savigny that the *Journal* had received the report but from the office of the minister of police.[15] Though this satisfied the minister vis-à-vis Savigny, it petrified DuBouchage, who at once understood what Decazes was about. The minister of police sought to expose the tragedy as a political misdeed and he wished heads to roll.

DuBouchage hit back; in an article carried by both the right-wing *Quotidienne* and the liberal, or Bonapartist, *Constitutionnel* on Sunday, September 15, the minister questioned the veracity of the diverse reports about the tragedy that had appeared in different newspapers. He asked: "How can one describe one's feelings while reading the *Journal des débats* of the 13th of this month . . . in which one can't help but notice a certain malign insinuation which makes one doubt the exactitude of the facts? The author of this article should have thought that, above all, he would be answerable for his opinions at the Court Martial which will deliberate this affair. . . . How, in short, can the author be a witness if he has already gone public as an accuser?"[16]

Savigny, in turn, made a public declaration in *Le Moniteur universel* that was surprisingly picked up and reprinted as a reply to DuBouchage in the ultra *La Quotidienne.* The surgeon confessed to be astonished by the publication of his report in the *Journal,* claiming that, as he had arrived in Paris at eleven a.m. on the eleventh and spent only a few minutes at his lodgings before being conveyed to the Ministry of the Navy, where he handed over all the papers at his disposal, it would have been impossible for him to have made contact with the editor of the *Journal des débats* to whom he categorically denied having given the report. "After all the evils that have beset me," he continued, "nothing could have been worse than to be seen to have failed in my duty. I would have thought that such misfortune would have given me the sympathy of people rather than provoking a severe reprimand from my superiors."[17]

DuBouchage knew that, under the stringent censorship laws, newspapers were effectively controlled by the minister of police and so the secrecy he so urgently sought was unlikely to be respected. Indeed so good was the story that even the right-wing press seemed reluctant to let it go. On the front page of its September 22 issue, in pride of place, *La Quotidienne* printed a private letter reporting on the sailors, troops, and colonists who had been forced to trudge through the desert. It suggested that the establishment of a colony on Cap Vert had been delayed by one year because of the loss of essential instruments. Both *Le Constitutionnel* and the *Journal des débats* carried this item in much the same form on the following day. Clearly it was in Decazes's interest to keep the story alive outside the secret confines of a ministerial investigation and in camera court-martial.[18]

A board of inquiry had begun to sit on September 17 at Brest under Vice Admiral Saint-Haouen. The minister of the navy, meanwhile, solicited the opinion of Admiral de Rosily, the director of the Hydrographic Service, on some uncertainties relating to the wreck. A reply was received on September 25, confirming that Chaumareys had been mistaken in sighting Cap Blanc in the late afternoon of July 1, because at midnight the *Echo* estimated herself to be twelve minutes north of the cape. At the same time, Admiral de Rosily conceded that the route outlined in his *Nautical Description* was dangerous. However, as the current director-general of the Paris Depot, which had issued the maps for the expedition, de Rosily felt less comfortable about accepting Vénancourt's assessment that the Bellin map was not the best available, as it placed the coast between Cap Blanc and Saint-Louis thirty miles to the east of where in fact it was to be found.

The next official step was the commission of Rochefort, convened by Rear Admiral Maurville. It started to sit on November 7 in order to determine the time at which Cap Blanc had been sighted, the route that had been set by Chaumareys after that sighting, and what attempts had been made at salvage and rescue. By the end of the three-and-a-half-week investigation, it was clear that Chaumareys had indeed been guilty of negligence. Cap Blanc had not been doubled during the late afternoon or early evening of July 1, but at around two a.m. on the morning of July 2. The *Medusa* had been a good deal farther north than had been supposed and thus, when, at seven-thirty a.m. on the morning of July 2 she veered south-southeast in the direction of Portendick, assuming that she had cleared the dangerous shoal, she plowed straight onto the Arguin sandbank.[19] The day before the Rochefort commission concluded its investigations, on December 1, 1816, Hugues Duroy de Chaumareys, passenger on board the *Loire*, left Senegal for France. The tragedy that had resulted from the quality of his leadership had already become an international sensation.

Decazes bribed the London *Times* 10,000 francs a month to plant articles under the names of their own correspondents. Whether as a result of such interference or merely by virtue of its nose for news, the paper translated and printed Savigny's report on September 17. On the previous day, the *Times* had already picked up the morsel about cannibalism that had appeared in *La Quotidienne* on the eleventh.[20] Not only did these items astound British readers, but copies of the papers eventually arrived for the English administrators in Senegal, where Savigny's frank tale shocked Colonel Schmaltz and Lieutenant

Reynaud into issuing a strong refutation. Their fears were compounded when a French schooner, the *Flore,* arrived from Bordeaux with letters on board that informed the colonists about the "big sensation" that their misadventure had caused in France.

Schmaltz and Reynaud drew up a report that was conveyed to Corréard, who was still in the hospital. Corréard read the report, and finding it to be untrue he refused to sign his acceptance of the facts as it presented them. Several times, underlings were sent to change his mind. On one occasion, Schmaltz went himself to exert maximum pressure on the frail patient. Again Corréard refused to sign. Kummer, Corréard's friend, was dispatched to persuade the invalid to approve the document, saying that without his signature he would not be permitted to return to France. Such coercion, Corréard and Savigny observe, testifies to the urgent need felt by Schmaltz and Reynaud to suppress the truth. Their document claimed that the towrope had broken. It maintained that the words "We're abandoning them" were never spoken. It protested that Savigny's report was a defamation of the officers who had done everything in their power to save him. Understandably Corréard refused to sign.

At the bottom of the document, Corréard was surprised to see the signature of one of his companions in misfortune, Griffon du Bellay, whom Savigny himself had saved from drowning. Subsequently, it emerged that the secretary had signed the document when he had been in a weak and confused state. Shortly after the appearance of the first edition of Savigny and Corréard's book, Bellay wrote to the surgeon to beg his pardon for having acted on the "first impulse of a weak and exaggerated imagination." While Corréard remained unyielding, the governor's persistence and intimidation succeeded with other victims from the raft who were still in a delirious state. Captain Dupont, Lieutenant l'Heureux, Sergeant-Major Charlot, the workshop foreman Lavillette, and Jean-Charles, the black soldier, all signed—some to gain favor with the governor, others too weak to realize what they were doing. They blamed Savigny for the horrors that had taken place on the raft; it was, according to their statement, he alone who had incited violence. Lavillette subsequently signed a disclaimer on the very day that Savigny and Corréard's book appeared, becoming one of the four survivors to repudiate what he claims he had been encouraged to affirm while in a state of "mental derangement."[21]

By the end of November 1816, Corréard was just about well enough to make the journey home to France. On the twenty-third and twenty-fourth he was visited by Majors Peddie and Campbell, the two English officers who had shown him much kindness over the previous months. Under the auspices of the Royal Society in London, Peddie and Campbell were about to set off to explore the scientific aspects and commercial prospects of the interior of the continent, continuing, in effect, the work of the great explorer Mungo Park. Despite strained relations between the English and the French in Senegal during that unusually tempestuous autumn, the expedition stimulated a degree of cooperation. For whatever motive, Schmaltz promised "every assistance in his power." Kummer, Corréard's associate in the Philanthropic Society, joined the team and his "Journal of an Expedition into the Interior of Africa," written in perfect script and embellished with meticulous botanical and zoological pencil and watercolor drawings, survived the expedition. Sadly, Major Peddie did not.[22]

The English major felt concerned for Corréard and generously gave him 300 francs for his journey home, along with some sound advice, which Savigny and Corréard used to advantage in their narrative: "Without pretending to guess how your Navy Minister will act towards you, I nevertheless think myself justified in presuming that you will obtain no relief from him; a Minister who has committed a fault will never suffer it to be mentioned." Guided by such thinking, Peddie advised Corréard not to return to Paris but to go to London, where he would find "a number of philanthropists" who would help him. This kindly advice provokes an upsurge of patriotism in Corréard and Savigny, permitting them to contrast what they have done for their country, what they feel about France, and how they expect Frenchmen to act, with the malignity of the leaders of their expedition who "have nothing French about them but their dress." The touching episode also gave the authors the pretext for citing, in a footnote in the earliest editions and thereafter in the body of their text, some of the seven or eight other doubtful commands "who do no more honor" to the "choice or discernment" of DuBouchage "than the expedition to Senegal has done." They despair that "we have seen titles pass for knowledge, repose for experience, and protection for merit."[23]

It was, in fact, only through the intervention of English doctors that Corréard was able to escape from Senegal and save his life. It was the certificate that Corréard had been given at the English hospital that made it impossible for Schmaltz, who had not yet taken over as governor and who therefore remained under English jurisdiction, to refuse Corréard's passage home. On November 28, Corréard embarked on a coastal cutter that was to carry him out to the *Loire,* anchored in the roads. Weakened by five months of suffering, and exhibiting an intense psychosomatic revulsion to being on board a boat, Corréard was immediately seized by fever and vomiting. Becalmed, the cutter drifted under the noonday sun and Corréard, in his delirium, overheard a fellow passenger who was nodding in his direction: "There's someone who won't reach France." After many hours drifting in the burning heat, a welcome breeze blew up and the cutter was able to join the ship.

Setting sail on December 1 under the command of Gicquel des Touches, the cumbrous store ship was carrying a number of other survivors from the *Medusa,* including its captain, Hugues Duroy de Chaumareys, returning to France to give an account of his expedition. Also on board was the English governor Thomas Brereton, returning to England for reasons of health and carrying with him a menagerie of rare and beautiful animals that were, during the storms weathered between the Azores and Cap Finisterre, nearly all crushed by chests that had been inadequately secured between decks.

On board, des Touches found the attitude of Chaumareys very strange. He records that the *Medusa*'s captain spent no time preparing his defense for the forthcoming court-martial, could not understand how despicable his actions had been, and seemed rather pleased to have come out of it all as well as possible. Corréard, who encountered Chaumareys strolling on the quarterdeck, likewise found his attitude odd and inconsistent. The captain seemed dead set on establishing his innocence and shifting the blame onto Governor Schmaltz, whom he accused of stirring things up between himself and his second in command. He also recalled the unsympathetic attitude of his officers and insisted on his own qualities as a mariner, though his evidence was restricted to the very earliest years of his career. He praised the younger officers from Napoleon's navy, saying that he differed from them only in politics, lamenting the fact that France was full of "young Jacobins," and blaming the wreck of the *Medusa* on such men. So many of Chaumareys's attitudes and actions seem peculiar. He was either so dim as to be oblivious to the gravity of his errors and omissions, or he had, indeed, been unhinged by the events of early July 1816. It seems crazy, but Chaumareys thought that the case of the *Medusa* would demonstrate beyond all doubt that all the king's ships should be commanded by officers from the ancien régime. Arriving in France, Chaumareys wrote to DuBouchage asking for "several months' holiday in order to restore my health which is in a terrible state." By way of reply he was arrested.[24]

With violet-colored, scorbutic scars covering his body, Corréard was admitted to the officers' ward of the navy hospital in Rochefort. Savigny visited him each day and it was perhaps during this time that they planned to collaborate on a more extended account of their sufferings. Certainly, the frustrations of the ensuing months would provide them with a powerful incentive to produce such a text. What is more, Corréard had not yet benefited, as Savigny had, from the therapeutic effect of externalizing his misfortune. He told his companion in suffering about Schmaltz's trumped-up document and showed him his written refutation. Savigny immediately set about procuring similar disclaimers from the survivors François and Coudein. While his verbal report to Saint-Haouen had seemed to excuse those who dropped the towropes, passing over the thorny question of responsibility, Coudein's written testimony spoke, perhaps ambiguously, of Savigny's "prudence" being "of the greatest service . . . in suggesting to us the means by which to maintain good order." With these three certificates and an intention to further clear himself of any blame, Savigny sought permission to go to Paris in order to alert the minister about the mendacity of Schmaltz's plotting. He waited many weeks for a reply, eventually receiving a negative response in May 1817. The combination of the interminable delay followed by a blunt refusal so angered Savigny that he quit the navy.[25]

When he at last felt that his condition had somewhat improved, Corréard likewise wished to make for Paris. First he needed to clothe himself, for he had disembarked from his ill-fated voyage almost naked; and so, using the little that was left of Major Peddie's gift, he equipped himself for his journey. All too recently returned from the hot tropics and suffering from a lesion to his right ankle and gouty rheumatic pains that were particularly susceptible to cold and damp, he set out in the depths of the French winter on foot. After walking for three days and having covered nearly a third of his route, he was overcome by fever. He called on the mayor of a small village just outside Poitiers where he unsuccessfully sought lodgings, forcing him to slog on a couple of miles to an inn where he could rest. The following day, February 4, suffering great pains in his chest and spitting blood, he reached Poitiers, where he fainted in the street. Fortunately, the mayor of that city was more sympathetic and lodged him with a compassionate landlord by whom he was treated as something of a celebrity. Corréard rested and then completed his journey to Paris by coach.

Arriving in the capital, Corréard felt it his first duty to express his gratitude for the help he had received from the English officers in Senegal and thus addressed a letter to the British ambassador. The inclusion of this letter of March 4, 1817, in Savigny and Corréard's narrative stresses the fact that the survivors of the wreck received their most generous succor from the English, contrasting, by implication, the worth of Peddie and Campbell and the "wisdom of the government that appointed them" with the insufficiencies of France. Corréard's next step was to seek employment at the offices of the minister of the navy. On being refused, he was advised instead to make an application for a situation in the colonies. He spent the next three frustrating months attempting to obtain compensation for his losses on the *Medusa* and in fruitless requests for such employment.[26]

The court-martial of Chaumareys, which had started just before Corréard set out for Paris, was a largely perfunctory affair. There were no surprising testimonies or unexpected revelations but there was drama in the attitude of those who tried him, the sentence they pronounced, and the effect it had on the evolution of the public's understanding of the *Medusa* scandal. When the news had first broken, liberal elements of the government had made political capital out of the affair; it was now the turn of the conservatives in the navy hierarchy to minimize the penalties for those whose incompetence had resulted in the disaster. The court-martial began on January 22 at Rochefort under the presidency of Rear Admiral La Tullaye, in the presence of seven captains and with Le Carlier d'Herlye acting as the king's prosecutor. Twenty-three witnesses were summoned, culminating with the interrogation of Captain Chaumareys, whose testimony began with a demonstration of his capacity for error; when he was called to testify on February 3, he managed to miscalculate his age by three years, claiming to be fifty-one instead of his actual fifty-four.

Chaumareys attempted to justify his actions. He blamed the delays caused by the shortages in the shipyard at Rochefort and the different capacities of the ships in the convoy. Orders were to reach Senegal as swiftly as possible and Chaumareys had been acting under the pressure of Schmaltz's impatience. Elements considered as vital evidence in naval trials such as logbooks and charts had been lost in the wreck. Chaumareys was thereby guilty of a breach of discipline, for a captain is responsible for removing his log when he abandons his ship. As the officers on board the *Medusa* had also lost their diaries and watch reports, the log of the *Echo,* kept with precision and not without wry editorial comment by Vénancourt, was a vital document in the trial. Vénancourt's log clearly states that at eleven p.m. on July 1 he had not yet sighted Cap Blanc because it was still eighteen nautical miles off his port bow. Vénancourt records that he doubled the cape at three a.m. on July 2. Chaumareys was altogether less decided. In his written report of July 29, he had claimed an unmistakable sighting of Cap Blanc in the afternoon of July 1. He now stated that this sighting occurred at eight p.m.

The log of the *Echo* was likewise useful in establishing other errors. While Vénancourt kept setting off flares and hoisting more lights throughout the night of July 1–2, Lieutenant Reynaud, the officer of the watch on board the *Medusa,* had made no attempt to keep in contact with the corvette. During that night Vénancourt also recorded that he took soundings every hour. At eight a.m. on July 2, finding a depth of sixty-one fathoms, he took the precaution of steering farther west. At ten-thirty a.m., finding the depth increased to ninety fathoms, he set a course west-southwest, which he kept until he reached a latitude of 19 degrees north. By contrast, Chaumareys showed a cavalier attitude toward soundings: it emerged that those he recorded in his report of July 29 as having been taken at nine and ten a.m. on

July 2 were never done. Throughout his various statements and accounts, Chaumareys also revealed considerable confusion over the
exact location of the wreck; before the court, this captain, who had
been appointed by a minister of the crown to lead the all-important
convoy, indicated no less than three different points at which the
Medusa ran aground.

During the court-martial, the testimony of the officers of the
Medusa established four important points: first, that Chaumareys refused to take a sounding one hour before the catastrophe because it
would slow the ship down; second, that the *Medusa* was sailing south-
southeast at that time; third, that the raft was released because the efforts of the boats towing it were judged to be ineffective; fourth, that
as a number of men had voluntarily stayed on board the frigate, the
captain was not the last to leave his ship. In conclusion, the prosecutor added the following points: that Cap Blanc had not been accu-
rately identified and the course of the *Medusa* had been determined
according to this mistake; and that the abandoning of the raft was not
the sole fault of the captain. He insisted that, in violation of all rules
and usages, the captain had not been the last to leave his ship. Because
the legal consequence of this final fault was capital, La Tullaye, as early
as January 23, took the precaution of writing DuBouchage to secure
a stay of execution. The minister and the king responded favorably to
the arguments that the captain had not acted with evil intentions, noting
that, in the past, he had served the Bourbons well.

Chaumareys had lied to save his skin when he had been brought
before the revolutionary tribunal after the royalist attempt at Quiberon.
He had denied being a monarchist, denied his nobility, and denied
having participated in a military capacity in the Quiberon uprising.
His lies earned him a stay of execution and allowed him the chance to
escape and flee to England. At Rochefort, it is doubtful that he deliberately falsified the facts; it seems more likely that his testimony was
born of confusion, ignorance, and incompetence—all, in this instance,

damning. However, once again, it appeared that Chaumareys was to escape the death penalty. The captain showed skill in his defense, maintaining that he stayed on board the *Medusa* until he was beseeched to take command in a large lifeboat. Chaumareys had gone to the aid of the raft; he claimed that when those on board the platform saw him take command of the towing operation, heartwarming cries of "Long live the king" resounded. He spoke candidly about the abandoning of the raft, citing the impossibility of the task and the necessity of saving those in the lifeboats. On the advice of his defense counsel, Chaumareys added that when he left the *Medusa,* he was aware of the navy rule that he, as captain, should be the last to leave his ship, but that he was also aware of the Ruling of 1765, Article 1285, stating that in each situation an officer should behave so as to best serve his calling. "It was," he claimed, "this last article that motivated me."[27]

The trial to examine and pass judgment on the facts established at the Court Martial began on a gray, rainy February 24, on the admiral's ship, anchored in the Charente. The king's prosecutor, Le Carlier d'Herlye, presented his summary of the case on February 28. On the separation of the convoy near Finisterre, Chaumareys was held to be not guilty as he had been acting on orders to reach Senegal as speedily as possible. The prosecutor acknowledged the gross errors in the maps used by the expedition but observed that this had no bearing on the captain's negligence in respect of soundings. Chaumareys was thus guilty of the shipwreck of the *Medusa* through arrogance. However, he was not guilty of the loss of the frigate, as everything in his power had been done to save her. Nonetheless, he would have to be declared "incapable of serving," according to Article 39 of the Penal Code. Next, Le Carlier d'Herlye tackled the evacuation and the abandoning of the ship, which could result in the death sentence. Surprisingly, the attitude of the prosecutor appeared lenient. Suggesting that Chaumareys's actions resulted from an error of judgment rather than from treachery or cowardice, the prosecutor recommended that he be held in a military prison for five years rather than pressing the court for the ultimate punishment. On the subject of the abandoning of the raft, Le Carlier d'Herlye asked whether it and the lifeboats should be treated as an entity under a single captain or as separate entities. Favoring the latter, it was clear that if force of circumstances made it necessary to abandon any one of the boats or the raft, then Chaumareys would not be accountable. Finally, to cap such remarkable tolerance, Le Carlier d'Herlye gave a glowing report of the behavior of Captain Chaumareys after his arrival in Senegal.

At eleven-thirty on the night of March 3, after lengthy deliberations, the captain of the *Medusa* was led into a large cabin on board the admiral's ship, where, standing hat in hand by the light of low-burning candles, he received the astonishingly lenient judgment. Hugues Duroy de Chaumareys was condemned, by a majority of five out of eight, to be removed from the list of officers and never be allowed to serve again; to be imprisoned for three years; and to pay the costs of the trial. In the crowded confines of the admiral's quarters, braid surrounded by braid, how could Chaumareys have fared badly?[28]

The puzzlingly light sentence caused much controversy. The old guard thought it too severe and claimed that the prosecutor had been too indulgent toward the other officers. Those of a less conservative frame of mind wondered if there had not been some interference from above; during the exploratory court-martial and subsequent trial, rumors had been circulating in the naval community in Rochefort that DuBouchage had bribed the principal witnesses so that they would not prove too vehement in their condemnation of the captain.

In a letter to his minister, La Tullaye pleaded that the condemned man should not be forced to pay the costs of the case as his family would be ruined. On March 6, Chaumareys himself intervened, petitioning the king that to be struck from the list of officers and condemned to three years in prison was penalty enough, without being stripped of his decorations. DuBouchage, in his turn, successfully petitioned the king for a choice of open prison and relief from the costs of the case. Thus, on September 11, 1817, Hugues Duroy de Chaumareys was committed to the prison of Ham, from which, during the following month, he petitioned to be transferred to the prison of Mont-de-Marsan, closer to his family home.

While Chaumareys continued to seek the restitution of his medals and a pension for his family, neither of which was granted, the leniency of his sentence was considered outrageous in many quarters. Those who had suffered enormously in the aftermath of the wreck were appalled. They felt that the full horror of the *Medusa* must not be left to drift into oblivion like its captain. To add to the slew of inhuman horrors—which, thanks to the opportunism of the ambitious Elie Decazes, had already become the talk of the town—there was the new affront of Chaumareys's farcically inappropriate sentence. Those who had paid with their health, their sanity, and their careers felt cheated. Alarming facts had already come to light, gossip was rife, liberals and Bonapartists were eager to seize any opportunity for discrediting the monarchy, and the inhabitants of France, not to mention the appalled public of all the seafaring nations, deserved to know more.

Superficially, the French political situation appeared to have calmed. The elections of October 1816 had returned a more moderate chamber. The hope that it should be composed of "men who love the King with passion and respect the Charter with sincerity," as Decazes had urged in a handbill, had been largely realized. Out of 238 deputies, 146 members in the new chamber supported the government, whereas only 92 ultras had been elected. Elie Decazes had limited ultra extremism and the militant left had not, as yet, grouped itself into a palpable menace to the monarchy. However, while Decazes was feeling confident that all the steps he had taken to secure a working acceptance of the charter were coming to fruition, the ultras were out for his blood and left-wing elements were not, in point of fact, rallying around a monarchy that was attempting to accommodate them, but rather preparing, in one way or another and with varying time frames, for its overthrow. It was into this political ferment that Alexandre Corréard arrived in Paris in that frustrating and humiliating spring of 1817, and it was into this buzz that Théodore Géricault returned from Italy later in the year to find, like Corréard, that Paris once again had become a politically exciting city.[29]

In order to emerge from his troubles with something positive, Corréard sought the Légion d'Honneur, but his request seems to have been lost or blocked, perhaps deliberately, among the mass of paperwork at the Ministry of the Navy. At last he received a communication from DuBouchage, dated June 4, notifying him that all his applications would most probably come to nothing. Despite the support of twelve deputies, the authorities refused to be of any assistance in Corréard's attempts to secure a position as an engineer.

He had meanwhile learned that a councillor of state had indeed recommended him for the Légion d'Honneur, but that the minister of the navy himself had refused to put the request before the king. Corréard rightly felt it unjust that a victim of official incompetence should be blocked from receiving from his king some assuaging sign of "justice and benevolence." The indifferent Lieutenant Reynaud, the executioner himself, had been given command of the transport vessel the *Gironde,* while, by contrast, Corréard was still finding it difficult to walk and Savigny's fevers and pains made it impossible for him to work for two weeks out of every month. Having lost all his "resources in the course of duty," Corréard felt "disgusted" by the official attitude and, above all, "forgotten."[30] He had watched the men in braid, comfortably installed in their well-provisioned boats, pull away. He had been plunged into the abyss but had returned to the world a wiser man; should his health permit, he was ready to take it on.

The wreck of the *Medusa* as a news story and as a pretext for political change was still affective. On March 12, the *Journal des débats* carried the result of the trial of Chaumareys. On June 22, DuBouchage was forced to resign from the government. Having largely purged his ministry of liberal or Bonapartist sympathizers, he now provided Decazes, through his injudicious appointment of a particularly inept member of the old guard, with a tangible pretext for purging him. Decazes had never liked DuBouchage, so along with other unsympathetic elements in the government, DuBouchage was replaced.

Comte Matthieu Molé, the new minister of the navy, had served Napoleon as minister of justice and had even accepted a post during the Hundred Days. Molé immediately set about reversing the backward-looking policy of his predecessor. A royal ordinance appeared in the *Journal de débats* on October 22 announcing a reduction in navy personnel. From November 1, 1817, there would be six rear admirals, twelve commodores, sixty captains of warships, three hundred lieutenants, and four hundred ensigns. Although several esteemed monarchists were able to hold on to their commissions, the largest number of men retired were those who had been reappointed during the restoration after years of inactivity. Rear Admiral La Tullaye, who had served under Louis XVI and had proved a lenient president of Chaumareys's court-martial, was among those dispatched. The misadventure of the prestigious expedition to Senegal thus played its part in curtailing the careers of nine admirals and 173 captains.[31]

While the navy thus benefited from the tragedy, Corréard and Savigny were continuing to smart for their pains and suffer for their losses. As the gruesome complexities of the ordeal had not been adequately articulated, the affair had never altogether slipped from the public's interest. A letter written by Mlle. Schmaltz that was circulating in Paris fueled the disgust of survivors. In it, according to Savigny and Corréard, the young lady "confessed that the sight of the shipwrecked persons inspired her with a degree of horror. . . . 'It was really impossible for me,' she wrote, 'to endure the presence of these men, without feeling a sentiment of indignation.'" It was such lack of compassion along with the navy cover-up that finally convinced Savigny and Corréard to bring before the public the ugly sweep of their scandalous saga. In their narrative, they analyzed the source of Mlle. Schmaltz's repugnant aversion and exploited it politically with a honey-tongued irony.

> She could say to herself, "these men have in their hands the
> fate of my father. If they speak, if they utter complaints . . .
> if they are listened to (and how should they not be listened
> to in a country where a charter, the noble present of our
> august Monarch, causes justice and the law to reign) instead
> of being the daughter of a governor, I am but a wretched
> orphan; instead of these honours, with which it gives me so
> much pleasure to be surrounded, I fall into the degradation,
> and the oblivion which generally await the unhappy family
> of a great criminal."[32]

The conditions for exposing governmental faults were, however, difficult. Censorship and secrecy had become important and controversial political tools of the restoration. Pasquier, the *Garde des Sceaux*, the French lord chancellor, observed that it was indispensable to maintain surveillance on newspapers and periodicals "in a country emerging from a long period of political torment." Opponents of current repression, such as the baron Martin de Gray, maintained rather that "the manifestation of thought is the vital driving force of free and representative government" and that it is "to police tribunals that you hand over the limits of thought, you give them the right to say to human intelligence: 'You can't go any further.'" Decazes, supporting the law of censorship, which was, to all intents and purposes, an extension of his laws of autumn 1815, skillfully smoothed over the debate by claiming that the purpose of censorship was to "maintain a complete and just equality, to consign the past to oblivion, to extinguish hatred, to make power loved and respected, which is the aim of the government."[33] It was against the backdrop of this discussion about governmental control of politically inflammatory material that the bombshell *The Shipwreck of the Frigate, the Medusa* was first published. Although decidedly less politicized than later editions, it was not calculated to "consign the past to oblivion, to extinguish hatred" or to "make power loved and respected."

Registered at the *Bibliography of France* on November 1, 1817, this first edition was the only one that carried Savigny's name before Corréard's and it is the simplest and shortest of all the versions, the one that most closely resembles the original text that Savigny had written on board the *Echo*. The book was available at a cost of 3 francs from five shops in the capital, including that of its printer, François Hoquet, and that of the renowned legal and children's bookseller Alexis Eymery. Books at this boom time in French publishing were brought out by printers or booksellers and Savigny and Corréard's text was published by three people who owned establishments in the Palais Royal, that vital hub of Parisian life.[34]

That *The Shipwreck of the Frigate, the Medusa* would become a rallying point for the liberal cause was clear from the extensive review that appeared in the liberal *Mercure de France,* of which Alexis Eymery was an administrator. The moderate *Journal des débats* likewise carried an excellent review in which we read that

Nothing is more terrible than this tale, we tremble at each page, shudder at every line. The secret passages of Anne Radcliffe, and all the imaginary horrors of our melodramas and tragedies are nothing compared with the real horrors of this awful catastrophe. . . . [Savigny and Corréard] survived by a miracle! But intrigue and persecution awaited them ashore and it is more difficult to escape from the injustice of man than the fury of the sea. Everyone will read the tale that they are publishing; it is an historical piece that will give rise to stringent reflection and must find a place in all libraries.[35]

Le Journal du commerce, the rebaptized *Constitutionnel* that had been suppressed for its pro-Bonaparte stance in July 1817, carried a large, two-column review of *The Shipwreck* on November 29, significantly placed under Domestic News rather than Book Reviews. It claimed that there had been no event "so deplorable" as the wreck of the *Medusa* and spoke of a subscription fund being set up for the survivors by Etienne Jay, who had first announced the fact at the end of his lengthy review of *The Shipwreck* in the *Mercure.*

When *Le Journal du commerce* published a list of initial subscribers, it was obvious that sympathy for the ill-treated victims of government incompetence came from all levels of society and all walks of life: a member of the Académie Française, a lawyer, a doctor, the duc de Berry, the duc d'Orléans, the proprietor and regulars of a café in the rue St. Denis all gave. Sums ranged from the 500 francs given by the liberal banker Laffitte, to the touching two francs given by "Mademoiselle Caroline B., orphan."[36]

The disaster was reaching far and wide and stirring the hearts of many people. The scandal and the issues surrounding the wreck of the *Medusa* played into the hands of the ever-strengthening liberal faction—republican ideologues, reeling from the collapse of the empire, the fiasco of the Hundred Days, and the repressive measures of the ultras in the regressive *chambre introuvable.* Slowly, they were organizing an offensive with far-reaching consequences, and the *Medusa* scandals would play a crucial part in their story.

9

The Fualdès Affair and
the Love Affair

On March 20, 1817, a body was found in the waters of the Aveyron River in southern France. It was soon identified as being that of Antoine-Bernardin Fualdès, a magistrate and criminal prosecutor from Rodez who had served the revolution and the empire and who had come out of retirement during the Hundred Days. On the previous evening, Fualdès had left his house with a substantial IOU tucked in the pocket of his frock coat and was on his way to redeem the debt. He was followed into a rough part of Rodez where, at about eight p.m., he was ambushed at the corner of the rue Hebdomadiers, gagged with a handkerchief, and bundled off into a gambling den aptly named the Crooked House, a notorious haunt of smugglers and prostitutes. After the assassins had forced their hostage to sign letters of exchange for the IOU, Fualdès was stretched out on a table. Sawing with a blunt knife, his murderer opened a transversal section across his neck from the right to the left carotid arteries. Posted by the assassins at the corner of the street outside, hurdy-gurdy players ground out their eerie melodies, obliterating the screams of the victim. The murderer smeared the body of the ex-magistrate with a little of the blood he had let while the rest dripped steadily into a bucket. When full, this was given to a pig to drink. The animal, having gorged himself, subsequently died. At around ten o'clock in the evening, the bloody body of the hapless Fualdès was placed on two poles, wrapped in a sheet, covered with wool, tied, and then carried to the river by four individuals who dumped the corpse into the Aveyron and hence, they thought, into oblivion.

That is the gist of the official account of the crime as presented by the public prosecutor in Rodez. Despite lengthy trials, and an eventual verdict, the truth behind the murder of Antoine-Bernardin Fualdès has, until recently, remained an enigma. Certainly, it had all the ingredients of a very murky mystery: the roughness of the isolated, inward-looking town of Rodez, which was torn by the furious political quarrels that had afflicted France over the previous decades; the probability that the murder was the work of an avenging ultra-royalist gang; the rumors, lies, and faked convictions; above all, the barbarity of the crime itself, made to seem even more vicious by the official verdict that the murder was carried out by men who were among the victim's best friends.[1] It was also obvious from the start that the authorities in Paris, anxious about their judicial hold on the volatile south, took a special interest in the case.

After hearing hundreds of witnesses, confessions, and denials, a verdict was returned in early September, which was annulled by the appeals court in Montpellier a month later. A retrial opened in the spring of 1818, one year after the crime had been committed. By that time the Fualdès affair had become a media sensation with reporters from the large Parisian papers in attendance.

Considering Fualdès's lengthy career serving the Revolution, it was obvious that he would be a prime target for royalist revenge. The comte François Régis La Bourdonnaye, an ultra deputy for Maine-et-Loire, listed a thousand heads that should tumble; Antoine-Bernardin Fualdès was on that list.[2]

The intrigue surrounding the murder of Fualdès was, like the *Medusa* scandal, testimony to the running sores that plagued France after a quarter of a century of revolution and civil and foreign war. Yet though the *Medusa* scandal was brought before the public in order to discredit the ultra-royalists, the truth behind the Fualdès affair was hushed up in order to suppress evidence of civil strife.

The falsification of the Fualdès verdict was, to a large extent, made possible by the volley of lies, contradictions, and hysterical accusations that tumbled from the mouth of a celebrity-seeking woman named Clarisse Manzon. Just as Corréard decided to expose the *Medusa* scandal in print, so the mysterious and highly strung Clarisse Manzon published her version of the events in Rodez. She was the quintessential publicity seeker who understood that if you say something sufficiently shocking, however ill-advised or stupid, people will lap it up. The thirty-two-year-old Clarisse soon achieved her aim of making Rodez "famous from Gibraltar to Archangel."[3]

Unlike the *Medusa* investigation, which was conducted in camera, the Fualdès case was a civilian affair, providing flamboyant copy for an avid press. *La Quotidienne* observed that "no one thinks of greeting a friend without asking for the news from Rodez."[4] Indeed, as the trial became the preoccupation of salons throughout Europe, it attracted the attention of writers, painters, and printmakers and a mini-industry grew up around the spurious proceedings. In Paris, along the quays of the Seine, booksellers hawked numerous images and lithographs treating the murky affair.[5]

Théodore Géricault's interest in the Fualdès murder and his subsequent obsession with the *Medusa* scandal reflect his developing absorption with crime and catastrophe—with the violent and shocking phenomena that were the staple of broadsheets, and with their starkly embellished woodcuts dramatizing sinister events. Such publications fascinated people and fed popular literature with tasty morsels suitable to the Gothic novel, a genre that has been described as a "literature of cannibals that feeds on bits of human flesh."[6]

In the second half of 1817 the Fualdès affair had somewhat eclipsed the wreck of the *Medusa* as the talk of the town but, with the publication of *The Shipwreck of the Frigate, the Medusa,* once again the maritime atrocity seized the public's imagination. The sheer scale of the loss, the mortifying tale of selfishness, cowardice, cannibalism, and murder—to which must be added the resolve and courage of the authors of the book for getting their version of events into print—was simply staggering; Savigny and Corréard's narrative exposed nothing less than the government's failure in its duty to its subjects.

On his arrival in Paris in late 1817, Géricault would seem to have had the time neither for the top stories of the day nor for painting. The months in Italy had only exacerbated his desire for his aunt and mistress and he rapidly fell into the arms of Alexandeine-Modeste, the woman he had left France to forget. In his private sketches he now expressed more intimate and personal evocations of loving. Mythology had once provided a way to sublimate the sexual dilemma of his life; now he was producing works that expressed the intensity of coitus or those gentle moments of tender intimacy either before or after.

These drawings and washes are celebrations of sex in which the woman is active, and not, as is so often the case, a displayed object to delight the male voyeur.[7] The passionate hug of the woman on top in *The Embrace* reveals someone who clamors for, and enjoys sex. These are not titillating scenes, not confessions of psychological and physiological distress, but celebrations of the power and pleasure of physical union. Wash drawings such as *The Kiss* express the sheer exuberance of tenderhearted lovemaking, the sensual and spiritual rapture experienced by reunited lovers. Géricault revels in the plump form of his beloved. Their union was obviously intense and, as with all true love, supremely precious. Catastrophically, it was to prove short-lived.

For all their elation at being reunited, something occurred that crushed them. After more than a year without each other, they had plunged feverishly back into their affair. Within two months, Alexandrine was pregnant with Géricault's child. It would soon no longer be possible to conceal their intimacy. Within a matter of months the pregnancy would be obvious to Alexandrine's husband and her position in society, as a wife and mother, would be in jeopardy.

In the early decades of the nineteenth century, the upper classes of French society became obsessed by the subject of adultery. Alexandre Dumas dated this fixation from the 1804 civil code that abolished primogeniture, the right of the firstborn to inherit. Fathers, stewards of a family's fortune who were suddenly obliged to acknowledge all the children produced by their wives, naturally became anxious over the question of paternity; bastards, under the *Code Napoléon,* were entitled to the same privileges as legitimate children. When such concerns were brought to bear on marriages complicated by decades of difference between husband and wife, anxiety increased. The divorce law under Napoleon had allowed a husband to get rid of his wife for adultery but, in 1816, the *chambre introuvable* abolished divorce. In the case of Géricault and his aunt, the kindred nature of the relation did make it easier to contain the problem within the family, the preferred course at a time when the guilty woman and her lover, if he was a bachelor, faced imprisonment for a period of up to two years.[8]

By April 1818, with his aunt's womb swelling into scandal, Géricault had begun to play with the macabre subject of murder. After making a series of preliminary sketches, however, the Fualdès affair, already treated so well by the popular engravers of the day, appeared somehow wanting. Instinctively, Géricault was searching for a contemporary event of sufficient scale, energy, and universality to make a lasting impression. It was during this period, while his child was growing toward an uncertain life, that Géricault became interested in, and fixed on, a much grander tale of murder. It was a tale whose themes touched the deep and searching questions that the French were asking about their national identity, and it presented a particularly striking example of man's inhumanity to man.

The period between the breaking of the *Medusa* story and the publication of Savigny and Corréard's book, with its upsetting, in-depth revelations, had been a difficult time for Géricault. In early 1818, as a result of the calamitous twist in his secret relationship, he developed an even deeper engagement with suffering that would, in one way or another, transform him into a man who, for the rest of his short existence, would wrestle with questions of life and death. Géricault was facing the inevitable loss of his loved one along with the probable loss of his child. At this time, he decided to abandon the Fualdès murder for the horrors that followed the catastrophic loss of the *Medusa*.

10

Trips to the Morgue

I wander aimlessly now and always go astray. Vainly, I
search for any support. Nothing is solid, everything escapes
me, everything deceives me. . . . If anything is certain upon
earth, it is our pain. Suffering is real and pleasures are nothing but imaginary.

N o exact date can be placed on the letter from which these lines
are taken, but it seems likely, as Géricault also writes of the
"terrible difficulties" into which he has "rashly thrown himself," that it was written during the bewildering months after the discovery of Alexandrine's pregnancy.[1] Apart from his self-reproach, there
would have been a feeling of helplessness at not being able to be with
and console his beloved as her condition became increasingly evident.

While the pregnancy remained invisible, and seven months to
the day before Alexandrine gave birth to Géricault's child, her husband,
either by a cruel irony or by way of reaffirming and consolidating their
marriage, added his wife's maiden name to his own; henceforth he

would be known as Jean-Baptiste Caruel de St. Martin, to which, in 1819, he would add the title of baron. Preoccupied by business, over fifty, and already blessed with two male heirs, we can guess that sexual relations between Jean-Baptiste and his wife were rare or nonexistent, otherwise there would have been an obvious, if deceitful, solution to Alexandrine's dilemma. How culpable and forlorn she must have felt disclosing her condition to her generous husband, how awkward before her two children. Whether confined in the Château of Grand-Chesnay or sequestered in the depths of the country, how alone she must have felt without the comforting presence of her nephew. Would she have dared to admit the identity of the father? Would such a treacherous relationship prove more or less insulting to her husband than some chance dalliance?

As there is no record of subsequent visits made by Géricault, either to the Château of Grand-Chesnay or to the Caruel's Parisian establishments, it does suggest a permanent rupture, signaling the fact that the painter was indeed known to have been Alexandrine's lover. In light of the pregnancy, Caruel, the astute businessman, could not have failed to consider the intense relationship between his wife and nephew that had developed over the previous years and reflect upon its possible consequence. It was certainly not uncommon for women in upper-middle-class families, often married to much older men, to help a younger male in the advancement of a career, such intimate collaboration often plunging the pair into an emotional relationship that led to the young man's initiation into the pleasures of sex.

During the early part of the pregnancy, the *Medusa* scandal was once again in the news with the February 28 publication of Corréard and Savigny's entirely reworked second edition of *The Shipwreck of the Frigate, the Medusa*. With the addition of Brédif's notes and some further observations on West Africa, it was a much amplified text, embellished by a plan of the raft drawn by Corréard and a portrait of King Zaide somewhat surprisingly providing a frontispiece. The short, four-month interval between the first two editions suggests that the public's appetite was keen, and Corréard's name placed before Savigny's on the title page established the fact that the text had, by this second edition, become Corréard's baby.[2]

At five a.m. on August 21, 1818, a son was born to Alexandrine-Modeste Caruel at the house of the celebrated obstetrician Dr. Danyau, at 14 rue Pavée Saint André des Arts. In violation of Article 312 of the civil code declaring that any child born into a marriage, even one sired by a third party, was legally considered to be the husband's, the boy was taken away and registered as being "of unknown parents" at the town hall of what had been at that time the Eleventh Arrondissement.

Such declarations of anonymity were not uncommon; with the thirty thousand or so abandoned children and the seventy thousand illegitimate births registered in Paris each year, about one in three children was the fruit of an extramarital liaison. It was Dr. Danyau who registered the infant at the town hall and, seemingly under instruction from the father, gave him the name Georges-Hippolyte—Georges, in honor of Géricault's father, who had been consoling in a time of crisis, and Hippolyte, a Greek name meaning, "I release the horses." The unrecognized Georges-Hippolyte was first cared for by Danyau and then was sent to a nurse at the home of a Monsieur Dubois in Normandy, where he spent his childhood.[3]

As the pregnancy was coming to its term, Géricault had begun work on some studies to help him bring before the salon, some as yet unchosen moment from the *Medusa* saga. To capitalize on the interest generated by the enlarged second edition of *The Shipwreck,* Henri Savigny, in May 1818, published his *Observations on the Effects of Hunger and Thirst Experienced After the Wreck of the King's Frigate, the Medusa, in 1816.* This was a study of calenture, the delirium and fever that attacks sailors in the tropics. Although Savigny presented the work as a thesis at the Faculty of Medicine in Paris, it was hardly an original piece. It copied whole passages from a study of the phenomenon that had been published by Fournier de Pescay in 1812 and it added little to Pescay's more recently published work on the subject of March 1818.[4] Savigny's thesis was, however, useful to Géricault who, from the outset, craved facts about the catastrophe and assembled a file full of related documents. There were the first two editions of *The Ship-wreck* and clippings from the newspapers, to which he added Savigny's treatise on calenture. The painter supplemented these printed sources by securing interviews with certain survivors of the raft and by making a series of gruesome anatomical studies.[5] There was a modernity in his profound factual, intellectual, and emotional engagement with his subject, and such a depth of research had, at the same time, a palliative effect; Géricault was somewhat distracted from his own misfortunes through immersion in this horrific shipwreck. At last, a subject of sufficient size and pertinence had presented itself to him and it could not have come at a more welcome moment.

Géricault was drawn to several episodes on the raft: the mutiny of the soldiers and sailors against their leaders; the cannibalism; the sighting of the *Argus*; the approach of its lifeboat; and the moment of rescue. The actual abandoning of the raft proved unsuitable because of the complex problem of realizing a striking compositional drama with a glut of 147 people crushed onto a small platform. Such a throng would confuse and compromise the impact of personal suffering, which could be better expressed through the sparse incident attaching to a much smaller group. A similar excess of incident, albeit cunningly disposed, is apparent in an advanced sketch for the *Mutiny,* which also provides ample proof that Géricault was keen to make maximum use of Corréard and Savigny's account: the broaching of the barrels, the jettisoning of the casks, the ropes used to keep people from being washed away, the leader at the base of the mast repelling a hatchet attack, the axe-wielding mutineer who was plunged into the sea, the vulnerable stern, and the supplication of the frightened souls on board. Géricault soon came to understand, however, that the writhing turbulence of this scene also worked against the most profound message that could be extracted from the catastrophe.

A small seascape produced around this time reflects the artist's preoccupation with cataclysm. This gloomy marine disaster was Géricault's *The Deluge,* which reveals, in the foreground of the somber scene, scattered people hopelessly clinging to the small, barren rocks of a reef. A black block of cloud filling the top third of the canvas, bearing down on the shipwrecked victims like the wrath of God, perhaps expresses the plight of its tormented maker.

Géricault took himself out of circulation in order to work. He installed himself at No. 232 faubourg du Roule on the outskirts of Paris with the sole purpose of focusing on the *Medusa.* The list of welcome visitors was short: his close freiend Dedreux-Dorcy, his pupil Jamar, his disciples Montfort and Leroux, and those survivors of the raft whose brains he wished to pick. Géricault shaved off his hair so as to strengthen his resolve not to enter society. He slept in a room off the studio and his meals were brought to him. Most important, he had chosen a location only a short walk from the Beaujon hospital where he could go to observe human suffering and from which he would obtain severed body parts for private study.[6]

The hospital near Géricault's new and temporary work space had been founded in 1784 by Nicolas Beaujon as a hospice for orphans and the poor of the parish. Becoming a hospital in 1795, it slowly grew until, by 1816, the authorities crammed 140 beds into a space originally intended for 80. During the Allied occupation at the beginning of the restoration, typhus resulted in a death rate of nearly one in every four patients, but conditions began to improve in 1818, when the hospital was provided with facilities for washing laundry and supplying water to each floor. Although the mortality rate was in decline, there remained a sufficient supply of dismembered limbs and dead bodies for student study.

Géricault's interest in corpses and human fragments was not merely anatomical but also pathological; the *Medusa* project compelled him to observe the effects of deprivation and violence and he made arrangements with the interns and nurses at the Beaujon to allow him to follow the phases of suffering on site as well as to provide him with amputated limbs for studio study.[7] Because exhumation and dissection were, from October 1813, forbidden outside the Faculty of Medicine, Géricault may have had to come by his limbs and heads in a roundabout way. It is quite possible that Henri Savigny, through his medical connections, was instrumental in helping the painter obtain some of the amputated limbs.

The conditions that Géricault encountered on his visits to the dissecting theater would give him some insight into the state of the raft after the carnage of the mutinies. Hector Berlioz, who at that time was a young medical student, vividly described the scene.

> This human charnel house, scattered members, grimacing heads, skulls half open, the bloody cesspool in which we trod, the revolting odour . . . filled me with such fright that, jumping through the window of the amphitheatre, I escaped as fast as I could and ran panting to my place, as if death and its dreadful cortège were hot on my heels.[8]

Unlike Berlioz, Géricault felt compelled to accept such pursuit, inviting death into his studio.

The city also provided Géricault with an extensive site in which to study human misery. Pre-Hausmann Paris remained a densely packed warren of pest-ridden streets in which ordure, offal, and assorted rubbish were scattered by scavenging dogs, splattered by cart wheels, and further mired by the horses that circulated through the entrails of the city.[9] An anonymous English visitor noted that the "climate of the French metropolis is bad, unpleasant and unhealthy. It is subject to frequent and sudden falls of rain" so that the city was known, even by the French themselves, as the "chamberpot of France." This situation was compounded by the

> injudicious manner in which the drains are laid on for conveying the rain-water and filth of every description, which gradually amasses, from the roofs and gutters of the houses, and which, instead of being carried down, as in England, to the ground, project from the house to the distance of three or four feet, and consequently inundate the passenger who walks under them.

These dense, unhealthy spaces were littered with amputees, men whose lives had been saved by the celebrated seventeen-second disarticulations of Dominique Larrey on countless Napoleonic battlefields, cripples who now mooched an uneasy and impoverished existence in the capital. In these fetid streets, Géricault walked among the physical remains of rejection and disease and produced, during 1818–19, poignant and provocative lithographs that formed an elegy for the Napoleonic adventure: *The Retreat from Russia, The Cart of the Wounded,* and *The Swiss Sentry at the Louvre.* As with the artist's work on the *Medusa,* all of these explore different forms of betrayal, attest to the burgeoning of Géricault's political consciousness, and disclose the morbidity of his mood. His familiarity with the city's streets, his trips to the nearby Beaujon as well as to the Bicêtre hospital, and the morgue, all contributed to his researches for *The Raft of the Medusa.*[10]

Only a stone's throw from where Georges-Hippolyte was born, on the south bank of the Ile de la Cité near the Pont-Neuf, was a gaunt, freestanding rectangular structure, the Paris morgue. Inside the building bodies were laid out for display and fashionable visitors would come to spectate on the transitoriness of life or gloat over the wages of sin.

The morgue was just opposite the Académie Suisse, an informal studio where many of Géricault's friends came to draw. On the testimony of the regulars, it seems that Géricault worked across the road in the morgue for long hours, on and off, over a period of a year. The function of the morgue was to receive the unidentified cadavers that came under the jurisdiction of the police. Inside, the clothes they had been wearing when found were hung above the anonymous corpses in order to offer some aid to identification. Stillborn babies and miscarriages were displayed for a period of three days, during which they could be reclaimed by relatives, a mortifying sight, perhaps, for one who had so recently been forced to give up his son to an anonymous nurse.[11]

On occasion, Géricault's friends Charles-Émile Champmartin and Alexandre Colin joined the artist in his noxious studio to paint severed limbs and heads. In *Anatomical Fragments,* now in Montpellier, Géricault presents a tangle of limbs that recalls the human debris strewn about the raft. An intimation of cannibalism is suggested by the section cut above the shoulder like a choice offering on a butcher's block. The cut of the joint is presented as something potentially edible and lit in a manner that recalls Dutch still lifes that celebrate a brace of pheasants or a rib of beef. Delacroix, sounding the romantic artist's understanding of what Géricault was all about, called these studies "the best argument for Beauty as it ought to be understood," revealing as they do the transfiguration by art of what was odious in nature.[12]

After a two-day period of rigor mortis, which sets in six to twelve hours after death, the effect of the stiffening lactic acid wears off and the body softens and putrefies. Géricault kept cadavers and fragments for weeks and his closest friends, along with those few visitors who had not been on the raft, became afraid of infection.[13] By contrast, Géricault did not hesitate to handle these toxic fragments and touching and smelling death brought him closer to the world of those abandoned by Chaumareys and Schmaltz. If he was not about to eat the flesh that he brought home, the artist was prey to its odors, and the sense of smell accounts for much of what we "taste." Géricault felt the flesh becoming limp, he smelt the putrefaction, he all but tasted the meat. If not directly related to his sketches for the *Medusa* project, for which he used live models, we can attribute to these paintings and drawings of severed limbs the role of stimuli in his living with the raft.[14]

Installed in the new studio, skin-headed after discarding the thick locks of an earlier, happier self, Géricault set to work. Gone was the soft, blushing, elegant figure. Lebrun would no longer come upon an embarrassed, vain young dandy with hair in curling papers. The shaving of his head, a practical preparation for settling down to work undisturbed, was also perhaps an impetuous act of purification, a renouncing of sex.

Deprived of love, Géricault became a man of compassion. He dedicated himself to painting the cruelties of modern life. Amid the acrid relics littering his studio at St. Philippe du Roule, Géricault set out on his own short and fatal voyage. In the wake of separation and loss, he seemed to be saying, "I'll sorrow with the sorrowful, I'll repent among the dead. I will set myself adrift on a difficult sea."

11

The Raft of the *Medusa*

As the winter of 1819 progressed, Géricault was hard at work, intent on finishing his painting for the Salon, which would open in August of that year. He had won a gold medal with his debut in 1812, exhibited three works in 1814, but had missed the event in 1817 because he had been in Italy. It was high time to make his mark. The Salon was supremely important to painters; with an embryonic art market and with nonofficial or privately mounted exhibitions a rarity, it was their only established forum. Organized by the administrators of the royal museums, during the restoration the event had grown in size.

The 1819 Salon would be not only larger than its predecessors, it would be coupled with an Industrial Fair, proclaiming that France was emerging from the ravages of instability and beginning to embrace the modern age. The return of a good deal of Napoleonic plunder to its rightful owners had left gaping spaces in the Louvre's collection, now waiting to be filled with the best in modern French painting. The artists attracting the most official interest were those history painters who turned their backs on the large battle scenes that had been so popular during the empire in order to flatter the restored monarchy with illustrations from the lives of French kings.[1]

Ignoring this trend and having discarded other ideas, Géricault had finally settled on the most poignant moment in Corréard and Savigny's scandalous narrative, a moment of hope that would evaporate, leaving the enfeebled survivors in despair. Apart from their inherent technical difficulties, discarded episodes such as acts of mutiny or of cannibalism might have jeopardized the polemic of the painting by provoking questions about the culpability of his new friends Alexandre Corréard and Henri Savigny. What had been the two survivors' motives in giving an exhaustive account that repeatedly apportioned blame while praising and flattering its two authors? Had they, in order to survive, and in refusing the role of victim been guilty of actions that were as cowardly or egotistical as the leaders whom they accused?[2] In choosing to paint the first sighting of the *Argus,* when the brig remained too distant to notice the raft, Géricault subtly reminded spectators of the culpability of the leaders of the expedition. By freezing that moment, the painter presented his public with a scene of great suspense. The unsaved were fixed at a point before the happy ending, before, at the eleventh hour, rescue miraculously arrived.

On a political level, the image is a stern indictment. Géricault's decision to include, on the extreme right-hand side of his canvas, the blue, white, and red of a uniform trailing off the raft into the water, acts with its echo of the revolutionary tricolor like a requiem for republican French values. On another level, if the almost imperceptible *Argus* were to be read as a religious or spiritual metaphor, it suggests that salvation may simply not be forthcoming. The artist's search for a composition capable of conveying far-reaching meanings precluded any off-putting scene of Gothic horror. Géricault sought a potent image, not realism in all its awful excess.

Montfort, Géricault's young assistant, recalled the painter's complete need of quiet as he worked: "When I made a bit of noise with my chair, in the midst of the absolute silence in the studio, . . . Géricault, who was standing on a table in order to paint the top of his canvas, reproached me gently with a knowing smile, which let me know that the noise of a mouse was enough to stop him from painting." Géricault's pupil Jamar was, to that end, obliged to wear slippers. Concentration was intense and the hours were long; the artist would start early, so as to benefit from the morning light, and work on, uninterrupted, through the day until nightfall.[3] Even when he left the studio that he had littered with death, Géricault found himself attracted to the pallor of suffering. One day in Sèvres he encountered his friend Théodore Lebrun, who had succumbed to jaundice. Lebrun recalled that

> I had much trouble finding a lodging; my cadaverous face frightened all the inn-keepers; none of them wanted me to die at their place . . . one afternoon, I saw Géricault approaching with one of his friends . . . suddenly he recognized me and seized me in his arms: "Ah, my friend, you are really beautiful." I frightened myself, children ran away, taking me for dead—but I was beautiful to the painter who was looking everywhere for the color of death. He pressed me to visit him and to pose for the *Medusa*.[4]

Among the people who came to model for Géricault was the young painter Eugène Delacroix, who posed for the man facedown in the center foreground of the picture. Delacroix remembered that *The Raft of the Medusa* had a terrifying effect in its unfinished state and recalled that the "impression it gave me was so strong that, as I left the studio, I broke into a run, and kept running like a fool all the way back . . . to the far end of the faubourg Saint-Germain."[5] Generally, Géricault used professionals such as the popular model Joseph, who sat for the figure of Jean-Charles, the black man signaling. He also made numerous studies of survivors such as the ship's carpenter, Lauillette, and Savigny and Corréard.[6] They came to the studio to provide the artist with eyewitness accounts and they came to pose. Corréard, as a recognizable figure, first appears in the sketches for the scene of false hope that Géricault finally selected for his painting.

Since September 1818, Corréard had been running a bookshop in the Palais Royal that had become a meeting place for political activists. The publication of *The Shipwreck* had made him a celebrity, and unlike the retiring Savigny, who wished to put his difficult past behind him, Corréard capitalized on his success and went so far as to call his bookshop At the Victim of the Shipwreck of the Medusa. Corréard was trading on his misfortune as well as making a political point, alerting the authorities of his desire to publish and spread what they considered to be sedition.

Corréard exerted a considerable influence on the painter. Certainly, they became friends and even collaborators when Géricault produced engravings for the third edition of *The Shipwreck,* which, with additions such as an account of Corréard's trial, a list of the "Subscribers to the *Medusa* Shipwreck Fund," and a seven-page, indifferent ode, fell somewhere between a self-promoting gripe and a deluxe collector's edition. Although it was unlikely that Corréard could influence Géricault radically, he had by now a reputation to maintain. Elements of his narrative had already been contested by other survivors of the raft and Corréard could not afford to have his authority doubted. His credentials as an agitator needed to remain secure. If the scandal was, once again, to be brought to the public's attention, and particularly in such a prominent place as the Salon, would it not be in Corréard's interest that certain elements be sanitized so as to avoid embarrassing speculation about those actions that enabled him and Savigny to survive? Would it not be in his best interest that Géricault's painting stress the culpability of the leaders rather than the horrors of the raft? Corréard's cause would be served by a painting that made a grandly political statement, rather than one that presented a vision of bloody and controversial massacre or cannibalism.

In the finished *Raft of the Medusa,* Géricault placed Corréard in pride of place, positioning him almost centrally, on the line of the canvas's all-powerful golden section, with his side-lit face carrying the charged expression of one who has something to broadcast. He is looking at the swathed head of Savigny, his coauthor, as if saying, "There you have it. What we see in the distance is not a rescue vessel, it's nothing but a part of the same state machinery that is responsible for our present plight." His gesture is not one of exuberance at having glimpsed hope, but alarmist and accusatory. His outstretched arm against the dawn light takes the eye along the line from the dead son outstretched in his father's arms to the controversially placed black signaler at the apex of all their hope. Although this signaler is given a position of importance, Corréard pulls the eye as the key figure in the composition. The painting does not present Corréard as victim, but Corréard as messenger, Corréard the polemicist, the savior who would take up arms against a sea of troubles.

On April 21, 1819, still smarting from the lack of sympathy shown him and his fellow sufferers, Corréard presented a report to the chambers of the peers and deputies, attacking the inexperienced and unworthy men who to his mind had caused the tragedy of the *Medusa.* Corréard sought justice on behalf of the victims of the shipwreck who, nearly three years after the tragedy, were still struggling against slander, rejection, exhaustion, and pain. Corréard pleaded for even the smallest display of compassion from the authorities. Insisting on nothing for himself, and in the name of national honor, he beseeched the members of the chambers, those "moral guardians" of France, to observe the rights set out in the charter and punish the guilty parties to the fullest.

He attacked the ex–minister of the navy, vicomte DuBouchage, whose pride had prevented him from adequately pursuing and punishing his appointees. Corréard accused DuBouchage of concealing crime and encouraging it by impunity, having tried Chaumareys only for the loss of his ship. He further accused DuBouchage of having imperiled the lives of Frenchmen and other ships of his majesty by placing them under the command of like-minded incompetents.

Corréard urged the members of the chambers to consider whether Captain Chaumareys had been adequately tried for the two major crimes he had committed, the abandoning of his ship and the abandoning of the raft. Often citing the letter of the law and before proceeding to the capital crimes, Corréard lists the various misdemeanors of the Captain and the other officers: Chaumareys for allowing the convoy to break up; Chaumareys and the officer of the watch for abandoning a fifteen-year-old ship's apprentice who had fallen overboard on June 23, 1816; the officer commanding the boat that put in to shore at Santa Cruz on June 29 who refused to rescue six French prisoners; Chaumareys for having failed to recognize Cap Blanc; Chaumareys for having lost the *Medusa*. He then accused Chaumareys for not being the last to leave his ship but rather disembarking when there were still sixty-four men on board, which, according to Article 35 of the law of August 22, 1790, carried the death penalty. All the *Medusa*'s officers are accused of having abandoned the "152" people on board the raft; this "in the name of all the laws of humanity and Articles 36 and 37 under Heading 2 of the aforementioned law," which clearly stated that "All officers entrusted with commanding a convoy found guilty of having voluntarily abandoned it will be condemned to death." Corréard also chided Chaumareys for not having sent the *Argus,* the *Loire,* and the *Echo* to search for the raft as soon as he had reached Saint-Louis.

Corréard attacked Colonel Schmaltz for various crimes and misdemeanors: for having waited two days before liaising with the English governor over a possible search-and-rescue operation; for not accepting Colonel Brereton's offer of using all the ships at his disposal; for delaying the departure of the *Argus;* and for not punishing those who misappropriated government and personal property recovered from the *Medusa* two months after its wreck. He declared Schmaltz unworthy of representing the French government and stated that he should be indicted under clause No. 12 of Article 475 of the penal code, which condemns those who refuse or neglect to help the victims of a shipwreck or other accident. Most important, perhaps, Corréard openly questioned Schmaltz's behavior in relation to one of the most far-reaching and unpleasant aspects of the whole recolonization of Senegal, the abominable trade in human beings that was becoming a burning issue for liberals in France, and which would unite Corréard and Géricault. Without swearing that such rumors were true, Corréard urged the chamber to look into the possibility that Schmaltz was not only openly favoring but active in the slave trade.[7]

Corréard was still physically suffering from his ordeal, with painful scars covering his body, and he was not prepared to accept soft justice; Chaumareys had less than a year left in jail and Schmaltz was, by all accounts, profiting from the slave trade. Corréard was adamant that subsequent editions of *The Shipwreck* contain a printed record of the catalog of crimes that he had aired before the government and, henceforth, his attack would take on a larger target than mere reparation for past ills; it would begin to address this illegal trade in human flesh.

To place a black man in such a dominant position in his finished *Medusa* composition suggests that Géricault sympathized with Corréard's political struggle and was listening to the debates in the liberal circle around him. To place a figure who, because of his color, was generally considered to be subhuman at the summit of whatever hope *The Raft of the Medusa* may be said to express was daringly, dangerously, avant-garde.

Recent research shows that the three black figures in the finished painting were introduced at a late stage in the composition.[8] Their placing tells its own story. The one lying facedown, dead, over the haunch of the figure clammering from the deck speaks of past despair. The second, placed significantly between Savigny and the political agitator Corréard, looks up hopefully to the third, who is signaling optimistically. A counterpoint to the story of voyagers abandoned by their leaders, these three present the larger drama of a people passing from despair and victimization to hope for a brighter future. The artist had become not only a witness to the malfunctioning French administration, but also an advocate for a fundamental shift in human rights.

While working on the painting, Géricault made short excursions out of Paris. In late March 1819, he made a trip to Le Havre to study the effects of clouds over water. He also went with Horace Vernet and a retired officer on a short trip to visit English artists. The channel crossing afforded Géricault further opportunity to study the sea and the clouds and allowed him to experience the sensation of being on water.[9] Otherwise, the painter was hard at work in his studio on *The Raft of the Medusa,* which, as a result of his enforced isolation, he finished in the relatively short period of eight months. The painting was emerging darkly monochromatic. There was a lot of black, a color that, Géricault observed, "suits pain."[10]

The large surface of the canvas may have been dark, but it revealed something surprising, even revolutionary. Traditionally, seascapes painted in Holland, France, and England presented distant scenes of disaster on small canvases in which any human drama was relegated to tiny, almost meaningless detail. In the powerful northern romantic work of Caspar David Friedrich and J. M. W. Turner, human incident was dramatically subordinated to the force and grandeur of nature, but in Géricault's large painting, however much we feel the presence of threatening elements, the work focuses on the survivors on the raft.

Géricault's major paintings bring the spectator right up to the action, revealing the artist's early and persistent understanding of the power of the close-up. In *The Raft,* such a procedure insists on the terrifying distance between the seemingly futile agitation of the survivors and the almost imperceptible fleck of the *Argus* on the horizon. This symbolically asserts the gulf between the peril of the abandoned and the distant attitude of the leaders of the expedition. The *Argus* is seen from either the stern or the bow but it is impossible to say which, so those on the raft and the spectator have no way of knowing whether the ship is approaching or is about to disappear from sight. Furthermore, by making the ship a mere smudge, Géricault suggests that it may even be a delusion, a phantom of these severely tested men's delirious minds.

When, in July 1819, Géricault thought that he had finished his canvas, six men came to transport it to the foyer of the Théâtre Italien in the Place Boieldieu, where paintings were being assembled for the Salon. Seeing the canvas with a refreshed critical vision once it had been removed from the familiar surroundings of his studio, Géricault realized that the bottom right-hand corner was disturbingly empty. Increased tension could be given to the painting by filling the space with a dead figure being dragged from the raft into the sea. Géricault decided to reintroduce a figure that had appeared in a study for what may have been a scene of cannibalism.[11] He further modified his work by including another figure, lying dead on his back, at the extreme left.[12] These additions to a raft already too populous to match the numbers given by the official reports as well as by Corréard and Savigny demonstrate how Géricault discarded journalistic verisimilitude. He placed his figures and structured his groupings in order to sweep from despair in the foreground to the false hope of the gesticulating black man on the barrel. Bolstered by his researches, which had secured emotional depth and integrity, the painter dared to depart from the literal truth in his expression of a more profound meaning.

When Corréard faced the finished picture, it must have made a tremendous impact on his sense of himself. He must have felt redeemed, honored, rewarded. Here he was, in the middle of this vast painting, sending a wake-up call to France.

On September 18, 1816, a worried vicomte DuBouchage had written to Louis XVIII on the subject of the wreck of the *Medusa:* "I bemoan the fact that the journalists revel in disclosing details of deplorable scenes, the picture of which must never be brought before the eyes of the public."[13] When the generally lackluster 1819 Salon opened on the Feast of Saint Louis, August 25, nearly a year to the day after the birth of Géricault's son, there could be seen, hanging among the sixteen hundred items on show, *The Scene of the Shipwreck,* the compromise title devised by the Salon authorities in an attempt to deflect public attention from the true subject of Géricault's vast canvas. Ironically, in an exhibition intended as a political shopwindow for the recently restored monarchy, one of the most talked about paintings was this very work, which, despite its neutralizing new title, obviously called into question the competency of the Bourbon administration.

The 1819 Salon saw the first stirrings of the debate between the old, neoclassical school, which had dominated French art for the previous thirty years, and the new romantic artists who had grown up during that period of turmoil. The quarrel would erupt dramatically in 1824 when the two schools would be split into the classical "Homerians" and the younger romantic "Shakespearians." It was an argument involving questions of detachment versus immediacy, formality versus spontaneity, and it led eventually to a loss of confidence in Salon juries and the revolt against the academy and official art that would stimulate painting in nineteenth-century France. Géricault's gloomy shipwreck, painted on an unacceptably large canvas for its genre, provoked an early attack on the new school of painting, which appeared to reject good taste for what was ugly.[14]

Artistic affront to the establishment was a dangerous tactic and, although Géricault's private income allowed him to invest the time needed to produce a vast canvas, he could not ensure that the result would be accepted for exhibition; these Bourbons may have been more tolerant than their predecessors, but they faced a disgruntled populace. Certainly, with its controversial subject matter, no revolutionary or Napoleonic government would have admitted such a subversive painting as *The Scene of the Shipwreck*. In order to justify his selection and sounding a decidedly pro-romantic note, the comte de Forbin, the courageous and perceptive director of museums and organizer of the Salon, wrote to the comte de Pradel, the director-general of the royal household, that the "arts are the enemy of restraint."[15]

Hanging in the company of the large work commissioned by the monarchy, the Ministry of the Interior, and the duc d'Orléans and placed compromisingly high on the wall of the Salon Carré, above the doorway to the Grande Galerie of the Louvre, was No. 510, Théodore Géricault's *Scene of the Shipwreck*. From the opening of the Salon, reaction to the work seemed to be largely unfavorable. Géricault swiftly realized that this had much to do with its positioning. With the aid of his friend Dedreux-Dorcy, the painter managed to have his enormous canvas rehung so that its baseline was much nearer the floor. At this level, it took the spectator into what seemed like an extension of real space. Viewers were drawn into the upward thrust of the raft, an illusion that pulled them right on board. Not only was a moment of false hope frozen, the viewer had been made part of it.[16] Hanging at this height, the impact of the scale of the figures was considerable and lent both drama and dignity to the suffering portrayed.

Louis XVIII kept up the custom, initiated by Napoleon, of the head of state visiting the Salon. On August 28, he made his two-hour visit in a wheelchair and, accompanied by several people including Elie Decazes, now the minister of the interior, Louis XVIII met Géricault. The king spent considerable time studying *The Scene of a*

Shipwreck and, in a celebrated witticism, demonstrated the scope and agility of his political acumen. The king's remark to Géricault begins, as the French writer Jean Sagne has pointed out, with what seems like an accusation: "Sir, you have made a shipwreck . . . ," displacing the guilt that Géricault, Corréard, and Savigny had heaped on the shoulders of the administration onto those of the painter. Expecting the sentence to keep up its accusatory tone, we are suddenly disarmed by the wit of its conclusion: "which is not one for you." As Sagne suggests, complimenting a work that dared to challenge the regime was a powerful demonstration of regal magnanimity. Perhaps, studying the painting in the company of his favorite Decazes, the king remembered how the catastrophe had, in their concerted effort to neutralize the ultra threat, played right into their hands.[17]

Once more the wreck of the *Medusa* was the talk of the town. The ultra-royalist *Quotidienne* recorded that Géricault's painting created a "huge uproar" at the Salon. Surprisingly, ex–minister of the navy DuBouchage became enraged with the organizer, Forbin, not for accepting *The Scene of the Shipwreck* for Salon presentation, but rather for including the portrait by Jacques-Marie Legros of his nemesis Alexandre Corréard, an exhibit that indeed confirms that Corréard had become something of a celebrity.[18]

Géricault, who until the late summer and early autumn of 1819 had been a relatively unknown artist, suddenly became "the painter of the *Medusa*."[19] Not only was the public's interest in the subject matter lively, the painting itself also provoked a great degree of critical controversy. Its somber, monochromatic effect was repeatedly reproved. *La Quotidienne,* in the first of its six articles covering the Salon, actually called the work by its real name, *The Raft of the Medusa,* and lamented the artist's use of monochrome. On the other hand, the critic in *Le moniteur universel* noted that "the melange of red and gray tones produces a sinister effect which is in perfect accord with the spirit of the scene."[20] The critic of the *Gazette de France,* calling it a "monstrous painting," suggested that Géricault had sacrificed all the rules in order to catch man in the midst of a calamity that forced him to lose his dignity; there was "nothing touching, nothing honourable."[21] The critic of *l'Indépendant,* while admiring Géricault's draftsmanship, found nothing of Corréard and Savigny in the work, which he would have thought to be the intention of the painter.[22] Meanwhile, aesthetes considered the "majesty of the brushwork" belittled by the choice of subject.[23]

Géricault was upset by the generally unfavorable reaction to his masterpiece and irritated by the inanity of certain critics. Having painted a political work, he now became a victim of political and journalistic wrangling. He vented his exasperation in a letter.

> This year, our journalists have reached the heights of stupidity. Each painting is primarily judged according to the spirit in which it has been composed. Thus you hear a liberal article praise a patriotic touch in a work. . . . The same painting judged by an *ultra* will then be nothing other than a revolutionary composition governed by a general tint of sedition. The faces portrayed will all have an expression of hatred for the paternalistic government. Finally, I was accused by a certain *Drapeau blanc* to have slandered, by an expression on a face, the entire Ministry of the Navy. The unfortunate people who write such stupidities obviously haven't starved for 14 days, because they would then know that neither poetry nor painting are capable of rendering with sufficient horror all the sufferings experienced by the people on the raft.[24]

It is obvious that as the *Medusa* was a cause célèbre, critics would be likely to divide along party lines. Given the subject matter, liberals took the pretext of the painting to reconsider the scandal of the shipwreck. To many of them, the refined neutrality of the classicized figures and the disinfected conditions on the raft appeared as a wasted opportunity. In the *Courrier de Paris* a critic even asked, "Are they Greeks or Romans?" The question is apposite; to deny the brutality of the facts by using a lingering neoclassicism in the treatment of the figures was to make a costume drama of a contemporary event and compromise the political message implied by the clash of the classes and races who had been condemned to the raft. Yet to make a great and important painting for the Salon, the language of Michelangelo was still considered necessary. The overall effect of the canvas is darkly romantic, yet the figures retain a muscular monumentality that belies its story.[25]

Exhausted by pressures in his personal life and by his punishing work on *The Raft of the Medusa,* as well as being overwhelmingly discouraged by its reception at the Salon, Géricault caved in to depression and retreated to the country. On September 11, he went to Machault and Féricy, near Fontainebleau, with the liberal sociologist Auguste Brunet. Despite the sympathetic company and the late summer splendors of the countryside, within two weeks Géricault retreated to his bed. He had became irritable and appeared to be suffering from persecution mania. By mid-October, he was taken back to Paris to undergo treatment.

It was decided that there should be no prize awarded for history painting in the 1819 Salon. Géricault's masterpiece, along with works by thirty-two other artists, won a gold medal, an award that was eventually bequeathed to Alexandrine's second child, Géricault's godson, Paul. Meanwhile the canvas, having picked up an award but no buyer, was rolled up and stored in the obscurity of a fellow artist's studio.[26]

12

The *Medusa* Sails On

T hree days after Géricault was informed that he had won a gold
medal at the Salon, Hugues Duroy de Chaumareys was released from prison and retired to his family domain, the Château
de Lachenaud in Limousin. Meanwhile Alexandre Corréard's call for
justice before the chambers had made no impact and, even though
the left would continue to cite the catastrophe as evidence of ultra
misrule, the political potency of the scandal of the *Medusa* seemed to
be on the ebb.

Across the channel, however, the story was very much alive. Not
only had the *Times* carried a version of Savigny's leaked article of
September 1816, but two years later a full translation of Savigny and
Corréard's book was published. Savigny's name appeared first on this
English edition even though it is a translation of the second French
edition, which had come under Corréard's control. The English publisher was the much respected Henry Colburn, who was currently publishing the likes of Benjamin Franklin and Madame de Staël and acting
as an agent for the collection of English donations to the *Medusa*'s

subscription fund. The *Narrative of a Voyage to Senegal* proved a highly popular book. The part played by the late Major Peddie, whose kindness to Corréard when he had been hospitalized in Senegal stood in such heartwarming contrast to the callous indifference of the French leaders, endeared the saga to the British.[1]

The English relished a scandal that revealed weaknesses in French administration and the lack of discipline and moral fiber in their navy. French ineptitude reflected advantageously on English competence, and the gulf between the two forces was further highlighted by the impeccable behavior following the shipwreck of the British frigate HMS *Alceste* in February 1817. Returning home from the Far East with Lord Amherst, the British ambassador to the emperor of China, on board, the frigate, negotiating the imperfectly charted Straits of Gaspar to the north of Java, "struck with a horrid crash on a reef of sunken rocks, and remained immovable!" In complete contrast to the lack of adequate measures taken by Captain Chaumareys, the English Captain Murray Maxwell, had sailed through these straits with "the utmost precaution." He had posted men "looking out at the mastheads, yard-arms and bowsprit end." The "officer of the watch, on whom the charge of the ship at such a time more particularly devolves," along with all the other officers on board, were vigilantly up on deck. In contrast to the *Medusa,* the *Alceste* was fortunately only three and a half miles from the nearest island when she ran aground and a raft was constructed to transport stores and baggage. A barge took the ambassador ashore and then returned for members of the crew. During the ensuing days, while Lord Amherst made for nearby Java to summon help, food and water dwindled and the British were threatened by savage Malay pirates, who eventually set fire to the *Alceste* and harassed their camp on the overgrown island. The officers set an excellent example to those beneath them and under "all the depressing circumstances attending shipwreck; of hunger, thirst and fatigue; and menaced by a ruthless foe, it was glorious to see the British spirit staunch and unsubdued." Everybody survived the shipwreck, being rescued by HMS *Ternate,* which had been sent from Java. Captain Maxwell was acquitted and praised by the subsequent court-martial as having "conducted himself in the most zealous and officer like manner."

A book written from the notes kept by the ship's surgeon, John McLeod, was published in the same year that Savigny and Corréard's *Narrative* first appeared in English, and the conduct of the British officers appeared exemplary beside that of the likes of Reynaud, Schmaltz, and Chaumareys. So telling was the contrast between these eyewitness accounts that a volume, published in Dublin in 1822, brought together the story of the *Alceste* with a truncated version of the *Medusa* narrative. In some "Observations" accompanying these texts, the editor states that the tales were placed together "as they clearly point out the advantage to be derived from discipline, subordination and moral feeling, on the one hand; and hold forth, on the other, a lamentable picture of the vicious state to which men may be reduced, when uninfluenced by these."[2]

With the hook of international rivalry, the sympathetic role played by the English, and all the horrific ingredients of the inhuman tale, it was not surprising that a Barnum-like figure named William Bullock would wish to bring Géricault's picture over to London as a topical attraction.[3] Apart from financial gain and the possibility that a triumph in London would eradicate the memory of a disappointing Salon showing, there was considerable interest for a French artist in coming to, and being shown in, London. Despite the enduring rivalry between England and France, a lively cultural exchange had been taking place during the restoration.[4]

One reason for these growing ties between the two nations was the anglophilia of Louis XVIII. He had been well treated in exile by the British, who believed that peace in Europe would be secured if the French monarchy could be restored. After the upheavals of the Hundred Days, Louis kept a precautionary nest egg in Coutts Bank in

England and the French government turned to Barings of London, rather than to its own banks, for a loan to help pay off its final indemnity to the Allies. At the same time, to the more liberal-minded French, London seemed a natural alternative to Paris; while the ultras were enjoying their domination of the *chambre introuvable* in the early part of the second restoration, the liberal Benjamin Constant had fled to London, as had the duc d'Orléans.

To the French of the restoration, Britain—with its industrial and naval supremacy—seemed progressive and powerful. But there was another side, a dark and unstable aspect to the country to which Géricault and his *Raft of the Medusa* came in 1820. The end of the Napoleonic wars had plunged Britain into serious economic crisis exacerbated by bad harvests and wildly fluctuating food prices. Around four hundred thousand demobilized soldiers were unemployed, factories that had lost their military customers faced ruin, government finances strained under the huge debt incurred by the war, and an enormously unpopular monarchy all placed Britain in a vulnerable and volatile state. There was open revolt and the specter of revolution. What is more, it fell to the normally stable property owners, already protesting over excessive taxation, to pay the rates that financed poor relief. The government thus faced rebellion, not only from radicals and agitators who made their appeal to the working class but also from the wealthier members of society. Recent French history had provided a dangerous precedent, which prompted Lord Liverpool's Tory government to oppose reform lest it lead to revolution. In 1811, George III was declared unfit to govern and his politically incompetent and petulant son George became the prince regent. By the time this extravagant and narcissistic man was crowned George IV in 1820 he was detested.

Géricault embarked for England on April 10, 1820. With life in Paris proving painful and disappointing, London offered a new horizon. Although Liverpool's reactionary government appeared to have successfully repressed revolt with the massacre at Peterloo in August 1819, its extensive network of government spies, and its six Gagging Acts, there was still revolutionary ferment in the air, rendering London an intriguing destination for the increasingly politicized artist.[5]

William Bullock, who was to exhibit Géricault's masterpiece, had been in France in September 1819 and may have seen *The Raft of the Medusa* at the Salon. The entrepreneur undertook to handle all the arrangements for the London exhibition, elected to pay all costs, and offered Géricault a third of the profits.[6] The lack of state or private patronage for history painting in England meant that, unlike in France, there had been a tradition of commercial exhibitions in London during the previous half century. In contrast to the exceptional presentation of *Sabine Women Enforcing the Peace* mounted by its painter, Jacques-Louis David, as a commercial venture in Paris in 1800, London had seen many celebrated artists such as John Singleton Copley, Benjamin West, and James Ward present their own large-scale works in exhibitions to which they charged admission.[7] Just prior to Géricault's arrival in the capital, Benjamin Robert Haydon "engaged the great room upstairs at Bullock's Egyptian Hall in Piccadilly, for a year from March 1, 1820." For £300, a sum that he did not possess when he signed the contract, Haydon secured the space in which to show his *Christ's Entry into Jerusalem.* As the exhibition overlapped with Bullock's presentation of *The Raft of the Medusa* the entrepreneur was praised by the *Literary Gazette* for creating the opportunity to compare French and English works.[8]

Shortly after Géricault's arrival in the English capital, he was joined by his friend Auguste Brunet and by the portraitist Jean-Baptiste Isabey, who crossed the channel to escape the unwanted attentions of the French police who suspected him of circulating seditious drawings. If one adds to this little nest of expatriate radicalism the fact that William Bullock, a member of several liberal scientific societies, was involved in antislavery activities, then Géricault's English adventure takes on a political as well as a personal and financial dimension. Abolitionists often cited African artifacts to help refute slave traders' arguments about the subhumanity of their cargo, and Bullock's London Museum was a startling showcase for ethnic dexterity. Even the dates of the exhibition of *The Raft of the Medusa* may have been deliberately chosen to coincide with increased English concern over France's clandestine continuation of the slave trade in Senegal.

Although Géricault was in London to see the *Raft* presented before a less hostile public, any excitement at the prospect of a more favorable reaction does not seem to have dislodged the depression that had settled over him six months earlier. Professional success and private happiness had eluded him at home, and on the streets of London, moving through the thick industrial air, he experienced a misery perhaps even more pronounced than that which he had known in Paris. The image of death haunted him and he wrote his will, an act that his traveling companion Nicolas Charlet took as a prologue to a suicide attempt. With such fears in mind, when Charlet returned to their hotel late one night and found that Géricault had not gone out that day, he feared the worst. He rushed to Géricault's room, banged on the door, burst in, and found his friend stretched out on the bed, unconscious. He revived him and, deploying his often brutal humor, attempted to jolt him out of his depression.[9]

Savigny and Corréard's translated *Narrative* created generous advance publicity for the London exhibition of *The Raft of the Medusa*. Interest had been further stimulated by the opening, on May 29, 1820, at London's Royal Coburg Theatre, of William Moncrieff's *Shipwreck of the Medusa, or, the Fatal Raft! A Drama in Three Acts*. It was a spectacle that boasted the most extravagant and newfangled scenic effects: "various Panoramic views of the Ocean & Red Deserts of Zaara" and a "View of the Raft sailing amidst Novel & Extensive

Moving Scenery." The play is remarkable for the fact that the *Medusa* suddenly found herself with a British botswain, Jack Gallant, whose primary function was to emphasize the honorable and fearless qualities of the British seaman. The introductory remarks to the printed text of the play strike that censorious note that the English so readily applied to the tragedy: "Owing to a very relaxed state of discipline, and an ignorance of the common principles of navigation, that would have disgraced a private merchant ship, this frigate was suffered to run aground . . ." Of the play itself, one can only hope that the language barrier would have protected Géricault from its chauvinistic froth.[10]

London was going *Medusa* mad. Publicity for Bullock's exhibition of the painting began with announcements for the private view on the front pages of the *Times* and the *Morning Chronicle* on Friday, June 9, 1820.

> The Private Exhibition of Monsieur JERRICAULT'S GREAT PICTURE (from the Louvre), 24 feet by 18, representing the surviving Crew of *The Medusa* French Frigate, after remaining thirteen days on a raft without provision, at the moment they discover the vessel that saves them, will take place at the Egyptian Hall, Piccadilly, on Saturday, and will be opened to the public on Monday next.

From the press we know that "the Marquis of Stafford, the Bishops of Ely and Carlisle, and a number of the most eminent patrons of the Fine Arts together with several members of the Royal Academy" were present at the private view. As for Géricault, perhaps his experience was much like that of Benjamin Haydon, who only a few weeks earlier had, on the day of the private view of *Christ's Entry into Jerusalem,* installed himself at Hatchett's Coffee Room where he spent the time wondering whether anybody would turn up.

When the exhibition of *The Raft of the Medusa* opened to the public, visitors streamed into the outrageous building; through the doors sided by lotus columns and surrounded by hieroglyphs, down the passage to the main exhibition hall, through a "Pasaltic cavern" resembling the Giant's Causeway, and through rooms that until the year before, when Bullock had auctioned off his own marvelous collection of objects and stuffed animals, had housed the most remarkable exhibits. Through these spaces of the newly established Bullock's Egyptian Sale Room they moved, lured by the proprietor's promise of a large and dramatic picture that portrayed the recent and ghastly shipwreck and that had created "universal interest . . . at the last exhibition of the Louvre." Driven to spy on their recent enemy in its most abject hour, the public surged into the large Roman Gallery where *The Raft of the Medusa* was hanging, cunningly close to the ground, so that their approach would seem to continue on into the horrific scene. If Géricault had suffered from the first positioning of his work at the opening of the 1819 Salon, or from his compatriot's wish either to forget the tragedy it portrayed or to use his painting as a pretext for political wrangling, then in London, in the hands of a consummate showman, he certainly fared better. As with Haydon's exhibition, the "rush was great and went on increasing."[11]

For the most part, the reviews were intelligent and sympathetic. In the *Globe,* on June 12, the reviewer noted that

> Monsieur Jerricault . . . has selected for his first great historical effort a subject of the utmost difficulty, and with a singular absence of the national vanity ascribed to his countrymen, one which it would be well for the naval character of France to have blotted from her maritime annals. The story of the shipwreck of *The Medusa* . . . records a narrative of the most criminal ignorance, pusillanimity, and individual suffering which has no parallel in modern history.[12]

The reviewer in the *Morning Post* on June 13 commented, "This work far excels anything we have seen of the school to which it belongs. . . . There is more of nature, of the grand simplicity of art, and of true expression than is usual with the highest of modern French painters." This was a view that was elaborated in the *Times* of June 22: "Though the painting bears marks of that cold pedantic school of which David may be considered the founder, yet the powerful talent of the artist has broken through the trammels of this system. . . . The expression is energetic, true, and full of pathos."[13] In contrast to the carping of many Parisian critics, two intelligent reviews appeared in the *London Literary Gazette: Journal of Belles Lettres,* noting, "The Morgue seems to have been studied as far as it could without exciting horror" and "the bold hand of the artist has laid bare the details of the horrid facts, with the severity of Michael Angelo and the gloom of Caravaggio . . . the whole of the colouring is so well suited to the subject."[14]

The exhibition having opened with great success, Géricault returned to France. He arrived in Dieppe on June 19 and went on to Paris. Across Europe there were stirrings of liberal discontent. In Spain, there was a successful revolt against the Bourbons. In July there were insurrections in Naples and Sicily, followed in 1821 by stirrings of subversion in Portugal and Greece. There was liberal agitation in German universities but in France, as one English visitor remarked, "Since the assassination of the Duke de Berry, all has been distrust and suspicion." Indeed, after that assassination on February 13, 1820, which forced the resignation of Decazes, blamed for his tolerance of dissent, the government shifted markedly to the right. Henceforth there would be no question of reconciliation, only of two opposed parties. Louis XVIII's worst fears were realized as the country became bitterly divided. In March 1820, more laws enforcing press censorship and curtailing individual liberties were passed. In April there was a control imposed upon the publication and distribution of engravings.

In May and June, medical and law students led the liberal reaction against the repressive measures and, in early June, they clashed with royalists outside the chamber of deputies where a twenty-three-year-old law student named Nicholas Lallemand was killed. The young man became a liberal martyr and, after his funeral, student demonstrators incited the workers of the faubourg Saint-Antoine to riot, crying, "Long live the charter!" and "Down with the royalists!" A rebellious crowd formed and began to move toward the Tuileries. Louis XVIII, sensing the tension and the danger to his throne, had not, as had been his habit, removed his court to St. Cloud for the summer. The crowd swelled to cries of "Down with the king!" and "Long live Napoleon" until, to the relief of the government, the mob was dispersed by a downpour. Over the following weeks, tension mounted and there was, by late summer, a general anxiety that the king and the benign institutions of his reign might be overthrown. The fact that the bourgeoisie felt as threatened by such outbursts as the ultras consolidated the country's move to the right; in the elections in early November 1820, the left captured only 80 out of 430 seats, whereas the ultras obtained 160, of which 75 had been held during the ill-famed *chambre introuvable*.

Against this deteriorating political situation, Alexandre Corréard was found guilty of publishing seditious material.[15] He had already brushed with the law and had pamphlets confiscated, but this time he was fined and imprisoned. As the third edition of *The Shipwreck of the Frigate, the Medusa* was to be published by Corréard in July of the following year, embellished by eight engravings made by Géricault and others, it seems inevitable that during the artist's six-month stay in Paris they would have met to discuss the project and Géricault would have become further involved in the struggles of active French liberals.

On December 30, 1820, Bullock's exhibition of *The Raft of the Medusa* closed. It had been a sensational success, drawing up to fifty thousand visitors. Géricault's share of the London takings was between 17,000 and 20,000 francs, three to four times as much as the sum that might be offered by the French establishment when purchasing canvases of this size and importance. Spurred on by success in London, where Bullock had exploited the similarities in size between Géricault's painting and the tremendously popular contemporary entertainment, the panorama, the impresario took *The Raft of the Medusa* to Dublin, where the commercial success of the venture was ironically compromised by competition from an immense panorama shrewdly capitalizing on the current interest in the horrors of the raft. Shortly after Bullock's exhibition opened at the Rotunda, on February 5, 1821, a notice appeared in a Dublin newsletter announcing that

> Messrs. Marshall respectfully beg leave again to solicit the kind patronage of the Nobility, Gentry and the public of Dublin, and its vicinity, for their lately finished, entirely novel *Marine Peristrephic Panorama of the Wreck of the Medusa French Frigate and the Fatal Raft*. Also the ceremony of crossing the line. Each view accompanied by a full and appropriate band of music. The picture is painted on nearly 10,000 sq. feet of canvas, under the direction of one of the survivors, in a superior style of brilliancy and effect—the figures on the Raft and on the boat being the size of life.[16]

A month into the exhibition of Géricault's painting, Bullock's presentation was obviously struggling in the face of the loud, popular "peristrephic," or revolving, panorama. He was forced to reduce his entrance fee from 1 shilling, 8 pence to a more competitive 10 pence, "In order that all ranks may have the opportunity of viewing this stupendous production of the pencil."[17] Although Bullock was now offering Géricault at the same price as the cheapest ticket sold by the Marshalls for their panorama at the Pavilion, by the end of March the

Géricault exhibition was forced to close whereas the panorama continued to play in Dublin thrice daily to packed houses until June 9.
Géricault's oblique, 430-square-foot indictment of the leaders and or-
ganizers of the Senegal expedition, his grand metaphor for the fragility
of the human condition, could not compete with an extravaganza that
sensationally plunged the public visually and aurally into the event.[18]

Géricault had not been in London for the closure of his exhibition
at the end of December 1820, but he returned to England shortly afterward for a stay of about a year. During the winter of 1821, the painter
lodged near fashionable Hyde Park where he was able to ride.[19] Although
he was participating in the equestrian pleasures of upper-class London,
Géricault's continuing depression led him to seek out and explore the
lower depths of the industrialized city. He observed those whose lives
had been wrecked by the changing order, the castaways along the
wharves and in the crippled byways of the city. Vestiges of classicism
that in certain critics' eyes had compromised the appalling horror of
the *Raft* could have no place here; classicism was a style incapable of
depicting the personal misery and suffering he encountered. Through
his political awakening while working on the *Medusa,* Géricault's subject matter had become man's inhumanity to man, and here, on the
streets of London, was an appalling parade of destitution and abuse. While
the *Medusa* was foundering in Dublin, Géricault was hard at work. He
collaborated with the lithographer Charles Hullmandel on a series of
twelve images contrasting aspects of life in the capital; workhorses and
thoroughbreds, industrious blacksmiths and farriers were treated along
with uncompromising images of the urban poor.[20]

Although it has been observed that Géricault was working in the
tradition of Hogarth, in his attitude to the destitute there is none of
that artist's overt didacticism. Géricault's view is objective, though not
unsympathetic. In the muted compassion of his lithographs, in their
elucidation of the shameful state of affairs, Géricault emerges as the
first great visual critic of the industrial revolution.

While devoting himself to an art that "was a novelty in London," Géricault wrote to Dedreux-Dorcy on February 12, reporting that he had been "extremely sick." He was also far from happy. The circumstances surrounding the otherwise flattering attentions shown to him by a married "woman of great fortune who was not in her first flush of youth" can only have acted as a painful echo of his complicated relations with his uncle and Alexandrine. This mysterious woman fell head over heels in love with Géricault, calling him the "God of painting," but the affair, in a mocking reminder of his uncle's early generosity, was made awkward by the "thousand kindnesses" her husband extended to the young man, even offering lodgings in his house so that Géricault could work. Otherwise, the painter admitted to his friend that "I don't amuse myself at all, my life is that which I led in Paris, working a lot in my room and then prowling the streets to relax myself where there is always such movement and variety that I'm sure that you wouldn't tire of it."

Although at the end of September Géricault wrote that his health was better, during this time in London he suffered an attack of sciatica, provoked by a boat trip on the Thames. When the architect Charles Cockerell, whom Géricault had met in Rome, went with the artist to view some paintings on December 1, he noted in his diary that Géricault looked "ill and consumptive"; bidding good-bye to him eleven days later, Cockerell summarized the painter's questionable style of life: "lying torpid days and weeks, then rising to violent exertions. Riding, tearing, driving, exposing himself to heat, cold, violence of all sorts." Cockerell concluded that he feared the artist was "in a bad way." Indeed, during his time in London, Géricault began to suffer from the first phases of what eventually developed into tuberculosis of the spine.[21]

On December 13, the artist traveled to Dover and embarked for France on the following day. He wrote of the crossing in a letter to a fellow French painter who had been living near him on the Edgware Road, perhaps gently mocking the current enthusiasm for nautical disaster.

I could easily give you a description of a marvelous storm, paint a picture of sails ripped, the masts swept by the furious waves, the captain up against it, abandoning the rudder and the sailors, petrified, fallen on their knees to invoke St. Veronica. I would rather first put you at peace and tell you simply that there was no real disorder except in our stomachs, that all the basins were used; we arrived at Calais well purged and very pale.

Géricault found absolutely nothing changed in France "except the ministers, but—they don't last long."[22]

Indeed, on December 14, the very day Géricault crossed the channel to return home, a new ultra ministry came to power. Its use of the police would differ little from the previous, more moderate administration, but this new right-wing government proved more determined in its application of repressive measures. Louis XVIII was growing weaker and this new government had the support of the ultra duc d'Artois, who was moving, daily, closer to the throne.

Two things, however, had changed in France while Géricault was away. First, the death of Napoleon on May 5, 1821, on the island of Saint Helena, had brought the various factions opposing the monarchy closer together; there were no longer Bonapartists and liberals and Orléanists but merely an antimonarchical left, united in opposition. Second, the English abolitionist William Wilberforce had begun to make efforts to enlist French liberals in his cause.

Work on *The Raft of the Medusa,* his association with Alexandre Corréard, and some disturbing news emerging from the colony in Senegal swept Géricault up into an issue that would preoccupy him for the rest of his short life. The residue of the *Medusa* fiasco was leading to the exposure of one of France's greatest scandals.

13

A Larger Struggle

"My Second Shipwreck"

In the early 1780s, the father of Louis-Philippe, the last king of France, built an oblong, arcaded quadrangle enclosing a garden divided by graveled paths. It was the Palais Royal. Having ruined himself gambling, this duc d'Orléans turned the place into an immense "temple of impurity—a den of Desperation," where "you can see everything, hear everything, know everything" and where, within its precincts, "you may eat, drink, sleep, bathe, . . . walk, read, make love, game and, should you be tired of life, you may buy powder and ball or opium to hasten your journey across the Styx."[1]

Haunting its galleries were pickpockets, con men, prostitutes, gamblers, procuresses, thieves, and spies. During the restoration, there were visitors of every class and nation; one English tourist remembered that "the military costume of every army in Europe, glared and rattled in the crowd." The Palais Royal was to the Paris of the restoration what Piccadilly Circus or Times Square have been to London or New York—the center of things. It was a focus for excitement and buzz, and tourists would make for its riot of "unsanctioned dissipation," where, in its gambling dens, thousands would suffer "shipwreck of fortune and character." As night fell, within and behind its brilliantly lit arcades, the Palais Royal became a "laboratory of Venus," "a world in itself . . . the temple of animal gratification," full of "the most disgusting scenes of debauchery and vice." There, as Balzac observed in his novel *La Peau de chagrin,* "orgies began with wine and ended with suicides in the Seine," going on to remark that if "Spain has its bullfights, if Rome had its gladiators, Paris is proud of its Palais Royal."[2]

On three sides of the quadrangle, in the arcades under the stone galleries, were about 180 shops where tradesmen of every sort sold their goods and services at inflated prices. There were restaurants, florists, jewelers, print sellers, and an early incarnation of the Paris stock exchange, where bankers and brokers met between four and five in the afternoon to buy and sell shares. The forth side of the structure terminated in a double row of wooden galleries that had been constructed as a temporary space and contained tall, windowed shops lit generously by natural light. These premises were largely occupied by milliners and booksellers. The sale of books and prints was an important aspect of trade in the Palais Royal, which, despite its proximity to the Tuilieries palace and the Louvre, was a hotbed of anti-Bourbon protest. It had been in the Palais Royal that the first revolutionary meetings had been held in 1789. The first tricolor had been hoisted in its garden and it was there that the attack on the Bastille had been organized. More recently, during the Hundred Days, its Café Montansier was a hub of Napoleonic fervor. Other cafés, such as the Corazza, were also meeting places for the politically active, and, in the twenty-odd reading rooms scattered about the quadrangle, such people, "for a very moderate monthly or weekly subscription," were able to keep up to date by consulting "all the ephemeral productions of the press . . . the different public journals, magazines, reviews and pamphlets of every description."[3]

In the temporary wooden galleries there were about 125 shops, the occupiers of which, since 1807, had been under notice to quit so that the passage could be rebuilt in stone. While shopkeepers in the other arcades were subject to high rents, premises were cheaper in this temporary section, which may well account for the fact that it was here that Alexandre Corréard, when he obtained his licence on September 9, 1818, set up shop at No. 258, Galerie de Bois, an address that rapidly became an evening rendezvous for literary and political men hostile to the crown.

If the Palais Royal, this "Babylon in miniature," was not only a honeypot of licentiousness but also a nest of sedition, then "swarms of spies and informers" were sure to be prowling. Relatively indulgent toward moral offenses, the police nonetheless kept a very keen eye on political agitators. This extensive spy network was a Napoleonic legacy, and these snoops, informers, letter interceptors, and plants were now, ironically, employed by the restoration government to keep tabs on Bonapartists and liberals. Corréard, having set himself up in the center of things, had also raised his cantankerous profile, rendering his subversive activities highly visible to the police.[4]

Corréard had bounced back. From penniless, uncompensated, and semi-invalided shipwreck victim, he had, within three years, co-authored a best-selling book and started up as a bookseller. Clearly, having lost everything on board the *Medusa,* he would have needed some kind of support or sponsorship.

One way in which the liberals scored public relations victories against the authorities was to set up subscription funds for anyone who had been exiled or imprisoned for their political views, for military widows, or for the victims of disasters caused by government incompetence. The fund created by the editors of the *Mercure de France,* Etienne Jay and Benjamin Constant, in favor of the victims of the

Medusa had grown rapidly. When, because of governmental persecution, the *Mercure* cleverly rebaptized itself *La Minerve française* in February 1818, it was able to announce a response to the appeal totalling 18,278 francs. Not only was the sum substantial, the lists of donors published over the previous months in the *Mercure* and *Minerve* provided a demographic insight into liberal sympathy, with money pouring in from the professional and merchant classes as well as from the disaffected military and working class. Indeed, the cause met with such national support that no self-respecting celebrity seeker such as Clarisse Manzon, the star witness in the Fualdès affair, could abstain from making a donation.[5]

During February, a notice was placed in the *Minerve* summoning the shipwreck victims to their offices on March 5. With typical French bureaucratic wariness, they were requested to bring proof that they had been on the raft along with a second document proving that they were indeed the person they claimed to be. The fund was to be divided among the survivors. One such, Colonel Schmaltz's secretary, Griffon du Bellay, having apologized to Savigny for the document he had signed in Saint-Louis, now accused Corréard of pocketing a large part of the money. With several of the survivors dead, several still in Senegal, and one gone off to the West Indies, there were only a few left in France to benefit from the cash. Though that would provide a considerable portion for each claimant, it required the further support of the wealthy liberal banker and deputy Jacques Laffitte, one of the administrators of—and largest and first contributors to—the *Medusa* fund, to provide Corréard with the extra finance necessary to establish himself as a bookseller and publisher in the Palais Royal.[6] The shipwreck victim was thus able to become one of the most vociferous private advocates for the liberal opposition. Publishing was, as Corréard recalled, "a profession that, in giving me liberty, permitted me to serve the cause of that same liberty."[7]

Happily, the book trade was flourishing; in the first years of the century, improvements in the production of paper had reduced costs, and one result of this was that the number of titles published annually in France nearly doubled between 1812 and 1825.[8] Despite the three hundred–odd booksellers in Paris, Corréard, already a famous writer, chose a promising and lucrative line of business. Early on in his new career, however, he was forced to pursue three men who had pirated *The Shipwreck* by inserting twenty-nine pages of its text into a collection entitled *History of Shipwrecks*. Corréard lost the case, the judgment somewhat spuriously maintaining that because *The Shipwreck* was four hundred pages long and the *History* eleven hundred, the twenty-nine pages copied represented only a trifling act of piracy. Furthermore, the judge ruled that Corréard's narrative was historic and belonged to everybody and could only be recounted with the same words. Astoundingly claiming that the accused had no intention of piracy and even took the trouble to praise the original work, the judge suggested that there was no cause for protest. Although, as Corréard noted in summarizing the affair, the accused had actually confessed to having taken all the words from his text, the guilty parties were absolved by what seems a decidedly unjust ruling and Corréard was ordered to pay costs.[9]

From early on in his new career, Corréard was harassed as a bookseller and publisher. In 1819, the author of one of the first works that he published, Claude-Henri de Saint-Simon, was called before the tribunal for offenses against the Royal family. The author was cleared by a judgment of the Assize Court but the work was ordered to be destroyed and new proceedings were directed against him for his follow-up pamphlet, which Corréard also published. Between 1819 and 1822, Corréard went on to publish several inflammatory and contentious works by Saint-Simon. A typical proposition offered by the author was that if France kept its craftsmen, its thinkers, or its artists but lost all its rulers, it would hardly be affected. Corréard's publication of such material drew not only police attention but menacing anonymous letters:

Publisher Corréard, you are a madman and a scoundrel. . . .
I warn you that the authorities are watching you; make sure
that they do not remain unsatisfied by just seizing the absurd inanities of the vile and contemptible Saint-Simon.[10]

Corréard was in obvious danger and set on a collision course with the
new law of May 17, 1819, which ruled for the suppression of books
that were offensive to God, to the crown, and to public and religious
morality. In 1820, with the resurgence of the right after the assassination of the duc de Berry, it was obvious that agitators such as Alexandre
Corréard would be hounded. What is more, in the face of this deteriorating situation, Corréard was expanding his activity. In the spring
of 1820, his list of projected publications ran to over 150 brochures,
priced at 50 centimes each, and among which could be found such provocative titles as: *Let's Defend Our Rights; The Wake-Up Call; Let's Speak,
They'll Shut Up; The Alliance of the Government with the Ultras; What's
Bred in the Bone Will Come Out in the Flesh; Does the Government Have a
System?;* and *The Sleepwalking Minister, a Tragedy in Five Acts.*

Corréard was also rashly distributing seditious texts in the royalist south; a bookseller in Montauban, instead of selling works that he
received from Corréard, took them straight to the police. The district
attorney of Toulouse wrote to the director of criminal affairs, insisting on Corréard's audacity in "spreading the poison of false doctrines,
disorder and rebellion everywhere." The authorities, at last, decided
to bring Corréard to trial.[11]

On June 14, 1820, Corréard and the twenty-three-year-old
Jacques Bousquet-Deschamps were tried as publisher and author of a
pamphlet entitled *Questions of the Day.* On April 11, the king's attorney had seized ninety-three of the thousand copies of the work at
Corréard's bookshop as well as the manuscript at Dupont, the printers. Consistent with Articles 1, 3, and 6 of the law of May 17, 1819,
Bousquet-Deschamps was accused of provoking the destruction of the

government and Corréard was arraigned as an accomplice. With the challenging winged head of a snake-haired Medusa printed boldly on the title page above a garland reading, "At the Victim of the Shipwreck of the Medusa," it appeared as if Corréard was indeed the publisher of the work. However, the printer testified that Corréard had told him that he was only its vendor. Furthermore, the bookseller maintained that he had not even read the pamphlet. Given its mere sixteen pages, its subject matter, and the fact that Corréard's establishment sought to attract and serve the liberal opposition, this claim seems farfetched, if not downright mendacious.

"The moment that a government threatens liberty," we read in the pamphlet, "its relationship with society ceases to be legitimate." Although the defense counsel sought to establish that such passages were merely philosophical considerations and not incitements to violence, and despite an impassioned plea for Corréard that played on his sufferings and his valor during the *Medusa* crisis, the author was sentenced to a year in prison and a fine of 3,000 francs for encouraging civil disobedience and the alleged publisher to four months in prison and a fine of 1,000 francs.

The authorities, keen to wipe "At the Victim of the Shipwreck of the Medusa" off the face of the capital, had Corréard back in court nine days later. His codefendant was, once again, Bousquet-Deschamps, this time accused of having written a pamphlet called *Attention!,* which had been published a year to the day after the law censoring books had come into effect. Designating the ultras as "the mortal enemies" of France, the work reflects upon the considerable cost of the revolution and asserts that, in France, "there are today a million of our young men, children of the Revolution, who have sworn to defend to their dying breath, our constitutional liberties."

Corréard, the vendor of the work, appeared in court without the young writer. Having already been arraigned before the assize courts twice, Bousquet-Deschamps had fled to England to escape his penalties.

On this occasion, the authorities charged the author and publisher with the provocation of an attack against the person of the king. The assistant public prosecutor pointed out that since the restitution of the laws of censorship governing newspaper and periodical publication, several writers or publishers had adopted the tactic of launching a series of pamphlets in quick succession with the intention of exciting public opinion and insulting the government. He insisted that the cheapness and frequency of such pamphlets allowed the author and publisher to disseminate articles that would be censored if written for the press. The long list of the titles offered cheaply by Corréard suggests that this was exactly his tactic. The assistant public prosecutor, anticipating Corréard's ruse of disclaiming knowledge of the pamphlet's contents, drew attention to the brevity of the document. It was unlikely, given Corréard's political sympathies, that he would have failed to enjoy the contentious passage, restricted as it was to just eleven lines on the final page. Corréard was found guilty, sentenced to four months in prison and fined 1,200 francs. Bousquet-Deschamps, in his absence, received the stiff default penalty of five years in prison and a 6,000 franc fine.

Five days later Corréard was back in the same court, accused, once again with Bousquet-Deschamps, author of *As Things Are,* of having outraged public and religious morality. This time the bookseller was awarded three months in prison and a fine of 400 francs, and the writer a year in prison and a fine of 500 francs. The court ordered the destruction of the brochure as it had done with the previously condemned publications.

Just under a month later, on July 26, Corréard was charged, along with the booksellers Béchet and Mongie, with having distributed *History of the First Fortnight of June* by Bousquet-Deschamps. They were accused of producing a work that provoked rebellion and disobedience. The printer testified that the writer had instructed him to place the names of the three booksellers on the title page. Although the two

other vendors were acquitted, Corréard, dubbed by the assistant public prosecutor "a great entrepreneur of sedition," was condemned to
four months in prison and a 500 franc fine, while the absent author
piled on another two years in prison and another 4,000 franc fine. Maintaining his innocence in the face of the charges, Corréard claimed that
the work in question had never appeared in his catalog but that, as a
bookseller, it was his job to sell books and, therefore, he would accept what was offered to him. In answer to observations about the
unhealthy relationship between himself and the accused author, Corréard simply responded that, as a bookseller, he necessarily met men
like Bousquet-Deschamps when they came to buy and sell.

The following day, July 27, as a result of a complaint made at the
end of May by the ambassador of the king of Portugal and Brazil against
a pamphlet entitled *Political Documents,* Corréard found himself back
in the assize court. The assistant public prosecutor demonstrated that
the pamphlet contained the libelous contention that the aforementioned ambassador, the Marquis de Marialva, benefiting from the lack
of a legitimate sovereign, was plotting to install a new family on the
Portuguese throne. Taking Corréard to task as "no ordinary editor,"
the assistant public prosecutor seized on the scam behind the announcement in the bookseller's brochure, promising "a political pamphlet per
day." The prosecutor again stressed that this was nothing other "than
a Daily in another format." Corréard was really a newspaper publisher
and therefore responsible according to the laws governing journals.
The result of the hearing was that Corréard was handed down another three-month prison sentence and a 400 franc fine.[12]

Within forty-three days, the public prosecutor's office had initiated five proceedings against Alexandre Corréard. Not only was he
being targeted as a dangerous and key subversive, he was also extremely
active. Lithograph portraits of Spanish revolutionary generals who
had risen up against the Bourbons were displayed in his bookshop.

He published documents in support of the parliamentary candidature of the abolitionist and supposed regicide Abbé Grégoire. Seventeen works in all had been seized from his shop that year, and, hounded by the justice, Corréard went to prison.[13]

In a back street on the Left Bank of the Seine, surrounded by thick, high walls, stood Saint-Pélagie, an ancient convent and refuge for prostitutes, which was serving as a prison for debtors and political offenders. It was the third largest prison in Paris with a population, in the year that Corréard was committed, of nearly 650 inmates. It was split into four divisions, including a section for young offenders between eight and sixteen years old, some of whom were serving prison terms of up to six years. To the left as you entered, there was the debtors' prison; on the ground floor to the right was the *Détention,* which held two hundred thieves and crooks "with names like *Massacre* and *Quatre-Sous.*" When not silently "familiarizing themselves with the Penal Code" so that when they got out they could "specialize in crimes that carried low maximum penalties," they were loudly clattering about in their clogs, chorusing obscene songs. Above their cacophony was the *Corridor Rouge,* home to political prisoners, a "paradise" compared with the other parts of Saint-Pélagie. In 1820 these inmates—men of letters, journalists, booksellers, printers, and soldiers from the imperial army—were free to wander as far as the prison's inner grill and they ceded the exercise yard to the debtors only in the hottest part of the day. They were not locked up in their cells at night and had the privilege to be visited at all hours. Indeed, the freedom enjoyed by these inmates meant that the political discussions of the Palais Royal could continue, their activities merely frustrated in the short term by their inability to turn words into actions. For a price, better food was available than elsewhere in Saint-Pélagie. Certain prisoners imported their own effects and furniture to make their stay more comfortable, Corréard among them, to judge from the Motte engraving of his cell printed in the later editions of *The Shipwreck.*

During the period of Corréard's incarceration, numbers grew after the failure of the Bazar Conspiracy of August 1820, which had aimed to overthrow the Bourbons by capturing the Château de Vincennes and other strategic points around Paris before instituting a provisional government led by the Marquis de Lafayette. A delay resulted in the discovery of the plot and many conspirators were subsequently committed to Saint-Pélagie.

Despite the privileges and relative comfort, Corréard's time in prison was not one of uninterrupted calm; at six a.m. on the morning of August 30, Police Commissioner Valade burst into his cell and seized works that were considered to be seditious. Forty-eight hours later, Corréard spent the day before the magistrate answering an unrelated police accusation. Two weeks later, on September 14, he was issued with the order that he would be detained in prison until he had paid the fines imposed upon him.

Since the beginning of his detention, Corréard had been petitioning to be transferred to a nursing home. Supported by a letter from Dr. Piron at Saint-Pélagie, Corréard claimed that scorbutic wounds from his thirteen days on the raft reopened frequently and that he was prone to rheumatism. These pleas were in vain and he was left in Saint-Pélagie with his fines unpaid. He wrote to the lord chancellor claiming that his shop had hardly been open before his enemies earmarked him as an opposition bookseller just because he sold, as did many of his competitors, works from across the political spectrum. He noted that five works of which he had not been the publisher were seized in 1819. The seventeen works already seized in 1820 had not been, with one exception, confiscated from the shops of his competitors. He also appealed an unjust fine of 3,700 francs, which it would, in any case, be impossible for him to pay.

Providentially, another subscription fund came to his rescue. The text accompanying the appeal's launch pointed out that "since 1814, magistrates have not pursued booksellers"—that is, "until the judgment against Corréard." Persuasive in its appeal to French patriotism, the subscription fund provided Corréard with the wherewithal to terminate his imprisonment on November 28. Summing up his incarceration for allegedly publishing seditious works, Corréard called it his "second shipwreck."[14]

Yet Corréard remained undaunted. In 1820, as the ultras once again became a force to reckon with, the liberals, anxious about the future, became increasingly militant in their behavior. By the spring of 1821 a network of secret cells of resistance was set up, known as the *Charbonnerie*. According to a police report, it was at "Corréard's bookshop in the Palais Royal" that, every evening, "a Jacobin circle met and shared news." Corréard was marked by the police as an influential member of the *Charbonnerie,* as well as being a man who had links with other known subversives and agitators.[15]

By naming his bookshop At the Victim of the Shipwreck of the Medusa, Corréard had effectively created a trademark for sedition. The *Medusa,* and all that name had come to signify, was now the flagship of the liberal opposition. Corréard was selling and publishing his own book in its third, fourth, and fifth editions and he was the champion of those writers and thinkers who sought to bring down the monarchy.

Whatever he pleaded before the courts, so long as Corréard kept his bookshop open, he sold and published material critical of the Bourbon regime. During this period, he claimed that he was the victim of a "permanent police initiative":

> I had works seized 130 times. I was accused 36 times and condemned 9 times to a total of 8 years in prison. Unjustified action never stops, and although the confiscation of belongings had been abolished, the authorities ordered the closure of my book shop in the Palais Royal. I was hunted. My door was sealed and it was guarded for more than a

month by the gendarmes. In 1823, I was again expelled from
my premises, and pressured to sell all my merchandise for a
base price.[16]

Though his skirmishes against a suspicious and threatened establishment undoubtedly furthered the liberal cause, during the militant
years between the opening and closing of his shop Alexandre Corréard
also involved himself with the greatest humanitarian crusade of the
epoch. Born of his knowledge of what was in truth going on in Colonel Schmaltz's Senegal, Corréard became a force in the fight against
slavery.

The Condemned and the Dying

In Géricault's *Raft of the Medusa,* the outstretched hand of Alexandre
Corréard leads the spectator's eye toward the signaling arm of the black
man standing on the barrel. Corréard is, in a sense, confirming the
selection and positioning of the figure, as if he himself had something
to do with the decision to show a black optimistically heralding a new
dawn. There are certainly elements in his book *The Shipwreck of the
Frigate, the Medusa* suggesting that such a reading of Corréard's gesture is justified. In the narrative, the would-be colonist shows himself
eager to understand the cultures of various African peoples. He questions earlier writers such as Adanson who noted that "the Moors . . .
either made captives, or killed, such Europeans, as had the misfortune
to be shipwrecked on their coast." By contrast, Savigny and Corréard's
account of the interview that the naturalist Kummer had with the
Moorish king Zaide revealed the ruler's civilization, his self-interested
but intelligent curiosity about Napoleon and the Hundred Days, and
his fair-mindedness. Furthermore, Corréard's choice of a portrait of King
Zaide for the frontispiece of the second edition was surely a provocative act, suggesting that it was this comparatively enlightened ruler

rather than the barbarian Frenchmen Chaumareys or Schmaltz, or even Louis XVIII, who deserved to preside over the events that occurred along the West African coast. The juxtaposition of Zaide's seemingly impeccable leadership with the maelstrom of French incompetence and cowardice that litters the pages of *The Shipwreck* acts as a strong reproach to Corréard's malefactors.[17]

Savigny and Corréard's text, even in its earliest editions, made it clear that the eventual health and success of any colonial project depended on the abolition of slavery. When they published the information that the slave trade was thriving in Senegal, it was a provocative and somewhat surprising revelation. Although reports were beginning to circulate that French slave ships were active along the West African coast, there was, at the time, little talk of slavery. Their narrative, therefore, makes a trailblazing contribution to the burgeoning abolitionist critique of the French government's continued and devious complicity with the trade. The timely appearance of the third edition of *The Shipwreck* just weeks after Benjamin Constant made a celebrated abolitionist speech to both chambers, again demonstrates Corréard's ability to exploit opportunity. Abolitionism, with the growing awareness of the persistent flouting of France's antislave trade laws, was newsworthy and Corréard's text would capitalize on the growing concern about what was actually going on in Senegal.[18]

England had dominated the slave trade in the second half of the eighteenth century. But under increasing pressure from humanitarian thinkers, coupled with a commercial desire to exploit the natural resources rather than the manpower of West Africa, the English abolished the slave trade in 1807. Although in France slavery and the slave trade had ended with the convention in January 1794, Napoleon had reversed the decree in May 1802. With the return of the Bourbons, England urged France, once again, to renounce the trade, but the artful Talleyrand, the principal architect of the Treaty of Paris, negotiated a five-year delay in implementing the ban, a period during which tax incentives were actually made available to stimulate the lucrative activity. As the French abolitionist Abbé Grégoire noted in a tract published in England,

> it is stipulated, that, for five years longer, the French shall
> be allowed to . . . steal or buy the natives of Africa, to tear
> them from their native country, from every object of their
> affections, to transport them to the West Indies, where, sold
> as beasts of burden, they shall moisten, with their labour,
> that soil, the fruits of which shall belong to others, and shall
> drag out a painful existence, with no other consolation at
> the close of each day, than that of having taken another step
> towards the grave.

When Napoleon returned for the Hundred Days, seeking to appease England, he declared the trade illegal and, on his second return to the throne, Louis XVIII, much indebted to the English, could hardly do anything but maintain abolition.[19] However, while his Ministry of Foreign Affairs was attempting to mollify the English, DuBouchage was besieged by shipbuilders, ship owners, and the chambers of commerce in ports such as Nantes and Bordeaux who were anxious not to lose so abundant a source of income. About thirty of the naval officers who, at the outset of the restoration, had been forcibly retired on half pay and thus denied their livelihood had turned to the slave trade, and in 1816 at least thirty-six slaving ships left French ports.[20]

Contemporary accounts of the appalling inhumanity and degradation of this commerce were appearing in English. The noted abolitionist Thomas Clarkson described the now infamous conditions of the transatlantic crossing.

> In the best regulated ships, a full-grown man has no more
> space allowed him to lie upon than sixteen English inches

in breadth, which gives him about as much room as a man has in his coffin, and about two feet eight inches in height. But there are very few vessels in which even this limited allowance is afforded. . . . Besides this they are naked; and they have nothing to lie upon but the bare boards: on this account they suffer often very severely from the motion of the ship, which occasions different parts of their bodies to be bruised, and which causes their irons to excoriate their legs.

But the situation is the most deplorable when it blows a heavy gale, and when the hatches or gratings are obliged to be fastened down. Their sufferings are, at this time, such as no language can describe. They are often heard, on such occasions, to cry out in their own language, "We are dying, we are dying."

Clarkson went on to describe that when they had "fainted from heat, stench and corrupted air," they were brought up on deck where, affected by dysentery, they covered the deck "with blood and mucous like a slaughterhouse."[21]

In March 1820, an English squadron patrolling the West African coast boarded *La Jeune Estelle* and discovered two slaves crushed into casks in an attempt to conceal them. Another twelve had been flung overboard in the barrels that Commander Sir George Collier had noticed bobbing about on the sea as they had approached the French ship, jettisoned by a captain hoping to escape the penalties of being caught engaging in the forbidden trade. The French were clearly continuing to participate in a traffic that they had, once again, outlawed in 1818.

The marquis of Lansdown stated in the House of Lords, in July 1819, that the slave trade was "carried on to a very great extent under the flag of France," and, three years later, a distressed Thomas Babington wrote from Paris, "No member of the Ministry cares a fig for the abolition of the Slave Carrying Trade, and many are really interested in its continuance." There were, however, voices beginning to be raised against what Benjamin Constant called "the unspeakable and sacrilegious commerce" that had, in the previous quarter of a century, carried off more than a million and a half Africans.[22]

The sheer barbarity of the trade had been recorded in Geoffrey de Villeneuve's *Africa,* which had appeared in Paris in 1814. He described how the tribes from the north side of the River Senegal would cross it on horseback in bands of about twenty well-armed men. When they drew close to a targeted village, they would watch and wait near a spring until the women and children came for water. Seizing them, they would carry their prize back to their horses, fixing their victims' fingers between their teeth, ready to bite if anyone cried out. Alternatively, they might attack by night, yowling savagely as they set fire to an entire village and capturing their prey as they fled the flames. Their prisoners were, at length, brought to the European trading posts in single file, necks bolted into six-foot-long, forked wooden yokes. The traders to whom the captives were sold inspected the merchandise thoroughly; if a tooth was missing or the eye dull, that would lower the price. They put the captives through their paces, making them run, jump, and speak and subjecting the women to a humiliating examination by a doctor. Breast size, held to be an indication of fertility, helped determine their price, while the stature of the men, often acquired for studding, determined their value. Once purchased, they would arrive in Saint-Louis or Gorée, where they were chained, branded, and left—sometimes for months—in dark, dank, and infected prisons in which dysentery was rife, awaiting transportation. While the European nations slowly became aware of the infamy of their actions, certain African tribes, obviously encouraged by local white slave traders, were reluctant to forgo the profitable commerce.[23]

When Julien Schmaltz eventually took possession of Senegal from the English on January 25, 1817, he was instructed to rebuild forts, strengthen trading posts, and reestablish relations with local chieftains.

He was to improve hygiene, combat disease, and spread Christianity. Slavery in the colony was to be terminated and blacks were to become hired labor, working to purchase their freedom. Schmaltz was, in short, supposed to transform what was little more than a commercial and military base into a tolerable settlement.

With severely depleted troops as a result of the shipwreck, and with disease devastating the camp on Cap Vert, Schmaltz set about reorganizing the remaining troops into two battalions, which, by mid-December, were strengthened by reinforcements arriving from France. He was then able to turn his attentions to costly and impractical projects for establishing plantations as well as to planning expeditions to explore and forge trading relations with the interior. But Schmaltz seemed to be curiously dilatory in carrying matters forward. It was not until the autumn of 1817 that an expedition, in which Brédif and Dechatalus were charged to assess the commercial interests of the natural resources around and about the Senegal River, was ready to depart. They made their way upriver until, after two months, they were forced to turn back because of Brédif's deteriorating health. Arriving in Saint-Louis on December 29, the man who had kept an eyewitness account of his first voyage, shipwreck, and survival in the Sahara was dead in a matter of weeks.

Procrastination, bluff, and a certain dissipation of his energies seem to have compromised Schmaltz's large plans and promises. A laxity was apparent in his sanctioning of the shameful plunder of the *Medusa* by the merchant ships of Saint-Louis, and once Senegal came back into French hands he unhesitatingly revealed his appetite for less arduous and more rapid ways to enrich himself and his colony.[24]

A series of letters from English observers to the directors of the African Institution in London leave us in little doubt that when Schmaltz took repossession of Senegal, "slave deals were waiting to be concluded as soon as the British quit the colony." By June a Mr. Macauley writes that "the coast is crowded with slave ships." In July, the slave trade was seen to be "raging dreadfully on the coast" and "Gorée is become quite an emporium." Writing from Saint-Louis on November 8, 1817, an Englishman gives a clear picture of how radically things had changed in the first nine months of Schmaltz's administration.

> To give you an idea of the extent to which this traffic has been carried on, I need only mention that four French vessels have been loaded here, the cargoes averaging, by the best information I can obtain, about 100 slaves each; and there are two schooners now in the river waiting for their cargoes which they have contracted for.

Lamenting that war had broken out between the peoples of the interior who had been unscrupulously armed by the slave traders, the correspondent continues:

> It must no doubt surprise you, as it does me, and the few English who remain in this settlement, that after the solemn manner in which the French Government engaged to Abolish the Trade, that it should be carried on here so openly without any interruption from the authorities.

In March 1818, the trade is seen to be "horribly increasing" and another correspondent noted that untold numbers of slaves are taken by Damiel, one of the most powerful kings in this part of Africa.

> Damiel destroys his country, and for the purpose of selling for Rum and tobacco the last of his people, he has established a residence at Gandiol, nine miles down the river. What are the natives to think of the promise so repeatedly made by us, of the Slave Trade being abolished.

Arriving in London later that year, one of the correspondents reported that he had been spurned by Colonel Schmaltz. When he had confronted him on the subject of slavery, the French governor snapped that it was none of his business and said that "he would receive no information from him on the subject." This eyewitness was convinced that the only time the administration interfered with the traders was when they were denied a portion of the profits.[25]

Coming under a good deal of pressure from the English during the winter and spring of 1818, the French pushed through an insufficient statute that punished a slave trader more leniently than a thief who had stolen a loaf of bread. The law, introduced by the minister of the navy, the comte Molé, provoked a thriving clandestine commerce and Molé's successor, the baron Portal, a Bordeaux merchant and anglophobe, appeared indifferent to increases in the traffic. Such an attitude was hardly likely to placate abolitionists and liberals in France, particularly as appalled French residents and visitors to the colony wrote that Governor Julien Schmaltz was encouraging and participating in the renewed trade.[26]

During the wreck of the *Medusa*, Schmaltz exhibited scant regard for human life. It now seemed that rather than proceeding industriously to establish a genuine agricultural colony in Senegal, he appeared content to live off the ruin of the indigenous population. The Corsican priest Jean-Vincent Giudicelly, apostolic prefect to Senegal and Gorée, was well placed to observe the activities of the governor. Giudicelly was unequivocal in his condemnation of both Schmaltz and his deputy. On the first page of an 1820 pamphlet, he writes of "the execrable commerce in human flesh . . . conducted in Senegal and Gorée under the administrations of Schmaltz and Fleuriau." After his arrival in the colony in 1816, and during Schmaltz's "calamitous administration," Giudicelly witnessed "hundreds of unfortunate blacks embarked."[27]

Schmaltz was temporarily recalled to Paris in late 1817, arriving with his depressed wife, Reine, who had succumbed to a fifth attack of mania. In Paris, the governor defended himself against accusations that emanated from the English press. Schmaltz reassured the minister of his "good faith," successfully whitewashing himself and deviously diverting blame onto Lieutenant Colonel Gavot, the commander of Gorée. Schmaltz secured more troops for the colony and steamboats to navigate the Senegal River. He also discussed plans to replace undisciplined soldiers, who were poorly adapted to the climate, with natives, slaves bought from their owners and press-ganged for a period of ten to twelve years as sappers and workmen.[28]

During Schmaltz's absence from the colony, the interim governor, Aimé-Benjamin Fleuriau selectively seized and intercepted certain ships suspected of slaving, while allowing the trade to continue elsewhere. The *Times* published a list of five French ships that were loaded in Senegal between November 9, 1817, and March 19, 1818—ships from ports such as Nantes, Marseille, and Bordeaux, noting that as of mid-March some were back, anchored in the Senegal River, waiting along with two other ships to be reloaded.[29]

By the end of June 1818 a French patrol route had been set up in an attempt to intercept and arrest slavers but, perversely, the inconvenience of eluding capture made the trade more difficult and therefore even more profitable for those who escaped the authorities. What is more, interception didn't lead to prevention as some ships carried two captains on board, and when one captain was arrested the other took over and the voyage continued.

When Schmaltz returned to Senegal, he pretended to make a stand against slavery by arraigning the owners and captain of the *Scholastique* who were guilty of carrying a secret cargo of twenty blacks.[30] But this was mere public relations and the traffic, as Giudicelly recorded, was allowed to thrive.

In the streets of the colony, as in the surrounding country-side, all unknown or unprotected blacks were arrested, sold, and embarked. . . . What then is Monsieur Schmaltz doing, who claims there is no slave trade? He goes every morning to spend four hours in the *captiverie* of Potin, his accomplice, his consultant, his preferred. . . . I heard publicly from several slave traders their complaints against Schmaltz who has given Potin an exclusive monopoly of the trade.

Corruption was evidently rife and Giudicelly even coined a word for letters, ready for dispatch from the colony, being tampered with or censored: *schmalisées,* or "Schmaltzified."[31]

There are reasons, perhaps, for questioning these reports about the extent and flagrancy of Schmaltz and Fleuriau's involvement in the slave trade. Giudicelly was angry with both men over the question of arrears of pay, as well as costs of his passage back to France. His anger may have led him to exaggerate the faults of men "who can better manage their own interests than the affairs of the king." Likewise, the British, who never doubted the desirability of Senegal, would not miss the opportunity to denounce or exaggerate a traffic that a good number of European governments had condemned as being "repugnant to the principles of humanity and universal morality."[32]

However, we also have the testimony of another witness—the agricultural botanist, Joseph Morenas—who arrived in the colony in July 1818 as part of a team that would explore the River Senegal. Between his arrival and his departure in November 1819, Morenas confirmed many of Giudicelly's observations, stating that "Saint-Louis continues to be a market where these unfortunate Africans are sold publicly." He noted that blacks are loaded for America from Potin's wharf, that the big traders such as the merchant Durécu go unpunished, and that Schmaltz and his aide-de-camp Gouraud are implicated in the trade. Morenas even claimed that a *captiverie,* or holding pen for slaves, was opened in the offices of the navy by Colbrant, a member of Schmaltz's administrative team, and he provides a harrowing vision of the state of affairs in Senegal.

> On 1 December, 1817, a mother arrived in Saint-Louis to free her ten year old son. His proprietor demanded eight and a half ounces of gold. The unfortunate woman had only six and promised to go and fetch some more. Even before leaving, she was captured in the streets of Saint-Louis. In her despair, she committed suicide by bashing her head against a wall. On 17 of the same month, the father, hoping to find justice under the flag of the King, came to Saint-Louis to ask about his son, his wife and his gold. The reply he received was to be clapped in irons. When they offered him food, he drove a nail into his heart, screaming, "God will avenge me in another world."[33]

The government, needing to protect French commerce while at the same time wishing to appear receptive to persistent international pressure, was facing a dilemma. In 1819 the baron Mackau was dispatched by the minister of the navy to refute the English accusation that slavery was thriving on the West African coast and to discredit the slanders heaped on the French governor of Senegal. Mackau's suppression of incriminating evidence and his contention that accusations over slavery were "odious calumnies" provoked Morenas to petition the government with an eyewitness account. He presented this "Petition Against the Slave Trade" before the chamber of deputies on June 14, 1820.

The fact that it did not quite create the stir that his fellow abolitionists expected—the minister skillfully dismissed it—did not deter men such as Giudicelly, Abbé Grégoire, and Lafayette from making themselves heard. Morenas had, in fact, penned the first French abolitionist petition and the text was published by Alexandre Corréard. During the summer of 1820, Corréard's bookshop in the Palais Royal—its proprietor already condemned to prison—was used as the address at which readers could participate in the abolitionist debate.[34]

In the face of growing concern over legal abuses in the colony, which were supported by a swelling volume of evidence, Schmaltz was soon removed. He left Saint-Louis on August 31, 1820, his departure having been delayed by his wife succumbing to yet another attack of mania. Although the slave trade was far from terminated, Corréard had helped to hound the inhuman commander who had done him and thousands of others untold damage. The accounts written by Giudicelly in 1820 and Morenas in 1820 and 1821 drew attention to the cause. Increased weight was added to the abolitionist movement by that important speech to the two chambers made by Benjamin Constant in June 1821 and by a lengthy address to the chamber of peers by the duc de Broglie in March 1822. Several years later, Morenas produced his *Short History of the Slave Trade,* a text that benefited from his knowledge of the writings of the British abolitionists Thomas Clarkson and William Wilberforce. Nonetheless, five hundred–odd slave ships set sail from France or from French colonial ports between 1818 and 1831, when a more rigorous law against the trade was passed. This was followed, seventeen years later, by a decree abolishing slavery in all French possessions.[35] During the years in which the transatlantic trade thrived, France transported fewer than half the number of slaves that England shipped, but it was in the last decades of that traffic that the pressure brought to bear by British abolitionists led to a rise in French consciousness. Slowly, a trade was suppressed that Morenas prophesied would "shock future generations," a trade that had ripped the heart and soul out of the peaceful residents of Senegal.[36]

★ ★ ★

Théodore Géricault's awareness of the international humanitarian liberal struggle had been stimulated by his close association with
the circle of intellectuals, artists, and soldiers who congregated in the
studio of his neighbor Horace Vernet and through his friendship with
Alexandre Corréard. His *Raft of the Medusa* had appeared before the
public as the abolitionist movement in France was just beginning to
coalesce. In June 1819, Lafayette spoke out on the subject. In August
of the same year, Benjamin Constant published a translation of *The
Thirteenth Report of the Directors of the African Institution* in *La Minerve,*
which revealed the true state of things in Senegal.[37]

As Géricault had distorted the facts of the raft by presenting bodies
less wizened and worn and by effacing the overt signs of cannibalism,
so he modified the truth to make his plea for blacks. The account
published by Savigny and Corréard speaks of only one black survivor
on the raft whereas Géricault includes three, two of whom are very
much alive. Writing about *The Raft of the Medusa* in 1845, Charles Blanc
observed of the black man signaling against the sky that he is

> not in the bottom of the hold but the one who saves every-
> body. Isn't it admirable how great adversity has, all at once,
> reestablished equality between the races? It's a poor slave
> who rescues these spurned and enslaved men and it takes
> place on the same coast where we go to take his brothers
> and put them in captivity.[38]

Spurred on by the gaining momentum of French abolitionism,
by his continuing friendship with Corréard, and by his now firmly
established habit of responding to the topical issues of the day, Géricault
embarked on the preparatory drawings for what would be a shocking
image, intended to bring home to the public the inhumanity of a

Senegalese slave market. Certainly, the way slavers split up families, carrying off children, tearing them from their mothers and their fathers, resonated deeply in the painter's own psyche.[39]

Sadly, *The Slave Trade* never got beyond the planning stage; Géricault's deteriorating health and finances took care of that. He had returned from his long English visit in a precarious condition; his sciatica remained uncured and he was suffering from an overwhelming weariness caused by the early phase of tuberculosis of the spine. This physical weakness was soon compounded by two riding accidents. The exact circumstances of the first of these vary in early accounts; Géricault was out riding, either alone or with Vernet, when his particularly feisty horse threw him head over heels and he came down on his back on either a stone or the knot of his belt. Whichever it was, the object pushed between two vertebrae, reactivating the infectious focus of the tuberculosis and provoking abscesses. Other accounts say that Géricault landed on his sciatic thigh, resulting in an abscess on his leg. Shortly afterward, when the painter was traveling by carriage, a horse bolted, leaving him stranded. Determined to finish his journey on horseback, which in his condition would prove extremely painful, the artist suggested lancing an abscess in order to make the journey less awkward. Fortunately, he was prevented by those who were with him. As if bent on self-destruction, shortly afterward he met with another accident that ended his days as a horseman. Galloping in the Champs-de-Mars, Géricault collided with another rider. The shock of the impact opened an abscess and confined him to his bed.[40] Accident and illness prevented him from preparing anything for the Salon of 1822, but he visited the exhibition and was struck particularly by Delacroix's debut, saying of the small, powerful *Barque of Dante* that it was a painting "I would like to sign."

An unsuccessful campaign to purchase *The Scene of a Shipwreck* for the king's own collection had been started shortly after the 1819 Salon by the sympathetic comte Forbin, director of museums. In 1822, Forbin renewed his efforts to persuade the government to purchase

Géricault's masterpiece for a sum of 6,000 francs. Forbin's plan was to place it in one of the large galleries at Versailles, arguing that it was a work highly esteemed both by French artists and by the general public in England. Perfectly aware that the subject matter would continue to prove a stumbling block for the government, Forbin unsuccessfully presented the canvas as revealing "man struggling against a cruel death, . . . a homage to Providence, which aided these unfortunate people" rather than "a critique of the incompetence which abandoned them to danger."[41]

By the beginning of 1823 Géricault's tuberculosis was firmly established. The disease, which had started with a bacterial infection in the lungs, had spread to other parts of the body where it lay dormant until it slowly destroyed his spinal column. Géricault was visited by the king's eminent physician Dupuytren, who diagnosed bone decay, and by another doctor, Laurent-Théodore Biett, who tended him regularly and, as a token of gratitude, was presented with a sketch for the *Medusa*. Géricault was not, at this stage, completely bedridden, but he was depressed by the delays surrounding the crown's purchase of his masterpiece.

The painter's melancholy and his delicate balance of health were not helped by the bankruptcy, in mid-August, of the stockbroker Félix Mussart, who fled Paris with about 78,000 francs of his clients' money, leaving behind him enormous debts. Mussart had undertaken investments on the stock exchange for a circle of liberal friends including Géricault. Much of the painter's considerable inheritance had been sacrificed to his expensive lifestyle, including the maintenance of several horses, as well as the purchase of the time in which to pursue his art. Left in dire straits after the added loss of the investment made by Mussart, Géricault, on the advice of his friends Colonel Bro and Dedreux-Dorcy, sold some work. The ailing painter was astonished that he raised 13,000 francs from the sale of small paintings, whereas the French government, when faced with a cost of 5,000 to 6,000 for

The Raft of the Medusa, seemed unable to come to any conclusion about its purchase.[42]

During the last weeks of 1823, Géricault's disease became agonizing. He was wasting away. On November 30 he made his will in favor of his father, Georges-Nicolas, who two days later made his own will in favor of Georges-Hippolyte, his unfortunate grandson, Géricault's illegitimate child. At the end of December, Delacroix described in his journal a visit he had paid to Géricault a few days earlier.

> He is dying; his emaciation is dreadful to see—thighs no thicker than my arms and a head like that of an ancient, dying man. I want him to live with all my heart but I dare not hope any longer. . . . To die in the midst of all this, which he has created in the full vigour and fire of his youth. And now, he cannot even turn in his bed without assistance![43]

In the early weeks of the new year, Géricault was close to the end. He had sufficient strength to make a drawing of his left hand with its transparent skin revealing sinew and bone, some morbid curiosity seeming to motivate him as it had done in his studies of the amputated limbs during his work on his masterpiece. Indeed, he was so thin that he had taken on the haunting look of a raft survivor. He had reached the state, starved of life, in which he appears in a posthumous portrait painted by his friend Alexandre Corréard, the fiery Jacobin, whom he had first met in a studio littered with death.

On January 17–18, Géricault suffered the excruciating pain of surgery. To no avail. He asked the lawyer Champion de Villeneuve to act as an adviser to his distant son, and as he drew near to death he repeated over and over again the phrase, "Nothing replaces the love of a mother." He may have been thinking of his own, supportive mother who had died before he was old enough to show her how truly he merited her encouragement, but most probably he was dwelling on the predicament of his son, estranged from his mother, Géricault's own beloved, Alexandrine-Modeste Caruel.

In the early morning of Monday, January 26, Théodore Géricault died, aged exactly thirty-two years and four months. Delacroix was painting the baby searching for the mother's breast in the *Massacre of Chios* when he heard the news the following morning: "I cannot get used to the idea. Although everyone must have known that we would inevitably lose him before long, I almost felt that we could conjure death away by refusing to accept the idea. But death would not relinquish its prey, and tomorrow the earth will hide what little remains of him."[44]

The funeral took place at the chapel of Saint-Jean-Porte-Latine on January 28. The oration was delivered by the lawyer Jean-François Mocquard, the man who had unsuccessfully defended Corréard in his trials of 1820. Mocquard spoke of the indefatigable dedication of those close friends who had attended the painter during his illness, most of whom had gathered on that bleak midwinter day to mourn. One striking member of the congregation was the shipwrecked Turk Mustapha, whom Géricault had found wandering the streets of Paris and taken on as a domestic. The howling man stood a little apart and, according to the custom of his country, flung fistfuls of cinders at his head in a sign of grief. Among the other mourners were the baron Jean-Baptiste Caruel de St. Martin and his wife, Alexandrine-Modeste. She had most probably not laid eyes on her handsome and beloved protégé since the early days of her pregnancy. Their son, Georges-Hippolyte, would now be left alone in the world, aged five and a half, prohibited by all the pressure of propriety from meeting his mother, denied by fate from ever knowing his father, and not even carrying his name.

14

The Shipwreck and
the Shipwrecked

While Géricault had been wasting away, the king's health had also been deteriorating. By the summer of 1824 Louis was blind and barely audible. Wet and dry gangrene attacked the base of his spine and his right foot, and on September 16 he died, leaving his younger brother, the ultra duc d'Artois, to become Charles X.[1] Corréard later summed up the ills of Louis's reign by stating that the Bourbons "gave all the jobs to . . . their old and new accomplices who immediately and throughout our territory started to vex, plunder and massacre the citizens." He might have added that Louis XVIII and his beloved Elie Decazes had skillfully used the *Medusa* catastrophe to their own political advantage, without doing anything for those people whose lives had been wrecked.[2]

A month after Corréard's license was revoked, he obtained permission from the commissioner of police to sell his stock. There were more proceedings against him in 1823 and 1824, and after a number of serious judgments Corréard at last took up the advice that had been offered to him by Major Peddie when he had been hospitalized in Saint-Louis—he fled to England, a decision that allowed him to escape the various sentences still pending.[3] The transportation of people by rail was only a few years away and Corréard, who had fled to a "country more of industry than of liberty," threw off the wearisome mantle of subversive publisher and busied himself with projects to construct railways. Not that this activity in any way stifled his spirits or made his passage through life any easier.

While he was building his new career as a railway engineer, the guilty architects of Corréard's misery fared less well. After being relieved of the governorship of Senegal in August 1820, Julien Schmaltz continued to work for the French administration, first in Mexico and then as a consul-general in Smyrna, where he died in 1827, apparently with little money to his name, a condition that suggests his profits from the illicit trade in Senegal had either been squandered or had not been spectacular.[4]

The man directly responsible for the shipwreck had a more pathetic fate. On release from prison, Hugues Duroy de Chaumareys retired to the small town of Haute-Vienne where he lived with his family in disgrace and poverty amid the fading beauty of the Château de Lachenaud. Consumed by remorse, it was rumored that he slept on vine shoots to atone for his failings. Although some sympathizers tried to obtain Géricault's painting of the raft in order to rip it up and efface the memory of the terrible event, the catastrophe pursued Chaumareys to the end. He was effectively forced to shut himself up in the garden of his château, as each time he walked abroad he was booed by peasants, whose children pelted him with stones. His wife, Sophie, died in 1837, and his younger son, who had refused to marry because he did not wish to perpetuate the line, died the following year. The older son did, however, marry and produced four children. Three years after the death of Chaumareys in 1841, this older son, crippled by debt, had his possessions seized and sold. He broke under the strain and committed suicide, his wife dying six months later, orphaning their four children, all of whom were under six years old.[5]

The other officers on the 1816 expedition to Senegal had varied fates. Joseph Reynaud, the man who was alleged to have cut the ropes, died in 1832 after contriving to remain largely portbound. The energetic, brave, and kindly Jean Espiaux died of tetanus in Brazil in 1835 after an illustrious career. Pierre-Joseph Lapeyrère retired as a captain of a frigate in 1827, having been much troubled by a herpetic infection contracted during his march through the Sahara in the summer of 1816. Joseph-Michel Maudet died in 1845 with the rank of captain of a corvette, as had Martin Chaudière in 1841, having contracted chronic dysentery during an expedition to Mexico. Sander Rang died of sunstroke in 1844 while he was governor of Nossi-Be in Madagascar. After a succession of commands, Gicquel des Touches, captain of the *Loire,* retired in 1845 to become director of the port of Brest. Captain Léon Parnajon of the *Argus,* the man who because of a change in wind direction had found the raft, rose to become a captain of a frigate by the time he retired in 1837. Jean-Daniel Coudein, whose behavior on the raft had been deemed "courageous and zealous" by the director of navy personnel, found himself involved in the shipwreck of the *Gloriole* in 1823. Surviving it, he went on to a long and successful career, reaching the rank of captain of a man-of-war in 1850 and retiring in 1853. Cornette de Vénancourt, despite the distinction of his seamanship, suffered after the July revolution of 1830, never making the rank of admiral, which should have been the obvious conclusion to his long and distinguished career.[6]

After producing a self-vindicating thesis on calenture in 1818, Henri Savigny distanced himself from any of the controversies that raged around the wreck and its aftermath. He married the girl he had left behind him in 1816, and between 1821 and 1829 he served as mayor of Soubise, a village near Rochefort. In 1831 he received the Légion d'Honneur from King Louis-Philippe, as did the other survivors of the raft. To his death in 1843, frequently ill and haunted by horrific scenes, Savigny remained embittered, melancholic, and racked by grief. When his wife died, the keepsake she had given to the surgeon as a "God-speed" before he set out on the doomed expedition, discolored by sea-water and stained with blood, was placed in her coffin.[7]

Alexandre Corréard's technique for survival was relentless action and agitation. Having returned to France by 1831, he found himself back in the role of protesting to the government on behalf of the victims of restoration injustice. Throughout the 1830s and '40s, however, he passed a checkered time developing projects for railways. In 1838 he found his competence questioned for grossly underestimating the cost of the Paris–Versailles route. In 1842 he found himself embroiled in a quarrel over who first carried out the surveys for the Paris–Bordeaux line. In the mid-1840s, seeking compensation for ten years' work and the considerable costs he had sustained, he learned that the government refused to grant him the concession on the project. Seemingly wearied by such endless struggles, he retired with his wife, Hortense, to the Château des Basses-Loges, a property of thirty acres of gardens and orchards situated in the middle of a forest at Avon, near Fontainebleau. It would seem that Corréard had, at last, found a haven away from the battles of the world. But not so. Finding cause to involve himself in lawsuits with his neighbors, he also, in 1848, proposed himself as a candidate for the chamber of deputies, advertising himself as "the engineer of the *Medusa*." Taking the historic opportunity offered in 1848 to shrug off the Bourbon yoke, Corréard predictably proposed a grand reform of the constitution, tax and budget cuts, and supported Louis Napoleon. His disposition remained embittered and his endless offensive zeal was one way of never allowing himself to become too much preoccupied with some of the unanswered questions surrounding the wreck and the raft.[8]

Among the officers, crew, and passengers on board the *Medusa*, there had been a number of people who, for a variety of reasons, personal and political, recorded their adventures. These notes or narratives are often contradictory. The various writers had seen things differently. What is more, their trudge through the desert or their drifting in the raft had resulted in a delirium in which actions and motives, like the hours and days, kaleidoscoped into one another. Charles-Marie Brédif is alone in having made on-the-spot notes. Otherwise, the only surviving record kept during the voyage was Captain Vénancourt's log. On board the *Echo,* Vénancourt could cast only a wary eye on the dubious maneuvers made by Captain Chaumareys.

Others who provided accounts of the voyage did so after the event. Charlotte Picard, who married Dard, the schoolmaster in Saint-Louis, and published under her married name, alleges that among her reasons for chronicling her adventure was the opportunity it offered of correcting "what is wanting in exactitude" in the famous narrative by Savigny and Corréard. Her corrections concern mainly her slog through the desert, and she quite justly asks, "How could they know from their raft what took place . . . in the Sahara?" To be fair to the authors, however, they did have access to the survivors of both desert marches, as well as the benefit of Brédif's notes, with which, as early as the second edition, they augmented their own story. In any case, Charlotte Picard's emendations are slight and one of the principal aims of her narrative is consistent with that of Savigny and Corréard; she berates Governor Schmaltz, who favored the rights of the large commercial enterprises of Saint-Louis over those of colonists seeking to establish plantations. Above all, she seeks to vindicate her father, who had received no help from the leaders whom he had criticized so frankly during the events of July 1816, a father who died in the colony in August 1819.[9]

The narrative by the royalist and protestant midshipman Sander Rang is not always to be trusted. He praises the efficacy of Colonel Schmaltz, and, on the subject of the evacuation of the *Medusa,* he writes that Chaumareys's barge had taken as many people as it could carry—

sheer self-exculpation, as he had been among the twenty-eight people on board a boat that could easily have accommodated fifty. Rang suggests that the cry "Long live the king," resounding from the various lifeboats, was a "cry of love, a sound that rallies all good Frenchmen," and that it "gave us strength and increased our desire to save everybody." This is either a naïve evaluation of the scene or empty bombast.

Like Rang, Anglas de Praviel and Schmaltz's secretary, Griffon du Bellay, are in their respective accounts, very much at odds with Savigny and Corréard. An annotated copy of the second edition of *The Shipwreck of the Frigate, the Medusa* in which page after page reveals Griffon du Bellay's refutation or contradiction of its authors does not, however, deny the principal circumstances of the events chronicled.[10]

Savigny and Corréard saw themselves, first and foremost, as victims of incompetent leadership, which, in turn, and particularly in Corréard's estimation, revealed the insufficiencies of the new regime. Yet they also had some bizarre events and dubious actions to explain away, and to that end, throughout their narrative, it was necessary for them to create impeccable characters for themselves. Of their choosing to go on the raft they write, "Monsieur Savigny . . . might have stepped on board a boat, but an invincible attachment to his duty made him forget the danger." Corréard, who, "among others, was to go in one of the boats," finding that his workmen were being forced aboard the raft, "thought that in his quality of commander of engineers, it was his duty not to separate from the majority of those who had been confided to him." Their noble blend of duty, compassion, and loyalty is pitched to contrast with the selfish character of the leaders of the expedition. Nonetheless, as if to preempt any charges that might be leveled against them for their actions on the raft, they grant a degree of sympathy to those who abandoned them while at the same time, leaving us in no doubt as to their guilt: "in forsaking the raft, the minds of those who did so were greatly agitated, and the desire of withdrawing themselves from danger made them forget that a hundred and fifty unfortunate men were going to be abandoned to the most cruel sufferings." Such unexpected empathy for their oppressors surely serves no other purpose than to encourage readers to be lenient in their judgment of the two authors for whatever atrocities took place on board the raft. By way of pleading their cause, Savigny and Corréard frequently crave the reader's indulgence.[11]

Savigny's explanation of calenture is deployed as an irrefutable defence. He claims that delerium seized the minds of those on board the raft as early as the second night. The "hallucinations," the "burning fever," the "insanity," the sensation of inhabiting a "horrendous dream" indemnified them for horrors of the following days: the slaughter, the cannibalism, the murder. As "darkness brought with it a renewal of the disorder in our weakened intellects," any aberration could be attributed to the debilitating affliction. The publication of his thesis on calenture provided further medical justification for the "insanity," "egotism . . . brutality," and "barbarous indifference" of those who were in command of the raft.[12]

When it comes to the fraught question of cannibalism, the authors preface their account with a guilt-drenched appeal to the reader, worthy of the narrator of a Gothic novel.

> We tremble with horror at being obliged to mention that which we made use of! We feel our pen drop from our hand; a deathlike chill pervades all our limbs; our hair stands erect on our heads! Reader, we beseech you, do not feel indignation towards men who are already too unfortunate; but have compassion on them, and shed some tears of pity on their unhappy fate.

Despite their remorse, Savigny and Corréard cannot conceal their powerful will and strong survival instinct. Inconsistencies between their narrative and other accounts are explained partly by their desire to whitewash their questionable roles on the raft and partly by their need to blacken the perceived villains of the piece in order to further their political aim.[13]

In their description of the soldiers from the Africa Battalion boarding the raft, they write that, although these men were forbidden to bring their muskets and cartridges on board, some managed to retain their carbines and sabers. Lieutenant Anglas de Praviel, who supervised this embarkation, incisively described the same scene.

> I watched with sorrow as these brave soldiers were forced
> to abandon their arms, and, despite what Monsieur Savigny
> says, I can confirm that none of them was carrying a saber
> or a rifle. This measure, which had such dire results, was
> undertaken through prudence; we were worried about over-
> loading the raft.

In discussing the so-called mutinies it served the interest of Savigny, whom some accused of having orchestrated the slaughter of the lower ranks on board the raft, that some soldiers should be seen to have been armed and therefore capable of initiating the violence against their leaders.[14]

Anglas de Praviel is immortalized by Corréard and Savigny as the officer whom the frenzied members of the Africa Battalion were seeking to kill on the raft. These soldiers were falsely convinced that he was on board and wished to destroy him because of his allegedly abusive behavior in the barracks on the Ile de Ré before departure. Thus maligned and even implicated as a pretext for the riot on the second night, it is hardly surprising that Praviel, in a text that was published after Savigny and Corréard's, should set out to discredit them. Praviel questions Savigny and Corréard's self-aggrandizing claims about their sense of duty, compassion, and loyalty, asking caustically, "What became of the twelve workmen for whom Corréard made such a generous sacrifice?"

An important discrepancy between their accounts is that Praviel took Schmaltz for a "man of honor" who was "ceaseless" in his rallying of the boats, despite the general perception that the governor's barge, along with the captain's barge and the pinnace, remained at some distance from the frigate. But in stark contradiction to these sentiments, it is Praviel whom Savigny and Corréard describe as taking aim at the governor's barge as it fled from the stricken frigate.

Surely, Praviel's rather pompous oath that he secured from the fifty-seven victims washed up on the shore at Cap Mirick, an oath in which he urged them to do nothing that would allow people to say that the French "have drunk the blood of their brothers . . . stuffed themselves with their flesh"—in short to say, "the French were cannibals"—is placed in his text as a blatant denunciation of what Savigny and Corréard guiltily confessed had necessarily taken place on board the raft. To that end, Praviel dwells on the Gothic horror of the platform when it was discovered—the survivors with their hands and mouths still dripping with blood, "their pockets stuffed with hunks of flesh on which they had fed."[15]

After returning home to France for health reasons, Praviel found that the celebrity of Savigny and Corréard had penetrated even to the depths of the country. When he eventually obtained their text, he exclaims,

> Imagine my surprise when this report was contrary to the facts of which I was witness, to the observations that I made, to the details that I collected. Alteration of the most essential circumstances, impardonable omissions, people blamed who, up to now, I had valued . . . I seriously asked myself if my shipwreck had not been a dream, an illusion, or if my

memory had not been weakened, deranged in the burning sands of the Sahara. . . . Recovering from this momentary uncertainty, I was unable to resist the desire to employ the leisure imposed by a long convalescence and write down the awful facts as I saw them.

In his own narrative Sander Rang records an observation of Honoré Thomas, the helmsman, which is at odds with Savigny and Corréard. He claims that the leaders had deliberately placed a barrel in the middle of the raft and broached it, leaving the soldiers free to drink their fill. Tempted by such largesse, they soon got drunk, which resulted in the inevitable disorder and the subsequent massacre.[16] This version of events is supported by Brédif. When he visited his old school friend Valéry Touche-Lavillette, who was lying in the hospital in Saint-Louis, the latter suggested that Dr. Savigny and two or three leaders behaved like brigands and committed murder when it was by no means necessary. He put it to Brédif that they had organized a sinister plan to nettle these ill-fated, frenzied people into destroying one another.

Lavillette, as a member of the Philanthropic Society, seems to have had no overt motive for questioning Savigny, and he would also have been one of the souls whom Corréard felt it his duty to accompany onto the raft. In any case, doubt is cast on Lavillette's own position by Honoré Thomas, who claims that Lavillette was a keen euthanasiast, helping those who were slowly drowning to die by thrusting them through with his saber, perhaps in collusion with the leaders on board.[17]

The health and judgment of these men were severely affected, not only during their ordeal but also in its aftermath. We can legitimately question statements, observations, and accusations made in the hospital in Senegal. Lavillette was, after all, one of the signatories of the Schmaltzified declarations brought to the sickbeds of the recuperating survivors in Saint-Louis. This declaration indeed names Savigny, "who, by his counsel and his discourse . . . was the principal provoker and executor" of the outrages on the raft.[18] But these letters were later refuted as the signatories claimed that they had been pressured to sign them and had not been altogether lucid when they had done so. Lavillette later went to Géricault's studio and made the painter a model of the raft. At whose invitation? Most probably through the Corréard connection, suggesting, perhaps, that any acrimonious differences had been patched up.

Certainly, Savigny has been accused of uncompromising brutality on the raft. But whose version of events can stand as truth? Savigny left Senegal in certain haste and wasted no time in getting his version of events down on paper. This was unexpectedly published and the surgeon went on to collaborate with Corréard on a full-length book. As this was the longest account of the tragedy to appear, it gave authority to Savigny's viewpoint. Midshipman Coudein, as senior naval officer on board the raft and therefore responsible for everything that happened, understandably followed Savigny and Corréard in his report to his minister. He suggested that the leaders had acted in legitimate defense and that Savigny's composure had been "very helpful in maintaining order" in that small, packed, and precarious space in which violence was certain to erupt.[19]

A tiny band of bourgeoisie, floating aimlessly on an impossible platform in the tropical heat with insufficient rations and dangerously outnumbered by cutthroats and brigands, would naturally be anxious. According to the mores of the period, the leaders on the raft felt themselves superior to the "scum of all countries, the refuse of the prisons" with whom they shared the makeshift space. The struggle on the raft, whoever initiated it, was inevitably a class battle in which the leaders believed that they had a greater claim to life, much as Schmaltz and Chaumareys had done.[20]

The least pardonable aspect of survival on the raft remains the self-confessed elimination of the weakest. It is of the same immoral order as the decision to cut the towrope, and Savigny and Corréard, sensing this, make an attempt to deflect their guilt by, once again, appealing to their public: "Readers, . . . recollect, at least, that it was other men, fellow countrymen and comrades, who had placed us in this abominable situation." Nonetheless, the tactical cull continues to haunt the story of the shipwreck of the *Medusa,* casting a macabre light across the all too human instinct for self-preservation.

Our inability to discover the truth behind the terrible events that have been variously recounted according to the interests of differing writers remains problematic. What comes down to us is, inevitably, a distortion of the truth—a mosaic of probabilities. Confusingly, in Savigny and Corréard's narration of the first days, the raft is one minute so crammed that no one can move and, the next, the mutineers are seen advancing against the leaders. If Savigny and Corréard were candid about eliminating those who were least likely to survive during their last days on the raft, why would they not be frank about the inescapable need to reduce numbers early on? Furthermore, we have to question whether it is not more likely that a murderous rout would have been started by a rabble of combustible professional killers than by a lone doctor, albeit a plucky and frightened one. And though it is true that Savigny rapidly distanced himself from the *Medusa* controversy, haunted by nightmarish memories, Corréard was less eager to let sleeping dogs lie. The polemicist and would-be politician had to live with an episode in his past that was inevitably blurred, and he most probably came to accept the version of the truth as given in *The Shipwreck,* not least because it served a larger political end.

The main elements of the catastrophe are universally agreed upon. It is a story in which the villains are obvious, heroes are few, and the chroniclers are not altogether to be trusted. At a time when tales of shipwrecks were commonplace, a particularly distressing example was presented to an appalled public in France and was manipulated by various parties, including, ironically, the king and his chief adviser, to drive one more nail in the coffin of the French monarchy. The burial process may have been slow, but the *Medusa* scandal played its part in disparaging the procedures of the ancien régime and toppling, albeit briefly, the ultra faction. The event was also used, through Géricault's painting, to present a new, romantic evaluation of the human predicament.

Much of the hard evidence surrounding the *Medusa* tragedy has perished in the sea, or on the desert sands, and what is left has been swirled and sifted by partial, prejudiced and imperfect narratives. Ultimately, what is of interest to perpetuity is not the exact truth of the contestable details but rather to what end the various versions of these errors and follies have been used. Parts of the *Medusa* story are lies, but lies that reveal truths.

In 1828, Arnold Scheffer called Géricault the "head of a new school," by which he meant the romantic movement in art. This was born in opposition and crisis and disturbed the models provided by religion and rigid hierarchy. The romantic often troubled readers or spectators by plunging them into the eerie or the ugly and denied redemption by placing them in an agony of endless longing. Themes of abandonment and false hope in Géricault's painting touch the wider romantic agony provoked by the loss of faith in religion.[21] Géricault's painting presents man grasping for salvation from a stinking, sinking, makeshift raft. His painting inhabits the same world as Caspar David Freidrich's *Wreck of Hope*[22] and Coleridge's "Ancient Mariner." Like the eponymous hero of Mary Shelley's *Frankenstein*, published at the time Géricault began working on the *Medusa*, the painter spent "days . . . in charnel-houses"[23] studying decay, pushing himself to the very edge in his preparations for his painting. But in its realization, transcending the Gothic horrors of the bloodied raft, Géricault resolved to be grandly romantic in his seizure of the large metaphor.

Famously, the historian Jules Michelet saw that the real subject of Géricault's painting is "France herself, our whole society . . . loaded on the *Medusa*"; Géricault, he believed, "paints the shipwreck of France." His viewpoint gains support from the fact that when the *Medusa* set sail from Rochefort, she carried on board a dangerous brew of jarring political approaches, a restoration France in miniature.

Géricault lived most of his short adult life through a time that is often dismissed as something that almost didn't happen, that is, the restoration, the sad coda to the eroica of revolution and empire. Yet in a sense the period was so tempestuous that it might just as easily be viewed as a chapter in the ongoing French Revolution. Certainly, down through the nineteenth century as the country continued to wrangle with the question of her political identity, *The Raft of the Medusa* remained a symbol of France riven. Even as the spectator stands before the painting, the composition seems to pull apart, flying off toward the corners, because the center cannot hold.[24]

In November 1824, there was a sale of works and effects from Géricault's studio, which achieved modest returns. Lot 66, including sketches and figure studies for the *Medusa,* went for 60 francs. The duc d'Orléans, for a total of just over 5,000 francs, bought lots 93 and 94, the magnificent *Officer of the Chasseurs* and *The Wounded Cuirassier.* Happily, at long last, the comte Forbin, who had been a persistent champion of Géricault's work, was able to purchase *The Raft of the Medusa* for the Louvre. The sum agreed, 6,005 francs, did not appear derisory when compared with the going rate for similarly sized works.[25]

On October 24, 1848, the year that saw the end of the Bourbon monarchy, a mason's ladder punctured *The Raft of the Medusa,* damaging some of the sky and the side of the hand of the sailor waving for rescue. The severely bubbling rectangular repair is visible today. In the late 1850s two painters, Guillemet and Ronjat, pointed out to the director of museums the extent to which Géricault's masterpiece had deteriorated. The bituminous paint was cracking and darkening and

Guillemet and Ronjat set about making a full-size copy using more stable paint. This now hangs in the Musée de Picardie in Amiens, where it provides a far better indication of how Géricault's masterpiece would have appeared to visitors at the 1819 Salon than the original, which hangs in the Louvre.

Its collection swollen as a result of Napoleonic plundering, the Louvre had been, in the first days of the restoration, a favored destination for visitors to the French capital; no other city boasted such a magnificent museum, and Géricault was heartbroken to learn that much of the pillage was to be restored to its rightful owners. One hundred and twenty years later, the fragile, unmovable *Raft of the Medusa* had to be carried off to spend six years hidden in the Château de Sarthe to avoid its falling into the hands of the plundering Nazis. After the Second World War, the masterpiece was back in the Louvre, where it remains to this day, one of that great museum's major attractions.[26]

As for the *Medusa* herself, beached on the Arguin sandbank with 90,000 francs in three strongboxes deep in the gunner's storeroom, she too has been the focus of considerable interest. Rear Admiral de Rosily, anxious to improve the faulty maps that had contributed to the shipwreck, ensured that a mission was swiftly undertaken to chart the dangerous West African coast. The 1817–18 hydrographic expedition under Commandant Roussin, contending with fogs, sandstorms, and mirages, established that Cap Blanc, which had proved so elusive to Captain Chaumareys, was actually four nautical miles farther south than it appeared on the existing map. The officers, attempting to protect themselves by duping their captain, had been sailing closer to the mark than they could have known.

On April 4, 1817, the hydrographic expedition spotted the carcass of the *Medusa* lying on its port side, with its starboard hull, still intact, withstanding the repeated battering of the ocean's waves. After that, the frigate broke up and disappeared beneath the shallow waters of the Arguin sandbank, lost until interest in its whereabouts was re-kindled, and determined efforts were made to find the wreck.

In 1960, the French Ambassador to Mauritania, Pierre Anthonioz, searched for the *Medusa* with navy divers. The following year, during a bathymetric survey of the sandbank, a team pinpointed the wreck at 19 degrees 53' 4" West and 19 degrees 18' 8" North. Under the direction of Professor Monod of the Research Group for the Identification and Exploration of the Wreck of the *Medusa,* a boat set sail from Rochefort in October 1980 to study whatever remained of the frigate. In early December, Jean-Yves Blot and his team found the wreck. Their search profited from the generous loan of sophisticated equipment. The fame of Géricault's painting persuaded companies that such support would, with industry's love of sponsoring established art, prove a fabulous public relations opportunity. Assisted by satellite positioning equipment and computers, they located the remains of the frigate. They also found an inexplicable mystery. There was no sign of the untraced 90,000 francs. Over the years, there had been theories about how Schmaltz or Chaumareys had managed to appropriate the fortune, perhaps before the *Medusa* had set sail, but, if that were so it seems strange that Schmaltz should die in reduced circumstances in Smyrna and that Chaumareys would die in debt, after decades of genteel poverty. Perhaps one of the enterprising commercial giants of Saint-Louis such as Valentin, Potin, or Durécu, unsatisfied by their fortunes made from the slave trade, managed to wrest the treasure from the frigate. Perhaps it lies there still, broken up, scattered, and swallowed in the shifting sands of the Arguin bank.[27]

Several survivors associated with the events and achievements surrounding the wreck of the *Medusa* lived on for decades. Corréard's determined agitation contributed to the eventual success of the abolitionist movement in France and to the eventual demise of the monarchy. To those ends, he lived most of his life under the perpetual burden of somebody in opposition. The failure of his attempt for public office can only have added to his misery at the end of his life. Still in pain from the numerous wounds he had sustained on the raft, he was grief stricken by the death of his wife. Indeed, such was his distress at her passing that he kept a dressmaker's mannequin sitting in the window of his house at Basses Loges. Every day he would change her clothes, dressing the life-sized doll in his dead wife's garments, a lonely, sorrowful fetishist, longing for things lost.

When Corréard died on February 16, 1857, he took the truth of what happened on the raft to his grave.[28] His struggle to keep the *Medusa* story before the public at a time when the establishment thought it best forgotten had been much aided by Théodore Géricault's decision to make a painting. Géricault had, of course, been drawn to the subject as a result of the dark mood that had displaced his youthful happiness. Painted at about the same time, a shipwreck scene entitled *The Storm* revealed a mother and her infant thrown up on a desolate shore. The painting hints at the dashed hopes of Alexandrine and her third son, Georges-Hippolyte, the child she was never allowed to know.[29]

Having negotiated the scandal of the illegitimate birth, Alexandrine continued to live as the wife of Baron Caruel de St. Martin in the relative isolation of the Château of Grand-Chesnay. In 1847 her husband died, aged ninety. Despite her impropriety, Caruel was generous to Alexandrine in his will, increasing her private annual income by twenty percent, as well as giving her 40,000 francs in gold, along with the silverware from his Paris mansion and all the books he owned, useful companions in her secluded life.[30]

Alexandrine-Modeste Caruel lived on, never able to meet her lost child, and reached the same ripe age as her husband by the time of her death in August 1875. Toward the end of her life she watched, perhaps with misgivings, when her younger son Paul, as his father had before him, finally married at the age of fifty. As Paul's unstable older brother, Louis-Sylvestre, had been placed under legal guardianship in 1845 and spent the last thirty-two years of his life in a mental institution at Ivry-sur-Seine, Paul inherited the Château of Grand-Chesnay. Producing only female children, the year after Paul's death, in 1889, the château, the place where the romance between aunt and nephew had flourished, was sold.[31]

Mental disturbance in the maternal line of Géricault's family claimed many victims. Not only had Jean-Baptiste Caruel's older son Louis-Sylvestre succumbed, but his nephew Théodore Géricault suffered a breakdown and severe depression after months of tortured emotional distress, augmented by the failure of his masterpiece at the Salon. While there is no evidence of treatable mental illness, it seems that Géricault's illegitimate son, Georges-Hippolyte, was overwrought and unable to forge a satisfactory life.[32]

There were resources to ensure that Géricault's child was brought up in comfortable circumstances, but from the outset things did not go well. Paul Clouard, Géricault's cousin, tricked the painter's father into changing the will that he had made in favor of his grandson, effectively cheating him out of most of his inheritance but nonetheless leaving him two farms in Normandy. Furthermore, Auguste Brunet, whom the dying Géricault had asked to act as a guardian to his son, met with an unexpectedly early death in February 1827, and so it fell to the families of other old friends to step into the breach.[33]

The wasted life of Géricault's son, a man vainly in search of the harbor of parental affection, played out its course over several sad decades. In September 1839, recently turned twenty-one, he successfully petitioned the lord chancellor for the right to bear the name Géricault. Shy, small, and dressed in a nondescript manner, Georges-Hippolyte spent the last twenty years of his life living in austere lodgings just beneath the attic in the modest Hôtel du Lion d'Or in Bayeux.

He had settled there in order to be near the source of his income, the farms at St. Martin. How piercing the sound of that name must have seemed, reminding him daily of his overwhelming desire to meet and get to know his mother, the baroness de St. Martin. At last, after years of silence, he managed through an intermediary to secure word from her. The message was brief. His mother insisted that they should not make contact. Her son must forget her—society would not permit otherwise.

His life dragged emptily, unhealthily on; his lodging seemed to a friendly visitor like a cell in which he waited for death to claim him. When he eventually died with the year, on December 31, 1882, his property fell to the state because he had no legal heirs. Georges-Hippolyte had outlived the mother whom he had never known by only seven years; their enforced separation was the only thing they had shared.[34]

It had been well over half a century since two scarred men met in an eerie studio in Saint-Phillipe du Roule, two men whose lives had been shattered—one in a senseless shipwreck with a particularly cruel and ghoulish aftermath, the other whose wreck had been emotional. Both had grown up amid the turbulence of revolutionary France and their respective fates had swept them up and set them on a course of political engagement that would involve them with the largest humanitarian issue of their time. Their meeting had proved fruitful; Corréard had become midwife to one of the great masterpieces of Western art, helping Géricault to crown his short but magnificent career.

For Corréard the wreck had been a rite of passage into the arena of political challenge. After his long and combative life, he was laid to rest in the cemetery at Avon, on the banks of the Seine, just a stone's throw from Féricy, where Géricault had gone to recuperate after completing *The Raft of the Medusa*. A short way downriver, in the celebrated Parisian cemetery of Père Lachaise, stands a memorial tomb to the romantic master. A bronze bas-relief of Géricault's most famous composition emblazons the front of the monument, reminding the visitor that the young man interred below had been someone of artistic genius who had kept the terrible story of the wreck of the *Medusa* alive. Around the base of the structure is a railing only eight inches high. In his will, Georges-Hippolyte had left money to embellish the tomb of his father and the wrought-iron railing remains as a son's acknowledgment of the parents he never knew. The discreet addition is a message from the unfortunate who occupies an almost anonymous grave nearby. The railing's repeating motif is a "G" embracing a heart transpierced by two arrows. It is a son's silent testimony to the brief love between Théodore Géricault and Alexandrine-Modeste Caruel, a secret witness to the shipwreck of lives caught up in an unrelenting passion.

Notes

Chapter 1

1. Benjamin Robert Haydon, *Life of Benjamin Robert Haydon, Historical Painter, from his Autobiography and his Journals,* ed. and completed by Tom Taylor (London: Longman, Brown, Green and Longman, 1853), vol. I, 238.

2. William Dorset Fellowes, *Paris During the Interesting Month of July, 1815, a Series of Letters* (London: Gale and Fenner, 1815), 22.

3. Monestier, Alain, and Jacques Cheyronnaud, *Le Fait divers* (Paris: Éditions de la Réunion des musées nationaux, 1982), 50.

Chapter 2

1. Philip Mansel, *Louis XVIII* (Stroud: Sutton Publishing, 1999), 119, 170, 186–87.

2. Alexandre Corréard, *Élections des représentants du peuple à l'Assemblée législative—Alexandre Corréard, Ingénieur (du Radeau de "La Méduse") aux électeurs du département de Seine-et-Marne* (Batignolles: n.d. [1848]); Jean-Paul Besse, *Compiègne dans l'histoire: une ville impériale et royale* (Paris: Éd. D.U.C, 1992), 2.

3. Guillaume de Bertier de Sauvigny, *La Restauration* (Paris: Flammarion, 1955; pbk. 1999), 11; Philip Mansel, *Paris Between Empires 1814–1852* (London: Phoenix Press, 2003), 4.

4. Haydon, *Life of Haydon,* 232, 237.

5. Mansel, *Paris Between Empires,* 16.

6. Bertier de Sauvigny, *La Restauration,* 63–64.

7. Louis XVIII qtd. in Jeanne Gilmore, *La République clandestine 1818–48* (Paris: Aubier, 1997), 9.

8. Corréard, *Élections des Représentants du Peuple à l'Assemblée Législative,* 2.

9. Edmond Hugues, *Alexandre Corréard de Serres, naufragé de la "Méduse"* (Gap, France, 1920), 5.

10. Charles-Pierre de Nazarieux, *Mémoire pour la Société coloniale philanthropique, présenté à son excellence Mgr. le Ministre Secrétaire d'Etat de la Marine et des colonies par MM. les membres composant la Commission administrative de la Société coloniale* (Paris, 25th November, 1816), 30; Alexandre Corréard and Henri Savigny, *Naufrage de la frégate la Méduse faisant partie de l'expédition du Sénégal en 1816,* 5th edition (Paris: Chez Corréard, Libraire, 1821), 64–65; Roger Mercier, "Le Naufrage de 'La Méduse'—Réalité et imagination romanesque," in *Revue des Sciences Humaines,* fasc. 125 (Lille: Université de Lille, Jan.–March 1967), 55.

11. Eugène Titeux, *Histoire de la Maison militaire du Roi de 1814 à 1830* (Paris: Baudry, 1890), 29; Mansel, *Louis XVIII,* 221.

12. *Le Moniteur universel,* 20 March 1815 qtd in Mansel, *Louis XVIII,* 227.

13. Mansel, *Paris Between Empires,* 80–81.

14. E. Chevalier, *Histoire de la Marine Française de 1815–1870* (Paris: Hachette, 1900), 8–9; Henri Legohérel, *Histoire de la Marine française* (Paris: Presses universitaires de France, 1999), 59–66.

15. Legohérel, *Histoire,* 68–77.

16. Present-day Java.

17. Georges Bordonove, *Le Naufrage de "la Méduse"* (Paris: R. Laffont, 1973), 18–21, 23–29.

18. Nazarieux, *Mémoire,* 8–9, 30.

19. Germain Bazin, *Théodore Géricault, étude critique, documents et catalogue raisonné,* vol. 1 (Paris: Wildenstein Institute, La bibliothèque des arts,

1987), 21, doc. 1; Jean Sagne, *Géricault* (Paris: Fayard, 1991), 15; Denise Aimé-Azam, *Mazeppa, Géricault et son temps* (Paris: Plon, 1956), 11–12; Gilles Buisson, *Géricault, de Mortain à Paris* (Coutances: OCEP, 1976), 22; Charles Clément, *Géricault, Étude biographique et critique* (Paris: Didier & Co., 1868), 15–16; Bruno Chenique, "Géricault, une vie," in *Géricault* (Paris: Éditions de la Réunion des musées nationaux, 1991), 263.

20. Louis Batissier, "Géricault," reprint from *Revue du dix-neuvième Siècle* (Rouen: n.d. [1842 is a mistake in many citations] 1824), 4; Michel Le Pesant, "Documents inédits sur Géricault," *Revue de l'Art* 31 (Paris: Flammarion, 1976), 74–75, 78; Clément, *Géricault,* 16.

21. Charles Blanc, *Histoire des peintres français au XIX siècle* (Paris: Cauville frères, 1845), 408–9; Clément, *Géricault,* 43.

22. See Blanc, *Histoire,* 408–9.

23. The posthumous inventory of Géricault's possessions included two copies of works by Ruysdaël and Wynants, artists included in Alexandrine-Modeste Caruel's dowry. See Philippe Grunchec, "L'inventaire posthume de Théodore Géricault," *Bulletin de la Société de l'histoire de l'art français* (Paris, 1976) 395–420; Bazin, *Théodore Géricault,* 178–94.

24. Bazin, *Théodore Géricault,* 32; Lorenz Eitner, *Géricault, Sa vie, son oeuvre* (Paris: Gallimard, 1991), 98; Stefan Germer, " 'Je commence une femme, et ça devient un lion': On the Origin of Géricault's Fantasy of Origins," in *Géricault, Conférences et colloques du Louvre* (Paris: La documentation française, 1996), vol. 1, 439.

25. Batissier, "Géricault," 6–7; Bazin, *Théodore Géricault,* 32–36.

26. Mansel, *Louis XVIII,* 204–5; Bertier de Sauvigny, *La Restauration,* 80.

27. Titeux, *Histoire,* 33; Frederick Antal, "Reflections on Classicism and Romanticism—III," *The Burlington Magazine* (London, Sept., 1940): 73.

28. See Mansel, *Paris Between Empires,* 27; Bertier de Sauvigny, *La Restauration,* 70–75; Irene Collins, ed., *Government and Society in France, 1814–1848* (London: Edward Arnold, 1970), 12; Mansel, *Louis XVIII,* 184.

29. Bertier de Sauvigny, *La Restauration,* 118, 124, 273; Mansel, *Louis XVIII,* 266–67; Alfred M. Nettement, *Souvenirs de la Restauration* (Paris: Jacques Lecoffre et Cie., 1858), 272–73, 275, 277; Edgar Leon Newman, *Historical Dictionary of France from the 1815 Restoration to the Second Empire,*

2 vols. (Westport, Conn.: Greenwood Press, 1987), vol. I, 300; Mansel, *Paris Between Empires,* 123.

30. Bertier de Sauvigny, *La Restauration,* 132–33; Collins, *Government and Society in France,* 19; Newman, vol. I, 275; Bertier de Sauvigny, *La Restauration,* 132–33; Pierre Darmon, *La Rumeur de Rodez* (Paris: Albin Michel, 1991), 14–15.

31. John Scott of Gala, *Paris Revisited in 1815, by way of Brussels* (London: Longman, Hurst Rees & Brown, 1816), 400, 401; Daniel P. Resnick, *The White Terror and the Political Reaction after Waterloo* (Cambridge, Mass.: Harvard University Press, 1966), 117–18; Gilmore, *La République,* 11–12; Bertier de Sauvigny *La Restauration,* 136; Newman, vol. II, 1125.

32. Bertier de Sauvigny, *La Restauration,* 79.

33. Terence Grocott, *Shipwrecks of the Revolutionary and Napoleonic Eras* (London: Caxton Editions, 2002), xv; Chevalier, *Histoire,* 1–3; E. H. Jenkins, *Histoire de la marine française* (Paris: Albin Michel, 1977), 334; Gicquel des Touches, "Souvenirs d'un marin de la République," parts I and II, *Revue des Deux-Mondes,* vol. 28 (Paris, 1905), 434.

34. Bordonove, *Le Naufrage,* 30–3; Philippe Masson, *L'Affaire de la Méduse* (Paris: Tallandier, 1989), 155–56.

35. J. Breillout, "La vie dramatique de M. de Chaumereix," in *Bulletin de la Société des lettres, sciences et arts de la Corrèze* (Tulle, 1933), 242–44; Bordonove, *Le Naufrage,* 34–36, 39–40; Masson, *L'Affaire,* 155–63.

36. Hugues Duroy de Chaumereys, *Relation de M. de Chaumereix, officier de la marine, échappé aux massacres d'Aurai et de Vannes, suivie de quelques observations sur l'esprit public en Bretagne* (London: J. de Bouffe, 1795), 3.

37. Ibid., 43.

38. Bordonove, *Le Naufrage,* 43.

39. Touches, "Souvenirs," 181, 434.

40. Corréard and Savigny, 5th edition (Paris, 1821), 65.

41. M. de Brisson, *Histoire du naufrage et de la captivité de M. De Brisson* (Genève & Paris, 1789), 14–25; René-Claude Geoffroy de Villeneuve, *L'Afrique ou Histoire, moeurs, usages et coutumes des Africains. Le Sénégal,* 4 vols. (Paris: Nepveu, 1814), vol. I, 9, 22–57.

42. Touches, "Souvenirs," 434.

43. Grocott, *Shipwrecks,* x–xi.

44. Bordonove, *Le Naufrage,* 75–76, 224; Vénancourt's log qtd. in Bordonove, 80.

45. Geoffroy de Villeneuve, *L'Afrique,* vol. I, 133.

46. Under her married name of Dard, Charlotte Picard left a detailed account of her voyage to West Africa: Mme. Dard (née Charlotte-Adelaide Picard), *La chaumière Africaine, ou Histoire d'une famille française jetée sur la côte de l'Afrique, à la suite du naufrage de la Frégate la Méduse* (Dijon: Noellat, 1824), 14–15.

47. Ibid., 6–12; Serge Daget, "France, Suppression of the Illegal Trade, and England 1817–50," in *Abolition of the Atlantic Slave Trade,* ed. Eltis and Walvin (Madison: University of Wisconsin Press, 1981), 195.

48. Charles-Marie Brédif, "Le naufrage de la Méduse, mon voyage au Sénégal," in *Revue de Paris* 11 (Paris, 1907), 636–37.

49. Ibid., 639–41; Dard, *La chaumière,* 18–19. There is a dating discrepancy between Brédif's and Dard's narratives; Mme. Dard writing eight years after the event seems more likely to have mistaken a date, whereas Brédif, given to taking measurements and recording events as he goes along, is more trustworthy.

50. Brédif, "Le naufrage," 641; Jean-Yves Blot, *La Méduse—Chronique d'un naufrage ordinaire* (Paris: Arthaud, 1982), 90–91; Aimé-Azam, *Mazeppa, Géricault et son temps,* 225.

51. Brédif, "Le naufrage," 643; Serge Daget, "France, Suppression of the Illegal Trade," 194; Service historique de la Défense—Vincennes: BB 3 432—letter of March 17, 1816, from the director of construction at Rochefort; Corréard and Savigny, 5th edition (Paris, 1821), 396.

52. Geoffroy de Villeneuve, *L'Afrique,* vol. I, iii., and vol. II, 156–57; Bordonove, *Le Naufrage,* 46; Parson, *Premier rapport de M. Parson, chef de la délégation envoyée au Cap-Verd par la Société coloniale philanthropique à l'effet de reconnoître les lieux les plus propres à la fondation des colonies agricoles,* 2e édition avec des notes par M. Sevigny (Paris: Au bureau de la Société coloniale philanthropique, 1817), 19; Darcy Grimaldo Grigsby, *Extremities* (New Haven and London: Yale University Press, 2002), 171.

53. Service historique de la Défense—Vincennes: Dossier marine, François-Marie Cornette de Vénancourt (b. 1778); Bordonove, *Le Naufrage,* 66–7; Daget, "France, Suppression of the Illegal Trade," 195.

54. Touches, "Souvenirs," 184–86, 417, 425–26, 428.

55. Service historique de la Défense—Vincennes: Dossier marine, Léon Henry de Parnajon; Bordonove, *Le Naufrage,* 67.

56. Service historique de la Défense—Vincennes: Dossier Marine: Jean

Espiaux (b. 1783, Carcassonne), including the evaluation of his commander aboard the *Medusa* in 1814; Bordonove, *Le Naufrage,* 44–45, 49, 51.

57. Service Historique de la Défense—Vincennes: Dossier marine, Joseph Pierre André Reynaud (b. 1786); Bordonove, *Le Naufrage,* 54, 56.

58. Corréard and Savigny, 5th edition (Paris, 1821), 23; Gaspar Mollien, *Découverte des sources du Sénégal et de la Gambie en 1818* (Paris: C. Delagrave, 1889), 20.

59. Parson, *Premier rapport,* iii–iv; Henri Savigny and Alexandre Corréard, *Narrative of a Voyage to Senegal in 1816* (London: Henry Colburn, 1818), 4–5.

60. Brédif, *"Le Naufrage,"* 644; Dard, *La Chaumiére,* 20–22.

61. Savigny and Corréard (London, 1818), 12; Mollien, *Découverte,* 20–21; Brédif, "Le Naufrage," 783–84.

62. Bordonove, *Le Naufrage,* 84.

63. Chevalier, *Histoire,* 4.

64. Brédif, *"Le naufrage,"* 785; Service Historique de la Défense—Vincennes: BB 4 3 93; Bordonove, *Le Naufrage,* 85.

65. Corréard and Savigny get this date wrong, claiming it to be the 27th, which, if you follow their text through, would make the arrival in Tenerife the 30th and not the 29th, which was not the case, as 29 June is St. Peter's Day and the island bells were tolling for the festival. Viz. Brédif, "Le Naufrage," 785–91; Bordonove, *Le Naufrage,* 87.

66. Corréard and Savigny, 5th edition (Paris, 1821), 28–29.

67. Brédif, "Le Naufrage," 786–87; Savigny and Corréard (London, 1818), 13–16; Bordonove, *Le Naufrage,* 87.

68. Savigny and Corréard (London, 1818), 16; Paulin d'Anglas de Praviel, *Relation nouvelle et impartiale du naufrage de la frégate la Méduse* (Nîmes: Paulin d'Anglas de Praviel, 1858), in *Relation complète du naufrage de la frégate la Méduse* (Paris: J. de Bonnot, 1968), 275; See M. Adanson, *A Voyage to Senegal, the Isle of Gorée and the River Gambia* (Dublin: Ewing, James & Bradley, 1759), 22; Sander Rang (Alexandre Rang des Adrets, dit Sander Rang), *Voyage au Sénégal, Naufrage de la Méduse* (Paris: Editions E.P.I., 1946), 13–17. According to Brédif it was at eight a.m. (788). Though Rang was on the boat, Brédif was keeping a diary. It was at ten a.m., according to Charlotte Picard: Dard, *La chaumière,* 24; Brédif, "Le Naufrage," 788.

69. Bordonove, *Le Naufrage,* 91.

70. Brédif, "Le Naufrage," 787; Dard, *La chaumière*, 24–27.

71. Dard, *La chaumière*, 27–28.

72. Based on an account given in a popular anonymous fictional treatment, *Le Naufrage de la Méduse* (Paris: Delarue, 1842), 2–8; Brédif, "Le Naufrage," 789–90.

73. Brédif, "Le Naufrage," 790.

74. Charles Cochelet, *Narrative of the Shipwreck of the Sophia on the 30th May, 1819, on the Western Coast of Africa* (London: Sir Richard Phillips and Co., 1822), introduction; Geoffroy de Villeneuve, *L'Afrique*, vol. 1, 9; James Riley, *Loss of American Brig "Commerce" wrecked on Western Coast of Africa in the month of August 1815* (London: J. Murray, 1817), 55, 72.

75. Savigny and Corréard (London, 1818), 24; Corréard and Savigny, 5th edition (Paris, 1821), 38, 40–41; Dard, *La chaumière*, 28; Mollien, *Découverte*, 21.

76. Corréard and Savigny, 5th edition (Paris, 1821), 44–46; Bordonove, *Le Naufrage*, 93, 99–102.

77. Corréard and Savigny, 5th edition (Paris, 1821), 41–43; Savigny and Corréard (London, 1818), 30; Dard, *La chaumière*, 30–31; Praviel, *Relation*, 276; Bordonove, *Le Naufrage*, 96, 176–77.

78. Savigny and Corréard (London, 1818), 31; Rang, *Voyage*, 20; Brédif, "Le Naufrage," 791; Dard, *La chaumière*, 32, 34–35; Praviel, *Relation*, 278; Mollien, *Découverte*, 22; Bordonove, *Le Naufrage*, 102.

79. Mansel, *Louis XVIII*, 330, 340, 411; Mansel, *Paris Between Empires*, 110; Savigny, *La Restauration*, 128, 138; Bazin, *Théodore Géricault*, vol. V, 50.

80. Blanc, *Histoire*, 415.

81. Benjamin Constant, speaking in 1822, and qtd. by Alan B. Spitzer, *The French Generation of 1820* (Princeton, N.J.: Princeton University Press, 1987), 4.

82. Blanc, *Histoire*, 415.

83. Chenique, "Géricault: une vie," in *Géricault*, 275.

84. Ibid., 276.

85. Théodore Lebrun to Batissier, 6 April 1836, qtd. in Clément, *Géricault*, 79–81; Bazin, *Théodore Géricault*, vol. I, doc. 1, 22.

86. Clément, *Géricault*, 77–78; Chenique, "Géricault, une vie," in *Géricault*, 276.

Chapter 3

1. Rang, *Voyage au Sénégal,* 25; Praviel, *Relation nouvelle,* 278; Brédif, "Le Naufrage," 792–93; Corréard and Savigny, 5th edition (Paris, 1821), 50; Savigny and Corréard (London, 1818), 35–36; Mollien, *Découverte,* 22–23; Bordonove, *Le Naufrage,* 111–12.

2. Savigny and Corréard (London, 1818), 36–37.

3. Auguste Bailly, *Le Radeau de la Méduse* (Paris, 1929), 27–28.

4. Royou in his *La Biographie pittoresque et contemporaine des hommes de mer et d'eau douce* (1811), qtd. in Corréard and Savigny, 5th edition (Paris, 1821), 278ff.

5. L. Jore, "La vie diverse et volontaire du Colonel Julien Désiré Schmaltz . . . Consul Général de France à Smyrne (Turquie) 1771–1827," in *Revue d'histoire des colonies,* vol. XL, 2nd trimestre 1953, 265–312 (Paris: 1953), 269–70; Bordonove, *Le Naufrage,* 60.

6. Etienne Esquirol, *Des maladies mentales considérées sous les rapports médical, hygiénique et médico-légal* (Paris, 1838), vol. II, 172–73.

7. Jore, "La vie," 272–76; Esquirol, *Maladies,* vol. II, 172.

8. Jore, "La vie," 278–83; Masson, *L'Affaire,* 21–22.

9. Esquirol, *Maladies,* vol. II, 173; Erwin H. Ackerknecht, *Medicine at the Paris Hospital 1784–1848* (Baltimore: Johns Hopkins Press, 1967), 48, 168–70; Corréard and Savigny, 5th edition (Paris, 1821), 50.

10. Grocott, *Shipwrecks,* ix–x; Dard, *La chaumière,* 35–37; Corréard and Savigny, 5th edition (Paris, 1821), 56; Savigny and Corréard (London, 1818), 35–38; Mollien, *Découverte,* 24–25.

11. Savigny and Corréard (London, 1818), 39–41; Corréard and Savigny, 5th edition (Paris, 1821), 56–57.

12. Service Historique de la Défense—Vincennes, Dossier marine, Jean Espiaux; Rang, *Voyage au Sénégal,* 79–80; Dard, *La chaumière,* 36; Savigny and Corréard (London, 1818), 56–59.

13. Dard, *La chaumière,* 41–43; Praviel, *Relation nouvelle,* 279.

14. Marie Antoine Rabaroust, "Récit inédit du naufrage de La Méduse," in *L'Intermédiaire des chercheurs* (Paris, January 10, 1902), column 45; Dard, *La chaumière,* 42; Brédif, "Le naufrage," 793; Savigny and Corréard (London, 1818), 43–44.

15. Dard, *La chaumière,* 46–50; Brédif, "Le Naufrage," 793–94; Praviel, *Relation nouvelle,* 280.

16. Dard, *La chaumière,* 49–51; Rang, *Voyage au Sénégal,* 81; Praviel, *Relation nouvelle,* 281–82; Rabaroust, "Récit," column 46; Savigny and Corréard (London, 1818), 50–51, 71–72.

17. Brédif, "Le naufrage," 793–94; Corréard and Savigny, 5th edition (Paris, 1821), 69–70.

18. Dard, *La chaumière,* 51; Brédif, "Le Naufrage," 793; Corréard and Savigny, 5th edition (Paris, 1821), 71.

19. Dard, *La chaumière,* 53–56.

20. Rabaroust, "Récit," column 46; Rang, *Voyage au Sénégal,* 37–39; Praviel, *Relation nouvelle,* 280–82; Savigny and Corréard (London, 1818), 52, 60–67, 71; Corréard and Savigny, 5th edition (Paris, 1821), 87–94; Dard, *La chaumière,* 59–63; Mollien, *Découverte,* 27–28.

21. Dard, *La chaumière,* 61–64.

22. Brédif, "Le naufrage," 795.

Chapter 4

1. Praviel, *Relation nouvelle,* 284–85; Mollien, *Découverte,* 28; Brédif, "Le naufrage," 795. They give conflicting numbers for those who stayed on board. Praviel gives the figure as forty-three but Brédif, who was on board and writing at the time, has twenty-seven.

2. Brédif, "Le naufrage," 796–99; Rang, *Voyage au Sénégal,* 66; Mollien, *Découverte,* 28–31.

3. Dard, *La chaumière,* 68, 77–95; Mollien, *Découverte,* 31; MacDonald Critchley, *Shipwreck-Survivors, a Medical Study* (London: J. & A. Churchill, 1943), 30.

4. Dard, *La chaumière,* 95–104; Brédif, "Le Naufrage," 799; Rang, *Voyage au Sénégal,* 69–70.

5. See Cochelet's impression, Cochelet, *Narrative,* 5.

6. Jean Baptiste-Léonard Durand, *Voyage au Sénégal* (Paris: Chez Henri Agasse, 1802), 2.

7. Frank Lestringant, *Cannibal: The Discovery and Representation of the Cannibal from Columbus to Jules Verne* (Cambridge: Polity Press, 1997), 80–86.

8. G. H. von Langsdorff, *Voyages and Travels in Various Parts of the World during the Years 1803, 1804, 1805, 1806, and 1807* (London: Henry Colburn, 1813), 141.

9. Cochelet, *Narratives,* 4.

10. Louis-Marie-Joseph Ohier, comte de Grandpré, *Voyage à la côte occidentale d'Afrique fait dans les années 1786 et 1787*, 2 vols. (Paris: Dentu, an IX—1801), vi–xi; Grigsby, *Extremities*, 185–86.

11. Geoffroy de Villeneuve, *L'Afrique*, vol. II, 18–20.

12. Brédif, "Le naufrage," 799–800; Mollien, *Découverte*, 32; Mollien, *Travels in the Interior of Africa to the Scources of the Senegal and Gambia Performed by Command of the French government in the year 1818* (London: Colburn & Co., 1820), 3–4; Adanson, *Voyage to Senegal*, 79; Critchley, *Shipwreck-Survivors*, 31; Andrew Boorde, *Dyetary*, ed. F. J. Furnivall, Early English Text Society e.s. 10 (London, 1870).

13. Dard, *La chaumière*, 100–19; Brédif, "Le naufrage," 799–800; Rang, *Voyage au Sénégal*, 70; Savigny and Corréard (London, 1818), 163–64; Mollien, *Découverte*, 33–85; Adanson, *Voyage to Senegal*, 46.

14. Dard, *La chaumière*, 119–129; Brédif, "Le Naufrage," 800–2; Mollien, *Découverte*, 39.

15. Brédif, "Le naufrage," 803; Dard, *La chaumière*, 129–132; Mollien, *Découverte*, 39.

16. Mollien, *Travels*, 3–4; Brédif, "Le naufrage," 802–3.

17. Brédif, "Le Naufrage," 803.

18. Dard, *La chaumière*, 133–36; Brédif, "Le naufrage," 803–4.

19. Dard, *La chaumière*, 137–158; Brédif, "Le Naufrage," 804.

20. Jacques-Joseph Le Maire, *Les Voyages du Sieur Le Maire aux Isles Canaries, Cap-Verd, Sénégal et Gambie* (Paris, 1695), 51; Mollien, *Travels*, 3–4; Praviel, *Relation nouvelle*, 287–88.

21. Praviel, *Relation nouvelle*, 289–91; Critchley, *Shipwreck-Survivors*, 28–30.

22. Praviel, *Relation nouvelle*, 292–93; Geoffrey de Villeneuve, *L'Afrique*, vol. I, 6, 40; Mollien, *Découverte*, 47–49; Critchley, *Shipwreck-Survivors*, 33–34.

23. Praviel, *Relation nouvelle*, 293–95; Geoffrey de Villeneuve, *L'Afrique*, vol. II, 43–44.

24. Praviel, *Relation nouvelle*, 296–98; Mollien, *Découverte*, 47–50; Adanson, *Voyage to Senegal*, 46.

Chapter 5

1. Savigny and Corréard (London, 1818), 60–61, 68, 72–77, 100–1; Corréard and Savigny, 5th edition (Paris, 1821), 99–102; Rang, *Voyage au*

Sénégal, 82; Critchley, *Shipwreck-Survivors,* 24, 42; Denis Escudier, *L'affreuse vérité de M. Savigny: second chirurgien de la frégate la "Méduse," naufragé du radeau, miraculeusement sauvé par l'Argus' le 17 juillet 1816* (Saint-Jean-D'Angely: Bordessoules, 1991), 16, 62; Henri Savigny, "Relation Manuscript," reproduced in Escudier, *L'affreuse,* 67; Jean Griffon du Bellay, *Les Griffon pendant cinq cent ans* (Garnes: privately printed, 1979), 26ff.

2. Savigny and Corréard (London, 1818), 78–80; Corréard and Savigny, 5th edition (Paris, 1821), 103–5.

3. Savigny and Corréard (London, 1818), 80–104; Corréard and Savigny, 5th edition (Paris, 1821), 105–29; Jean-Baptiste Savigny, "*Observations sur les effets de la faim et de la soif éprouvées après le naufrage de la frégate du roi la Méduse en 1816,*" (Paris 26 mai, 1818), reproduced in Escudier, *L'affreuse,* 101–16;. Griffon du Bellay, letter to his uncle from Senegal, reprinted in *Les Griffon pendant cinq cent ans,* 26–27.

4. Fournier de Pescay, "Notice sur la Calenture, maladie particulière aux gens de mer," in *Annales des faits et des sciences militaires: faisant suite aux "Victoires et conquêtes des Français de 1792–1815,"* ed. Jean Denis Barbié du Bocage, 4 vols. (March, 1818).

5. Corréard and Savigny, 5th edition (Paris, 1821), 125–33; Savigny and Corréard (London, 1818), 104–11; Langsdorff, 142–43; *The Book of Deuteronomy* XXVIII v. 53; Brian A. W. Simpson, *Cannibalism and the Common Law: The Story of the Tragic Last Voyage of the Mignonette and the Strange Legal Proceedings to Which it Gave Rise* (Harmondsworth: Penguin, 1986), 114–16, 123–25; Critchley, *Shipwreck-Survivors,* 44; John Graham Dalyell, *Shipwrecks and Disasters at Sea* (London: George Routledge and Sons, 1866), 198–202; Grigsby, *Extremities,* 186; Savigny, "*Observations,*" 101–2.

6. Critchley, *Shipwreck-Survivors,* 26, 49; Eric Martini, "Treatment for Scurvy not Discovered by Lind," *The Lancet,* vol. 364 (London, December 18/25, 2004), 2180; Savigny and Corréard (London, 1818), 111–15, 129; Corréard and Savigny, 5th edition (Paris, 1821), 133–38, 149.

7. Savigny and Corréard (London, 1818), 116–20; Corréard and Savigny, 5th edition (Paris, 1821), 139–42.

8. Savigny, "*Observations,*" 103–4; Corréard and Savigny, 5th edition (Paris, 1821), 142, 147–48; Savigny and Corréard (London, 1818), 121–23, 127–28; Critchley, *Shipwreck-Survivors,* 25.

9. Savigny, "*Observations,*" 104; Savigny, "Relation," ms. reprinted in Escudier, *L'affreuse,* 30; Savigny and Corréard (London, 1818), 123–29.

10. Service historique de la Défense—Vincennes: BB4393—Parnajon to Schmaltz, 19 July 1816; Savigny, *"Observations,"* 104–5; Critchley, *Shipwreck-Survivors,* 31, 44–45, 47; Savigny and Corréard (London, 1818), 126–45; Corréard and Savigny, 5th edition (Paris, 1821), 142–45, 147–66; Bordonove, *Le Naufrage,* 170–71, 265; Escudier, *L'affreuse,* 132.

Chapter 6

1. Rang, *Voyage au Sénégal,* 42–52, 53–57.
2. A. W. Lawrence, *Trade Castles and Forts of West Africa* (London: Jonathan Cape, 1963), 30, 41, 78; Bordonove, *Le Naufrage,* 47; Durand, vi–xx.
3. Major John Peddie, letter of 3 August 1816, in the National Archives, CO 2/5.
4. Governor Brereton to Governor-designate Schmaltz, 9 July 1816, in Service historique de la Défense, BB4 393.
5. Dard, *La chaumière,* 154–55, 174–75; Geoffrey de Villeneuve, *L'Afrique,* vol. 1, 63–96; Map of Saint-Louis, National Archives, M.P.G. 220.
6. Dard, *La chaumière,* 65–66, 156–57, 162–63, 165–67; Rang, *Voyage au Sénégal,* 63.
7. Brédif, "Le naufrage," 138; Dard, *La chaumière,* 162–63; Savigny and Corréard (London, 1818), 203–4.
8. Service historique de la Défense—Vincennes: BB4394—Vénancourt's report on Cap Vert; Le Maire, 57–58; Geoffrey de Villeneuve, *L'Afrique,* vol. I, 114; Brédif, "Le naufrage," 148; Bordonove, *Le Naufrage,* 173–75; Praviel, *Relation nouvelle,* 301; Mollien, *Découverte,* 43, 50–51.
9. Geoffrey de Villeneuve, *L'Afrique,* vol. I, 103; Savigny and Corréard (London, 1818), 232.
10. Rang, *Voyage au Sénégal,* 79; Brédif, "Le naufrage," 141–43; Savigny and Corréard, (London, 1818), 147.
11. Grigsby, *Extremities,* 190–91; Rang, *Voyage au Sénégal,* 78.
12. Brédif, "Le naufrage," 143.
13. Savigny and Corréard (London, 1818) 163–92; Corréard and Savigny, 5th edition (Paris, 1821), 215–43; Brédif, "Le Naufrage," 142; Rang, *Voyage au Sénégal,* 97–98.
14. Brédif, "Le naufrage," 143; Praviel, *Relation nouvelle,* 300.

15. Savigny and Corréard (London, 1818), 200, 213–26; Corréard and Savigny, 5th edition (Paris, 1821), 268–69.

16. Savigny and Corréard (London, 1818), 202–7; Corréard and Savigny, 5th edition (Paris, 1821), 244–61; Dard, *La chaumière,* 58–9; Escudier, *L'affreuse,* 27.

17. Savigny and Corréard (London, 1818), 210–13; Corréard and Savigny, 5th edition (Paris, 1821), 255–60; Claude Faure, "*La Garnison européenne du Sénégal et le recrutement des premières troupes noires (1779–1858),*" in *Revue de l'histoire des colonies françaises* 8, 3e trimestre (Paris: Société de l'histoire des colonies françaises, 1920), 17.

18. Service Historique de la Défense—Dossier marine: Cornette de Vénancourt, Report of Sept. 17, 1816; Parson, *Premier rapport,* vii; Savigny and Corréard (London, 1818), 232–24, 251.

19. This manuscript may well be the one in Bibliothèque Municipale de Saintes (donation du baron Eschasseriaux), a notebook of forty pages, which bears resemblance to the article eventually published in *Le Journal des débats;* see Escudier, *L'affrause,* 20, 29, 34.

20. Archive Nationales, Paris—Marine BB4 393 f° 122; Blot, 153–54; Bordonove, *Le Naufrage,* 186–87, 190–92.

Chapter 7

1. Clément, *Géricault,* 77–78.

2. Christopher Sells, "New Light on Géricault, his Travels and his Friends, 1816–23," *Apollo,* vol. CXXIII, no. 292 (London, June, 1986): 391; Géricault, letter of 18 October to Dedreux-Dorcy, qtd. in full in Chenique, "Lettres et documents," in *Géricault,* 318; Géricault, letter of 27 November to Dedreux-Dorcy, qtd. in Clément, *Géricault,* 84–85.

3. Pierre Courthion, *Géricault raconté par lui-même et par ses amis* (Vésenaz-Genève: P. Cailler, 1947), 89–90; Wheelock Whitney, *Géricault in Italy* (New Haven and London: Yale, 1997), 19.

4. Whitney, *Géricault in Italy,* 158, 161; René-Paul Huet, *Paul Huet d'après ses notes, sa correspondance, ses contemporains* (Paris: H. Laurens, 1911), 224; Lorenz Eitner, "Erotic Drawings by Gericault," *Master Drawings,* vol. XXXIV, no. 4 (New York, Winter, 1996): 375–77.

5. Whitney, *Géricault in Italy,* 158, 170–71, 181.

6. Montfort, qtd. in Bazin, *Théodore Géricault*, vol. I, 201; Mme. Meuricoffre, qtd. in Whitney, *Géricault in Italy*, 11; Régis Michel, "Le Mythe de l'oeuvre," in *Géricault*, 1991, 66.

7. Courthion, *Géricault racenté*, 93; Clément, *Géricault*, 111; Louis Batissier, 8.

8. Stendhal, *Racine et Shakespeare* (Paris, 1823), chapter III; Isaiah Berlin, *The Roots of Romanticism*, ed. Henry Hardy (London: Chatto and Windus, 1999), 14.

Chapter 8

1. Decazes, qtd. in Roger Langeron, *Decazes, ministre du roi* (Paris: Hachette, 1960), 76; Ernest Daudet, *Louis XVIII et le duc Decazes 1815–1820* (Paris: Plon, Nourrit et Cie., 1899), 142–43.

2. Bertier de Sauvigny, *La Restauration*, 150; C. L. Lesur, *Annuaire historique universel Pour 1818* (Paris: Thoisnier-Deplaces, 1825), 36; Irene Collins, "Liberalism and the Newspaper Press during the French Restoration, 1814–1830," *History*, vol. XLVI (London: RKP, 1961): 26; Langeron, *Decazes*, 97, 117–18; Louis Girard, *Les Libéraux français, 1814–1875* (Paris: Aubier, 1985), 61.

3. Decazes, qtd. in Daudet, *Louis XVIII*, 142.

4. Daudet, *Louis XVIII*, 132–33, 135.

5. Decazes, in notes to be used for his memoirs, qtd. in Langeron, *Decazes*, 71.

6. Decazes, qtd. in Daudet, *Louis XVIII*, 146–47; Ephraim Harpaz, *L'école libérale sous la Restauration, le Mercure et la Minerve, 1817–1820* (Genève: Droz, 1968), 68.

7. Service historique de la Défense—Vincennes: BB 4393.

8. Ibid.; Masson, 111–14; Bordonove, *Le Naufrage*, 187–89.

9. Service historique de la Défense—Vincennes: BB4393; Louis XVIII, "Ordinance Dissolving the Chamber," signed on September 5, Palais de Tuileries, and printed in *Journal des débats*, 8 September 1816; *La Quotidienne*, Friday, 6 September 1816; *Le Moniteur universel*, 8 September 1816.

10. Daudet, *Louis XVIII*, 148–49; Mansel, *Louis XVIII*, 344; Bertier de Sauvigny, *La Restauration*, 138–40; *La Quotidienne*, 13 September 1816; François-René de Chateaubriand, *Mémoires d'outre-tombe*, ed. Levaillant (Paris: Le Club français du livre, 1969), vol. III, 8.

11. *La Quotidienne*, Wednesday, 11 September 1816.

12. Corréard and Savigny, 5th edition (Paris, 1821), 305–8.

13. Collins, "Liberalism and the Newspaper," *History,* vol. XLVI, 21–22.

14. *Journal des débats,* 13 September 1816.

15. Corréard and Savigny, 5th edition (Paris, 1821), 307–9.

16. Vicomte DuBouchage, in *La Quotidienne,* 15 September 1816.

17. Savigny letter to *Le Moniteur universel,* 13 September 1816, reprinted in *La Quotidienne,* Monday, 16 September 1816; Corréard and Savigny, 5th edition (Paris, 1821), 306.

18. *La Quotidienne,* 22 September 1816; *Le Constitutionnel* and *Journal des débats,* 23 September 1816; Collins, *The Government and the Newspaper,* 14–16; Collins, "Liberalism and the Newspaper," *History,* vol. XLVI, 22.

19. Bordonove, *Le Naufrage,* 196, 197–98, 210–13.

20. Service historique de la Défense—Vincennes BB2152; Bertier de Sauvigny, *La Restauration,* 150; *Times,* (London, 16 September and 17 September 1816).

21. Service historique de la Défense—Vincennes: BB4393; Savigny and Corréard (London, 1818), 255–63; Corréard and Savigny, 5th edition (Paris, 1821), 309–17.

22. National Archives Ex 11/11; Parson, *Premier rapport,* v; Dard, *La chaumière,* 170.

23. Savigny and Corréard (London, 1818), 238–45; Corréard and Savigny, 5th edition (Paris, 1821), 288–93.

24. Service historique de la Défense—Vincennes: BB4393; Touches, 435; Savigny and Corréard (London, 1818), 247–49; Corréard and Savigny, 5th edition (Paris, 1821), 298–304; Bordonove, *Le Naufrage,* 206.

25. Savigny and Corréard (London, 1818), 249–50, 261–62; Corréard and Savigny, 5th edition (Paris, 1821), 314–17.

26. Savigny and Corréard (London, 1818), 263–68; Corréard and Savigny, 5th edition (Paris, 1821), 317–22.

27. Chaumareys, *Relation,* 31–32; Bordonove, *Le Naufrage,* 176–77, 188–89, 214–48; Masson, 131–43.

28. "Jugement de M. Hugues Duroys de Chaumareys," in Corréard and Savigny, 5th edition (Paris, 1821), 373–82; Masson, 145–54, 189–92; Bordonove, *Le Naufrage,* 248.

29. Ibid., 344; Bertier de Sauvigny, *La Restauration,* 141–42.

30. Savigny and Corréard (London, 1818), 270–77; Corréard and

Savigny, 5th edition (Paris, 1821), 323–29; Alexandre Corréard, letter to Decazes, June 27, 1818, in the *Archives Nationales,* F/18/1749.

31. Mansel, *Louis XVIII,* 356; Bertier de Sauvigny, *La Restauration,* 147; Chevalier, 3–4; Newman, *Historical Dictionary,* 341; Bordonove, *Le Naufrage,* 302–3; *Journal de débats,* 22 October 1817.

32. Savigny and Corréard (London, 1818), 200–1; Corréard and Savigny, 5th edition (Paris, 1821), 247.

33. C. L. Lesur, *Annuaire historique 1818,* 19–22.

34. A. Imbert, *Biographie des imprimeurs et des librairies* (Paris, 1826), 43, 48, 57; Jean de La Tynna, *Almanach du commerce de Paris, des départements de la France et des principales villes du monde* (Paris: Bureau de L'Almanach du Commerce, 1818 and 1822), 78, 98, 135; *Bibliographie de la France,* 1817, 602, entry no. 3404.

35. *Le Mercure de France,* November 1817, 340–55; *Journal des débats,* 4 November 1817.

36. *Le Journal du commerce,* 29 November 1817; Harpaz, *L'Ecole,* 156; Corréard and Savigny, 5th edition (Paris, 1821), 448–58.

Chapter 9

1. Darmon, *La Rumeur,* 21; Peter Shankland and the Rt. Hon. Sir Michael Havers, Q.C., *Murder with a Double Tongue* (London: Souvenir Press, 1990), 73; Lesur, *Annuaire historique,* 523.

2. Robert Simon, "Géricault and l'affaire Fualdès," in *Géricault, Conférences et colloques du Louvre,* vol. 1, 169–70; Darmon, *La Rumeur,* 14–15, 36, 137, 158–59, 206–7; Bazin, *Théodore Géricault,* vol. V, 50–51; Shankland and Havers, *Murder,* 26–28, 71, 89, 143–46; Mansel, *Louis XVIII,* 161.

3. Manzon, qtd. in Darmon, *La Rumeur,* 69.

4. *La Quotidienne,* 18 September 1817, quoted by Shankland and Havers, *Murder,* 137.

5. Darmon, *La Rumeur,* 142–43; Shankland and Havers, *Murder,* 158, 255.

6. Perrot qtd. by Simon, "Géricault and the fait divers," in *Géricault, Conférences et colloques du Louvre,* vol. 1, 258; E. Auger qtd. in M. Angenot, *Le Roman populaire: Recherches en paralittérature* (Montréal: Presses de l'Université du Québec. 1975), 16–18; Roland Barthes, "La structure du fait divers," in *Essais critiques* (Paris: Éditions Seuil, 1964), 188.

7. Linda Nochlin, "Géricault or the Absence of Women," *Géricault, Conférences et colloques du Louvre,* vol. I, 415.

8. Chantal Gleyses, *La Femme coupable* (Paris: Éditions Imago, 1994), 85; Patricia Mainardi, *Husbands, Wives, and Lovers* (New Haven and London: Yale University Press, 2003), 1–3, 7, 13, 16–19; Patricia Mainardi, "Husbands, Wives and Lovers. Mazeppa or Marriage and its Discontents in C19 France," in *Géricault, Conférences et colloques du Louvre,* vol. 1, 277–79, 280, 282–83; Patricia Mainardi, "Mazeppa," *Word & Image,* vol. 16, no. 4 (London: October 2000): 340; Bertier de Sauvigny, *La Restauration,* 236, 244.

Chapter 10

1. Batissier, "*Géricault,*" 8; Aimé-Azam, *La Passion,* 1956, 159.

2. Bazin, *Théodore Géricault,* vol. VI, 90, Vol I, 41–42; Donald A. Rosenthal, "Géricault's Expenses for the Raft of the Medusa," *Art Bulletin,* vol. LXII (New York: College Art Association of America, December, 1980): 639.

3. Buisson, *Géricault,* 40; Edward Planta, *A New Picture of Paris, or The Stranger's Guide to the French Metropolis* (London: Samuel Leigh, July 1814), 49; Mainardi, *Husbands and Wives,* 25, 193; Bertier de Sauvigny, *La Restauration,* 243; Chenique, "Géricault, une vie," in *Gericault,* 1991, 281, Le Pesant, "Documents," 76–78.

4. Jean-Baptiste Savigny, *Observations sur les effets de la faim;* Fournier de Pescay, "Notice sur la Calenture, maladie particulière aux gens de mer," in *Annales des faits et des sciences militaires;* Albert Alhadeff, *The Raft of the Medusa* (Munich: Prestel, 2002), 54–55.

5. Clément, *Géricault,* 129; Henri Houssaye, "Un Maître de l'école française—Théodore Géricault," *Revue des deux-mondes* (Paris, November 15, 1879), 384.

6. The present-day 80 rue de faubourg St. Honoré; Clément, *Géricault,* 137; Pierre Vallery-Radot, "L'anatomie et la psychiatrie dans la vie et l'oeuvre de Géricault," *La presse médicale,* 66, no. 27 (Paris: Masson, April 5 1958): 614; Eitner, *Raft,* 23–24.

7. Charles Fournel, *L'hôpital Beaujon. Histoire depuis son origine jusqu'à nos jours* (Paris: Dentu, 1884), 48–50, 82–87; Martial Guédron, *La plaie et le couteau: La sensibilité anatomique de Théodore Géricault, 1791–1824* (Paris: Kimé, 1997), 90; Bazin, *Théodore Géricault,* vol. VI, 29.

8. Vallery-Radot, "L'anatomie et la psychiatrie," 614; Hector Berlioz, *La vie de Berlioz racontée par Berlioz* (Paris: R. Juliard, 1954), 36, qtd. in Inken D. Knoch, "Une peinture sans sujet? Étude sur les fragments anatomiques," in *Géricault, Conférences et colloques du Louvre*, vol. I, 148.

9. Mansel, *Paris Between Empires*, 7, 49–50; Bertier de Sauvigny, *La Restauration*, 258–59.

10. Anon, *The Picture of the Palais Royal* (London: William Hone, 1819), 141–42; Pierre Vayre, *Les Larrey: Dominique, Hippolyte . . . et les autres* (Paris: Editions Glyphe, 2005). Disarticulation is different from amputation: the joint is simply dis-articulated; it is swifter and less dangerous on the battlefield than amputation.

11. C. Leymarie, "Michelet et Géricault," *L'Artiste* (1897), qtd. in Courthion, *Géricault*, 191–92; Guédron, *La plaie*, 90–92; Guillaume de Bertier de Sauvigny, *Nouvelle histoire de Paris: La Restauration* (Paris: Hachette, 1977), 190; Haydon, *Haydon*, 240.

12. Eugène Delacroix, qtd. by Eitner, *Géricault's "Raft of the Medusa,"* 36.

13. Clément, *Géricault*, 131–32; Vallery-Radot, "L'anatomie," 614; Jean-François Debord, "À propos de quelques dessins anatomiques de Géricault," in *Géricault—Dessins et estampes des collections de l'École des Beaux-Arts* (Paris: École nationale supérieure des Beaux-Arts, 1997), 65, n. 82.

14. Nina Athanassoglou-Kallymer, "Géricault's Severed Heads and Limbs: The Politics and Aesthetics of the Scaffold," *The Art Bulletin*, vol. LXXXIV, no. 4 (New York: December, 1992): 614.

Chapter 11

1. Marie-Claude Chaudonneret, *L'Etat et les artistes de la Restauration à la monarchie de Juillet (1815–1833)* (Paris: Flammarion, 1999), 55–57, 72–75.

2. Grigsby, *Extremities*, 232.

3. Montfort, qtd. by Clément, *Géricault*, 138–40.

4. Letter from Théodore Lebrun to Louis Batissier, April 8, 1836, qtd. in Bazin, *Théodore Géricault*, vol. I, 22.

5. Delacroix, qtd. in Eitner, *Géricault's "Raft of the Medusa,"* 34.

6. Clément, *Géricault*, 143–45.

7. Corréard and Savigny, 5th edition (Paris, 1821), 383–96.

8. Alhadeff, *The Raft*, 137, 163, 166–67.

9. Christopher Sells, "New Light on Géricault, his Travel and his Friends," 391–92; Clément, *Géricault,* 137.

10. Théodore Géricault, qtd. in Bazin, *Théodore Géricault,* vol. I, 73; Eitner, *Géricault's "Raft of the Medusa,"* 32.

11. See Bazin, *Théodore Géricault,* vol. VI, 16; Savigny and Corréard (London, 1818), 79 (printed between 96 and 98).

12. Clément, *Géricault,* 144–45; Eitner, *Géricault's "Raft of the Medusa,"* 38.

13. Vicomte DuBouchage, report to Louis XVIII, September 1816, in Service historique de la Défense—Vincennes BB4393.

14. Chaudonneret, *L'Etat,* 60, 80; Eitner, *Géricault's "Raft of the Medusa,"* 2, 5–6.

15. Chaudonneret, *L'Etat,* 76, 97.

16. Clément, *Géricault,* 147–48; Eitner, *Géricault's "Raft of the Medusa,"* 2, 5, 40.

17. Jean Sagne, "Géricault et l'opinion libérale," in *Géricault, Conférences et colloques du Louvre,* vol. II, 597–98; Bertier de Sauvigny, *La Restauration,* 152; Chaudonneret, *L'Etat,* 125; Bazin, *Théodore Géricault,* vol. 1, 44, where the remark seems to have come to painter Jean Gigoux via Gros, its authenticity questioned.

18. Houssaye, "Un Maître,"384; *La Quotidienne,* 30 August 1819, 4; Pierre Angrand, *Le Comte Forbin et le Louvre en 1819* (Lausanne-Paris: Bibliothèque des Arts, 1972), 172.

19. Aimé-Azam, *Mazeppa,* 169.

20. *La Quotidienne,* 30 August 1819; *Le Moniteur universel,* 12 October 1819; Eitner, *Géricault's "Raft of the Medusa,"* 40–41.

21. *Gazette de France,* 31 August 1819; Gustave Jal, *L'Ombre de Diderot et le bossu du Marais; Dialogue critique sur le Salon de 1819* (Paris: Corréard, 1819), 128.

22. *L'Indépendant,* 29 August 1819, 3.

23. Alphonse Rabbe, "Nécrologie, Géricault peintre d'histoire," *La Pandore, Journal des spectacles, des lettres, des arts, des moeurs et des modes,* no. 198 (Paris: January 29, 1824).

24. Géricault, letter to M. Musigny, qtd. in Batissier, "Géricault," 14; *Le drapeau blanc,* 26 August 1819, 3.

25. Eitner, *Géricault's "Raft of the Medusa,"* 52–54, 60.

26. Le Pesant, "Documents," 77; Eitner, *Géricault's "Raft of the Medusa,"*

61; Bazin, *Théodore Géricault,* vol. 1, 129; Sells, "New Light on Géricault, his Travels and his Friends," 395; Christopher Sells, "Two Letters from Gericault to Madame Horace Vernet," *Burlington Magazine,* vol. CXXXI, no. 1032 (London, March, 1989): 217.

Chapter 12

1. Paul Joannides, "The Raft of the Medusa," review of *Géricault's "Raft of the Medusa,"* by Lorenz Eitner, *Burlington Magazine,* vol. CXVII, no. 864 (London, March, 1975): 171–72.

2. John McLeod, *Voyage of His Majesty's late ship 'Alceste' along the coast of Corea to the island of Lewchew, with an account of her subsequent shipwreck in the straits of Gaspa,* compiled from the papers of John McLeod (London: John Murray, 1818), 3, 207–15, 220–21, 248, 253, appendix; John McLeod, *The Shipwreck of the Alceste, an English frigate in the straits of Gaspar; also the Shipwreck of the Medusa,* compiled from the papers of John McLeod and the narrative by Savigny and Corréard (Dublin: E. Tute, 1822), 157.

3. Houssaye, "Un Maître," 387.

4. Mansel, *Paris Between Empires,* 41, 44, 149–50; Mansel, *Louis XVIII,* 214.

5. Suzanne Lodge, "Géricault in England," *Burlington Magazine,* no. 753, vol. CVII (London, December, 1965): 617–18; Thomas Jessop, *Journal d'un voyage à Paris en septembre–octobre 1820,* edited by F. C. W. Hiley (Paris: 1928), 18–19; Bertier de Sauvigny, *La Restauration,* 331; Eric J. Evans, *Britain Before the Reform Act: Politics and Society, 1815–1832* (London and New York: Longman, 1989), 1–5, 15, 19, 22–24, 50; John Belchem, *Popular Radicalism in Nineteenth Century Britain* (London: Macmillan, 1996), 47–48; Mansel, *Paris Between Empires,* 142–44.

6. Sells, "New Light on Géricault, his Travels and his Friends, 1816–23," 390; Théodore Géricault, letter to Dedreux-Dorcy, April 23, 1820, qtd. in Courthion, 96; Lodge, "Géricault in England," 617; Clément, 189–90.

7. Christine Riding, "The Raft of the Medusa in Britain—Audience and Context," *Crossing the Channel, British and French Painting in the Age of Romanticism,* ed. Patrick Noon (London: Tate Publishing, 2003), 71.

8. Haydon, *Life,* 367, 378; Hugh Honour, "Curiosities of the Egyptian Hall," *Country Life,* vol. CXV, no. 2973 (London, January 7, 1954): 38–39; *Literary Gazette and Journal of Belles Lettres,* 1 July 1820, 427,

qtd. in Riding, "The Raft of the Medusa in Britain—Audience and Context," 72.

9. Although he was with Géricault at the time, Charlet's account has been strongly contested. On the advice of Dedreux-Dorcy, Clément discredited these stories and rather suggests that, although Géricault had his dark moments, "he was relatively happy and tranquil while he was living in England." Clément points out that a letter of April 23 to Dedreux-Dorcy shows no signs of despair; Chenique, "Géricault: une vie," in *Géricault*, 290–91; Clément, *Géricault*, 187–88; Houssaye, "Un Maître," 388; Sells, "New Light on Géricault and his Friends," 392.

10. W. T. Moncrieff, *Shipwreck of the Medusa, or, the Fatal Raft! A Drama in Three acts* (London, 1830), introduction and 17.

11. *Morning Post*, 13 June 1820; William Bullock, *Sale Catalogue of the Bullock Museum, 1819* (London: Johnson and Hewett, 1979); W. H. Mullens, "William Bullock's London Museum," in *Museums Journal*, no. 17 (London, October 1917): 54; Honour, "Curiosities," 38; Haydon, *Haydon*, 371–73; Johnson, "*The Raft of the Medusa* in Great Britain," *Burlington Magazine*, no. 617, vol. XCVI (London, August 1954): 250.

12. *Globe*, 12 June 1820, quoted in Eitner, *Géricault's "Raft of the Medusa,"* 64.

13. *Morning Post*, 13 June 1820, and *Times*, 22 June 1820, both qtd. in Johnson, "*The Raft of the Medusa* in Great Britain," 250.

14. *London Literary Gazette and Journal of Belles Lettres* 10 June and 1 July 1820, 427, qtd. in Johnson, "*The Raft of the Medusa* in Great Britain," 250–51.

15. Jessop, *Journal*, 65; Anon., *Souscription en faveur du libraire Corréard, condamné pour avoir vendu des brochures politiques, dont les auteurs et les éditeurs étaient connus* (Paris, 1820), 2; Alan B. Spitzer, *Old Hatred and Young Hopes: The French Carbonari against the Bourbon Restoration* (Cambridge, Mass.: Harvard University Press, 1971), 62–63; Mansel, *Louis XVIII*, 375; Mansel, *Paris Between Empires*, 172, 177–78; Bertier de Sauvigny, *La Restauration*, 163–66, 168, 172.

16. Johnson, "*The Raft of the Medusa* in Great Britain," 251–52 and quoting *Saunder's News-Letter*, 17 February 1821; *Times*, 12 December 1820.

17. *Saunder's News-Letter*, 5 March 1821, qtd. in Johnson, "*The Raft of the Medusa* in Great Britain," 251.

18. Johnson, "*The Raft of the Medusa* in Great Britain," 251–52.

19. Sells, "New Light on Géricault, his Travels and his Friends, 1816–23," 392; Bazin, *Théodore Géricault,* vol. VII, 20.

20. Sells, "New Light on Géricault, his Travels and his Friends 1816–23," 390; Michael Twyman, *Lithography 1800–1850* (London: Oxford University Press, 1970), 183, 185; Bruno Chenique, "Théodore Géricault, lithographe d'avant garde," in *Géricault—Dessins et estampes des collections de l'École des Beaux-Arts* (Paris: École nationale supérieure des Beaux-Arts 1998), 118.

21. Théodore Géricault, letter to Dedreux-Dorcy of February 12, 1821, qtd. in Courthion, *Géricault,* 98; Chenique, "Géricault: une vie," 295, 257; Cockerell's diaries qtd. in Lee Johnson, "Géricault and Delacroix seen by Cockerell," *Burlington Magazine,* vol. CXIII, no. 822 (London: September 1971): 547–51; Bazin, *Théodore Géricault,* vol. VII, 10.

22. Théodore Géricault, letter to Jules Auguste of December 27, 1821, qtd. in Bazin, *Théodore Géricault,* vol. 1, 65.

Chapter 13

1. Jessop, *Journal,* 70–71; Mansel, *Paris Between Empires,* 41–42; Major W. E. Frye, *After Waterloo—Reminiscences of European Travel 1815–19* (London, 1908), 59–60; H. Déterville, *Le Palais Royal ou les filles en bonne fortune* (Paris, 1815), ix, 15.

2. Lewis Tronchet, *Picture of Paris, being a complete guide to all the public buildings, places of amusement, and curiosities in that metropolis* (London: Sherwood, Neely and Jones, 1814), 160; Déterville, *Palais-Royal,* 15–17; Planta, *New Picture,* 54; Anon, *The Picture of the Palais Royal,* 25, 40, 151; Honoré de Balzac, *La Peau de chagrin* (1831) (Paris: Gallimard, 1974), 23–24.

3. Anon., *The Picture of the Palais Royal,* 14–17, 27, 29, 52, 60, 144–45; John Scott of Gala, 281–82; Bertier de Sauvigny, *Nouvelle Histoire de Paris: La Restauration,* 381.

4. Anon., *The Picture of the Palais Royal,* 21, 29–31, 83–84; Hugues, *Corréard,* 21; Jessop, *Journal,* 73; Frye, *After Waterloo,* 61; Jeanne Gilmore, *La République clandestine,* 30; *Archives nationales* F/18/1749.

5. *Le Mercure de France,* December 1817, 603; Harpaz, *L'Ecole,* 155–56; Shankland and Havers, *Murder,* 156.

6. Griffon du Bellay, *Les Griffon,* 28; *La Minerve française,* February 1818, 104.

7. Alexandre Corréard, *Élections des Représentants du Peuple,* 2.

8. Mansel, *Paris Between Empires,* 307; Bertier de Sauvigny, *La Restauration,* 340.

9. Corréard and Savigny, 5th edition (Paris, 1821), 398–405; Arnold Charles Scheffer, *De l'Etat de la liberté en France* (Brussels, 1818), preface.

10. Bruno Chenique, "On the Far Left of Géricault," in *Théodore Géricault: The Alien Body: Tradition in Chaos,* ed. Serge Guilbaut, Maureen Ryan, and Scott Watson (Vancouver: Morris and Helen Belkin Art Gallery, 1997), 73–75.

11. The copy of Jacques Bousquet-Deschamps, *Questions à l'ordre du jour* (Paris: Chez Corréard, April 8, 1820), in the *Archives nationales,* BB/18/999, along with the letter from the *Procureur Générale* of Toulouse, dated April 1820; Jean Sagne, "Géricault et l'opinion libérale," in *Géricault, Conférences et colloques du Louvre,* vol. 2, 605.

12. J-Lucien Bousquet-Deschamps, *Attention!* (Paris: Corréard, May 17, 1820), 15–16; Corréard and Savigny, 5th edition (Paris, 1821), 406–43.

13. Edmond Werdet, *De la librairie française: son passé, son présent et son avenir* (Paris, 1860) 178; Nina Athanassoglu, "Géricault and La Liberté des Peuples," 10–11; Hugues, *Corréard,* 21; *Archives nationales* F/18/1749.

14. Léonard Gallois, *Promenade à Saint-Pélagie* (Paris: Leroux, 1823), 6, 11–12, 14, 21–22, 31, 32–39; Newman, *Historical Dictionary,* 80–81, 939; Bertier de Sauvigny, *Nouvelle Histoire de Paris,* 47, 463; Collins, *Government and Society in France,* 27–28; Néret, 119; Corréard and Savigny, 5th edition (Paris, 1821), 443–47; Anon, *Souscription en faveur du libraire Corréard,* 1–3; *Je sais tout,* 15 July 1916, in the Corréard deposit in the Archives Départmentales, Gap; *Archives nationales* BB/18/999.

15. Spitzer, *Old Hatred and Young Hopes,* 2–3, 6–7, 58, 105–16; Bertier de Sauvigny, *La Restauration,* 180–81; Bordonove, *Le Naufrage,* 288–89.

16. Alexandre Corréard, *Élections des Représentants du peuple à l'Assemblée Législative,* 2.

17. Alhadeff, *The Raft,* 123–25; Savigny and Corréard (London, 1818), 179–84; Adanson, *Voyage to Senegal,* vii, 48–49.

18. Maureen Ryan, "Liberal Ironies, Colonial Narratives and the Rhetoric of Art: Reconsidering Géricault's *Radeau de la Méduse,*" in *Théodore Géricault: The Alien Body,* 30–31.

19. Henri Grégoire, *On the slave-trade and on the slavery of the blacks and of the whites, by a friend of men of all colours* (London: Josiah Conder, 1815),

2; Boime, "Géricault's African Slave Trade and the Physiognomy of the Oppressed," in *Géricault, Conférences et colloques du Louvre*, 567.

20. Chevalier, *Histoire de la Marine Française*, 7–8; Hugh Thomas, *The Slave Trade* (London: Papermac, 1998), 587; Savigny and Corréard (London, 1818), 311–17.

21. Thomas Clarkson, *The Cries of Africa to the Inhabitants of Europe; or, a Survey of that Bloody Commerce called the Slave-Trade* (London, 1822), 26–27.

22. James Walvin, *England, Slaves and Freedom, 1776–1838* (London: Macmillan, 1986), 126–27; *Times*, 10 July 1819; "De la traite des Nègres au Sénégal," a translation of the *13th Report of the Directors of the African Institution, London of March 24, 1819*, presented by Benjamin Constant in *La Minerve française*, 113, 116; J. Morenas, *Pétition contre la Traite des Noirs qui se fait au Sénégal, présentée à la Chambre des Députés le 14 juin, 1820* (Paris: Corréard, 1820), 10.

23. Geoffroy de Villeneuve, *L'Afrique*, vol. IV, 40–41, 44, 49.

24. Paul Marty, *Études Sénégalaise* (Paris: Société de l'Histoire des Colonies Françaises et Librairie Larose, 1925), 95, 101, 105, 157; Faure, "La garnison européenne," 17–18; Gabriel Debien, "J. E. Morenas à Saint-Louis en 1818–19," *Bulletin de l'Institut français d'Afrique noire*, series B, XXX, 2 (April, 1968): 692.

25. Letters from English observers in Sierra Leone and Senegal variously dated March 6, 18, 19, June 28, July 21, and November 8, 1817, in the National Archives FO/95/9/2.

26. Serge Daget, "L'Abolition de la traite des Noirs en France de 1814 à 1831," in *Cahiers d'études africaines II*, 1971, 28–29; Bertier de Sauvigny, *La Restauration*, 157; Thomas, *Slave Trade*, 620.

27. Jean-Vincent Giudicelly, *Observations sur la traite des Noirs en réponse au rapport de M. Courvoisier sur la pétition de M. Morenas* (Paris: Chez les Marchands de Nouveautés, 1820) 1, 12.

28. Marty, *Études*, 195–96; Faure, "La garrison," 19, 29, 30–31; Serge Daget, "L'Abolition de la traite des Noirs en France de 1814 à 1831," 27.

29. *Times*, 13 June 1818; Serge Daget, *Répertoire des expéditions négrières françaises à la traite illégale (1814–1850)* (Nantes, 1988), 32–33, 36, 52, 53, 55, 65, 87.

30. Daget, "L'Abolition de la traite des Noirs en France de 1814 à

1831," 30, 193; Serge Daget, *La répression de la traite des Noirs au XIX siècle* (Paris: Éditions Karthala, 1997), 69; Esquirol, *Maladies,* vol. II, 172–73.

31. Giudicelly, *Observations sur la traite des Noirs,* 22, 23.

32. Jean-Vincent Giudicelly, *Réponse de M. l'abbé Giudicelly, ex-préfet apostolique du Sénégal et de Gorée, à une lettre de S. Exc. le Bon Portal, ministre de la marine, 30 Avril, 1821* (Paris: Impr. de Mme Jeunehomme-Crémière, 1821), 10, 15; Gueye, "L'Afrique et l'esclavage," 202–3; Daget, "L'Abolition," 31; Thomas, 584; *Times,* 20 July 1818; Morenas, *Pétition contre la Traite des Noirs,* 5–6.

33. Morenas, *Pétition contre la Traite des Noirs,* 4–7, 12; J. Morenas, *Seconde Pétition contre La Traite des Noirs présentée a la Chambre des Députées le 19 Mars, 1821* (Paris, 1821), 55; Debien, "Morenas," 694.

34. Daget, "L'Abolition," 34; Debien, "Morenas," 693; Daget, "L'Abolition de la traite des noirs," 34; Gueye, *L'Afrique et l"esclavage* (Paris: Éditions Martinsart, 1983), 204.

35. Daget, "L'abolition," 36; M'Baye Gueye, "La Fin de l'esclavage à Saint-Louis et à Gorée en 1848," *Notes d'Histoire Coloniale,* no. 102, extract from *Bulletin de l'I.F.A.N.,* vol. 28, series B no. 3–4 (Dakar, 1966), 641; Alhadeff, *The Raft,* 155, 157.

36. Morenas, *Pétition* (1820), 12; Thomas, 805; Joseph Elzéar Morenas, *Précis historique de la traite des Noirs et de l'esclavage colonial contenant l'origine de la traite, ses progrès, son état actual et un exposé des horreurs produites par le despotisme des colons; ouvrage dans lequel on prouve qu'on a exporté d'Afrique, depuis 1814 jusqu'à présent, plus de 700 000 esclaves, dans un grande nombre sous pavillon français* (Paris, 1828), 176.

37. Jacques de Caso, "Géricault, David d'Angers, le Monument à l'émancipation et autres objets ou figures du racisme romantique," in *Géricault, Conférences et colloques du Louvre,* vol 2, 538; *La Minerve française,* 9 August 1819, 113–14.

38. Blanc, *Histoire,* 421.

39. Boime, *The Art of Exclusion,* 62–63.

40. Bro de Comères, *Mémoires,* 162; Clément, *Géricault,* 227–30; Chenique, "Géricault, une vie," in *Géricault,* 298–99, for extracts from all the early accounts of these accidents.

41. Chaudonneret, *L'Etat,* 40; Comte Forbin, qtd. in Chaudonneret, 40.

42. Bazin, *Théodore Géricault,* vol. I, 74, 83–85 and vol. VI, 20; Letter of Count de Forbin qtd. in Chenique, "Géricault, une vie," in *Géricault,* 303.

43. Eugène Delacroix, *The Journal of Eugène Delacroix* (London: Phaidon, 1951; pbk. 1995) 19.

44. Ibid., 24.

Chapter 14

1. Mansel, *Louis XVIII,* 399–404.

2. Alexandre Corréard, *Pétition des membres de la commission des condamnés pour causes politiques, adressée aux deux chambres* (Paris, 1832), 7–8.

3. Alexandre Corréard, *Résumé pour le sieur Corréard,* 2, 6; Werdet, *Librairie française,* 178; Alexandre Corréard, *Mémoire sur le projet d'un chemin de fer de Paris à Bordeaux* (Paris: Librairie Scientifique et Industrielle, 1838) 5; Alexandre Corréard, *Mémoire sur les différents moyens qui peuvent être employés par l'État pour intervenir dans l'exécution des chemins de fer en France, contenant des renseignements sur l'affaire du chemin de fer de Paris à Tours* (Paris: L. Mathias, 1837), 66.

4. Alexandre Corréard, *Mémoire sur le projet d'un chemin de fer de Paris à Bordeaux,* 5; Jore, *La vie diverse,* 306; Bordonove, *Le Naufrage,* 320–21.

5. Breillout, "La vie," 248–50; Masson, 233–34.

6. Service historique de la Défense—Vincennes: Dossier Marine: Vincent-Marie-Martin Chaudière, Francis Cornette de Vénancourt, Jean-Daniel Coudein, Jean Espiaux, Pierre-Joseph Lapeyrère, Joseph-Michel Maudet, Léon Henry de Parnajon, Alexandre Léonard Rang des Adrets, Joseph-Piere-André Reynaud, Jean-Baptiste-Henri Savigny.

7. Louis Robert, "Une odyssée atroce: le Radeau de la Méduse. La tragique Origine d'une thèse de médecine," *La Presse médicale,* 61, no. 51 (Paris: Masson, August 8, 1953) 1084; Michel Savigny, *L'Intermédiaire des Chercheurs,* no. 934 (Paris, May 30, 1901), column 1010.

8. Alexandre Corréard, *Chemin de fer de Paris à Versailles, rive gauche. Causes de la ruine de l'entreprise et réponses critiques aux attaques de la Compagnie* (Paris: L. Mathias, 1839), 3; Alexandre Corréard, *Chemin de fer de Paris à Bordeaux, par Chartres. Pétition sur l'usurpation par les Ponts et chaussées du projet de chemin de fer de Paris à Bordeaux, pour la partie comprise entre Tours et Bordeaux, présentée à la Chambre des Pairs par Alexandre Corréard* (Paris, 1842), 2– 8; Alexandre Corréard, *Élections des Représentants du peuple à l'Assemblée*

Législative; Alexandre Corréard, *Projet d'un barrage éclusé et mobile.* (Paris, 1856) 16–17; Hugues, *Corréard,* 20.

9. Dard, *La chaumière,* iii, 141, 226, 287; Mercier, 59–60; *La Minerve française,* 1819, 122; Debien, "Morenas," 692; Corréard and Savigny, 5th edition (Paris, 1821), 14–15: Brédif, "Le naufrage," 79.

10. Rang, *Voyage au Sénégal,* 39; Griffon du Bellay, *Les Griffon,* 27.

11. Savigny and Corréard (London, 1818) 46, 56, 69–70, 88, 100.

12. Corréard and Savigny, 5th edition (Paris, 1821), 121–24; Savigny and Corréard (London, 1818), 104; Savigny, "Observations de la faim et de la soif," in *L'affreuse vérité de M. Savigny: second chirurgien de la frégate la "Méduse,"* 112, 116; Bordonove, *Le Naufrage,* 161, 285.

13. Savigny and Corréard (London, 1818), 107–8, 119–20; Corréard and Savigny, 5th edition (Paris, 1821), 131.

14. Savigny and Corréard, 5th edition (Paris, 1821), 61–62; Praviel, *Relation,* 281.

15. Savigny and Corréard (London, 1818), 98; Praviel, *Relation,* 280, 283, 287–88, 309.

16. Rang, *Voyage au Sénégal,* 88; Bordonove, *Le Naufrage,* 155–56.

17. Brédif, "Le Naufrage," 143; Bordonove, *Le Naufrage,* 156–57.

18. Quoted by Griffon du Bellay in *Les Griffons,* 27.

19. Service historique de la Défense—Vincennes: Dossier Marine: Jean-Baptiste-Henri Savigny.

20. Savigny and Corréard (London, 1818), 94–95, 120; Grigsby, *Extremities,* 173, 176.

21. Arnold Scheffer, "Salon de 1827," *Revue Française,* 197, qtd. in Chaudonneret, *L'Etat,* 82; Berlin, *The Roots of Romanticism,* 15.

22. This is the traditional title of a painting now known as *The Polar Sea,* in the Kunsthalle, Hamburg.

23. Mary Shelley, *Frankenstein* (1818) (London: Wordsworth Editions, 1993), 41.

24. Jules Michelet, "L'Enfant du siècle," 5eme leçon quoted in Courthion, 112, 114.

25. Chaudonneret, *L'Etat,* 40; Clément, *Géricault,* 252–53, n.1; Philippe Grunchec, "L'inventaire posthume de Théodore Géricault," 406; Lorenz Eitner, "The Sale of Géricault's Studio in 1824," *Gazette des Beaux-Arts,* vol. LIII (Paris and New York: Presses universitaires de France), 122; Bazin, *Théodore Géricault,* vol. I, 92.

26. Ibid., 107, 110; Mansell, *Paris Between Empires,* 49.

27. Bordonove, *Le Naufrage,* 263, 265–66; Jean-Yves Blot, "Sur les traces de la Méduse," in François Bellec, *L'affaire de la Méduse,* Musée de la marine, Palais de Chaillot, 14 mai–21 juin 1981 (Paris: Musée de la marine, 1981).

28. *Archives départmentales,* Gap; Hugues, *Corréard,* 23; Bazin, *Théodore Géricault,* vol. VI, 84–85.

29. Sagne, *Géricault,* 272; Bazin, *Théodore Géricault,* vol. VI, 65.

30. Bazin, *Théodore Géricault,* vol. I, 106.

31. Ibid. vol. I, 116, 150.

32. Louise Becq de Fouqières to Georges-Hippolyte Géricault, July 19, 1863, qtd. in Bazin, *Théodore Géricault,* vol. I, 126; Bazin, vol. I, 129, 138, 186; Le Pesant, "Documents," 73, 77; Mainardi, "Husbands, Wives and Lovers," 285.

33. Le Pesant, "Documents," 77; Chenique, "Le Tombeau de Géricault," in *Géricault, Conférences et colloques du Louvre,* vol. II, 725–26.

34. Bazin, *Théodore Géricault,* vol. I, 122, 124, 126, 157–58, 160, 163.

Bibliography

Abrahams, Aleck. "The Egyptian Hall, Piccadilly," *The Antiquary* 42. London, 1906.

Ackerknecht, Erwin H. *Medicine at the Paris Hospital, 1784–1848.* Baltimore: Johns Hopkins Press, 1967.

Adanson, M. *A Voyage to Senegal, the Isle of Gorée and the River Gambia.* Dublin: Ewing, James & Bradley, 1759.

Aimé-Azam, Denise. *Mazeppa, Géricault et son temps.* Paris: Plon, 1956.

Aimé-Azam, Denise. *La Passion de Géricault.* Paris: Fayard, 1970.

Alhadeff, Albert. *The Raft of the Medusa.* Munich: Prestel, 2002.

Altick, Richard. *The Shows of London.* Cambridge, Mass., and London: The Belknap Press, 1978.

Angenot, Marc. *Le Roman populaire; recherches en paralittérature.* Montréal: Presses de l'Université du Québec, 1975.

Anglas de Praviel, Paulin d'. *Relation nouvelle et impartiale du naufrage de la frégate la Méduse* (Nîmes: Paulin d'Anglas de Praviel, 1858), in *Relation complète du naufrage de la frégate la Méduse.* Paris: J. de Bonnot, 1968.

Angrand, Pierre. *Le Comte de Forbin et le Louvre en 1819.* Lausanne-Paris: Bibliothèque des Arts, 1972.

Année, Antoine. *Le livre noir de Messieurs Delavau et Franchet, ou Répertoire alphabétique de la police politique sous le ministère déplorable; ouvrage imprimé d'après les registres de l'Administration.* Paris: Moutardier, 1829.

Anon. *Le Naufrage de la Méduse.* Paris: Delarue, 1842.

Anon. *Le Naufrage de la Méduse—Légendes populaires*. Paris: P. Martinon, 1863.

Anon. *Souscription en faveur du libraire Corréard, condamné pour avoir vendu des brochures politiques, dont les auteurs et les éditeurs étaient connu*. Paris, 1820.

Anon. *The Picture of the Palais Royal*. London: William Hone, 1819.

Anon. *The Shipwreck of the Alceste . . . The Shipwreck of the Medusa*. Dublin: E. Tute, 1822.

Antal, Frederick. "Reflections on Classicism and Romanticism," parts III, IV, and V, *Burlington Magazine*. London, Sept. 1940, Dec. 1940, and Jan. 1941.

Athanassoglou, Nina. "Géricault and La Liberté des Peuples," text submitted for publication in *Art History, n.d.,* copy in the Sackler Library, University of Oxford.

Athanassoglou-Kallmyer, Nina. "Géricault: politique et esthétique de la mort," in *Géricault, Conférences et colloques du Louvre,* vol. 1. Paris: La documentation française, 1996.

Athanassoglou-Kallmyer, Nina. "*Imago Belli*: Vernet's *L'Atelier* as an Image of Radical Militarism under the Restoration," *The Art Bulletin,* vol. LXVIII, no. 2. New York, June 1986.

Athanassoglou-Kallmyer, Nina. "Liberals of the World Unite: Géricault, his Friends and *La Liberté des Peuples,*" *Gazette des Beaux-Arts,* vol. CXVI. Paris, December, 1990.

Athanassoglou-Kallymer, Nina. "Géricault's Severed Heads and Limbs: The Politics and Aesthetics of the Scaffold," *The Art Bulletin,* vol. LXXIV, no. 4. New York, December 1992.

Bailly, Auguste. *Le Radeau de la Méduse*. Paris: la Renaissance du Livre, 1929.

Balzac, Honoré de. *La Peau de chagrin*. Paris: Gallimard, 1974.

Baron, Auguste. *Naufrage de la Méduse*. Limoges: E. Ardant, 1879.

Barthes, Roland. "*La structure du fait divers,*" in *Essais critique*. Paris: Éditions Seuil, 1964.

Batissier, Louis. "Géricault," reprint from *Revue du dix-neuvième Siècle*. Rouen, n.d. [1842 is a mistake in many citations], 1824.

Bazin, Germain. *Théodore Géricault, étude critique, documents et catalogue raisonné,* vols. I–VII. Paris: Wildenstein Institute: la Bibliothèque des arts, 1988–97.

Belchem, John. *Popular Radicalism in Nineteenth Century Britain*. London: Macmillan, 1996.

Bellanger, Claude et al. *Histoire générale de la presse française, Vol. II, 1815–1871*. Paris: Presses universitaires de France, 1969.

Bellec, François. *L'affaire de la Méduse,* Musée national de la marine, Palais de Chaillot, 14 mai–21 juin 1981. Paris: Musée national de la marine, 1981.

Berger, Klaus. *Géricault's Drawings and Watercolors*. New York: H. Bittner, 1946.

Bergot, François. *Géricault, tout l'oeuvre gravé*. Rouen: Musée des beaux-arts de Rouen, 1981.

Berlin, Isaiah. *The Roots of Romanticism,* ed. Henry Hardy. London: Chatto & Windus, 1999.

Berlioz, Hector. *La vie de Berlioz racontée par Berlioz*. Paris: R. Juliard, 1954.

Bertier de Sauvigny, Guillaume de. *La Restauration*. Paris: Flammarion, 1955; pbk. 1999.

Bertier de Sauvigny, Guillaume de. *Nouvelle Histoire de Paris: La Restauration*. Paris: Hachette, 1977.

Besse, Jean-Paul. *Compiègne dans l'histoire: une ville impériale et royale*. Paris: Éd. D.U.C., 1992.

Bjelajac, David. *American Art: A Cultural History*. London: Laurence King, 2000.

Blanc, Charles. *Histoire des peintres français au XIX siècle*. Paris: Cauville frères, 1845.

Blot, Jean-Yves. *"La Méduse," chronique d'un naufrage ordinaire*. Paris: Arthaud, 1982.

Blot, Jean-Yves. *"Sur les traces de la Méduse,"* in Bellec, *L'affaire de la Méduse,* Musée de la marine, Palais de Chaillot, 14 mai–21 juin 1981. Paris: Musée national de la marine, 1981.

Boime, Albert. "Géricault's African Slave Trade and the Physiognomy of the Oppressed," in *Géricault, Conférences et colloques du Louvre,* vol. II. Paris: La documentation française, 1996.

Boime, Albert. *The Art of Exclusion: Representing Blacks in the Nineteenth Century*. Washington, D.C.: Smithsonian Institution Press, 1990.

Boorde, Andrew. *Dyetary*, ed. F. J. Furnivall. London: Early English Text Society e.s. 10. 1870.

Bordonove, Georges. *Le Naufrage de "la Méduse."* Paris: R. Laffont, 1973.

Bousquet-Dechamps, Jacques-Lucien. *Attention!* Paris: Corréard, May 17, 1820.

Bousquet-Deschamps, Jacques-Lucien. *Pièces politiques*. Paris: Corréard, 1820.

Bousquet-Deschamps, Jacques-Lucien. *Questions à l'ordre du jour*. Paris: Corréard, April 8, 1820.

Brédif, Charles-Marie. "Le naufrage de la 'Méduse,' mon voyage au Sénégal," *La Revue de Paris,* nos. 11, 12, and 13. Paris, 1907.

Breillout, J. "La vie dramatique de M. de Chaumereix," *Bulletin de la Société des lettres, sciences et arts de la Corrèze,* 238–51. Tulle, 1933.

Brisson, M. de. *Histoire du Naufrage et de la captivité de M. De Brisson*. Genève & Paris, 1789.

Bro, Louis. *Mémoires du général Bro (1796–1844),* ed. Bro de Comères, Le Baron Henry. Paris: Plon-Nourrit et Cie., 1914.

Broglie, Achille-Charles-Léonce-Victor, Duc de. *Discours prononcé par M. le duc de Broglie, à la Chambre des Pairs, le 28 mars 1822 sur la traite des nègres*. Paris, 1822.

Brookner, Anita. *Romanticism and its Discontents*. New York: Viking, 2000.

Brown, David Blayney. "Literature and History: Shakespeare, Scott, Byron and Genre Historique," in *Crossing the Channel, British and French Painting in the Age of Romanticism,* ed. Patrick Noon. London: Tate Publishing, 2003.

Brown, David Blayney. *Romanticism.* London and New York: Phaidon, 2001.

Brunet, Auguste. *De l'Aristocratie et de la démocratie, de l'importance du travail, et de la richesse mobilière*. Paris: Corréard, 1819.

Buisson, Gilles. *Géricault: de Mortain à Paris*. Coutances: OCEP, 1976.

Bullock, William. *Sale Catalogue of the Bullock Museum, 1819*. London: Johnson and Hewett, 1979.

Byron, George Gordon, Lord. *Byron, A Self Portrait, Letters and Diaries 1798 to 1824,* vol. II, ed. Peter Quennell. New York: Charles Scribner's & Sons, 1950.

Carey, David. *Life in Paris*. London: John Fairburn, 1822.

Caron, François. *Histoire des chemins de fer en France,* vol. I. Paris: Fayard, 1997.

Caso, Jacques de. "Géricault, David d'Angers, le Monument à l'émancipation et autres objets ou figures du racisme romantique," in *Géricault, Conférences et colloques du Louvre,* vol. II. Paris: La documentation française, 1996.

Castel, René-Richard. *Lettres de René-Richard-Louis. Castel . . . au comte Louis de Chevigné.* Rheims: Delaunois, 1883.

Chateaubriand, François-René de. *Mémoires d'outre-tombe,* vol. III, ed. Levaillant. Paris: Le Club français du livre, 1969.

Chaudonneret, Marie-Claude. *L'Etat et les artistes de la Restauration à la monarchie de Juillet, 1815–1833.* Paris: Flammarion, 1999.

Chaumereys, Hugues Duroy de. *Relation de M. de Chaumereix, officier de la marine, échappé aux massacres d'Aurai et de Vannes, suivie de quelques observations sur l'esprit public en Bretagne.* London: J. de Boffe, 1795.

Chenique, Bruno. "Géricault posthume," in *Géricault, Conférences et colloques du Louvre,* vol. II. Paris: La documentation française, 1996.

Chenique, Bruno. "Géricault: une vie" and "Lettres et documents," in *Géricault,* ed. Régis Michel. Paris: Éditions de la Réunion des musées nationaux, 1991.

Chenique, Bruno. "Le tombeau de Géricault," in *Géricault, Conférences et colloques du Louvre,* vol. II. Paris: La documentation française, 1996.

Chenique, Bruno. "On the Far Left of Géricault," in *Théodore Géricault: The Alien Body: Tradition in Chaos,* ed. Serge Guilbaut, Maureen Ryan, and Scott Watson. Vancouver: Morris and Helen Belkin Art Gallery, 1997.

Chenique, Bruno. "Pour une étude de milieu: le cercle amical de Géricault," in *Géricault, Conférences et colloques du Louvre,* vol. I. Paris: La documentation française, 1996.

Chenique, Bruno. "Théodore Géricault, lithographe d'avant garde," in *Géricault, dessins et estampes des collections de l'École des beaux-arts.* Paris: École nationale supérieure des beaux-arts, 1997.

Chevalier, E. *Histoire de la Marine Française de 1815–1870.* Paris: Hachette, 1900.

Clarkson, Thomas. *The Cries of Africa to the Inhabitants of Europe; or, a Survey of that Bloody Commerce called the Slave-Trade.* London: Harvey and Darton and W. Phillipps, 1822.

Clément, Charles. *Géricault, étude biographique et critique.* Paris: Didier & Co., 1868.

Clinch, Dermot. "Hans Werner Henze—Profile," *New Statesman.* London: June 21, 1996.

Cochelet, Charles. *Narrative of the Shipwreck of the Sophia on the 30th May,*

1819, on the Western Coast of Africa. London: Sir Richard Phillips and Co., 1822.

Cohen, William B. *The French Encounter with Africans: White Response to Blacks, 1530–1880*. Bloomington: Indiana University Press, 1980.

Collier, Peter. "Newspaper and Myth: Migrations of the Romantic Image," in *Artistic Relations: Literature and the Visual Arts in Nineteenth-Century France,* ed. Collier and Lethbridge. New Haven and London: Yale University Press, 1994.

Collins, Irene, ed. *Government and Society in France, 1814–1848*. London: Edward Arnold, 1970.

Collins, Irene. "Liberalism and the Newspaper Press during the French Restoration 1814–1830," in *History,* vol. XLVI. London: RKP, 1961.

Collins, Irene. *The Government and the Newspaper Press in France, 1814–1881*. London: Oxford University Press, 1959.

Conservateur littéraire, Le, vol. II. Paris, 1820.

Constant, Benjamin. Introduction to *"De la traite des Nègres au Sénégal,"* a translation of "The 13th Report of the Directors of the African Institution, London of March 24, 1819," *La Minerve française*. Paris, 1819.

Constitutionnel, Le. Paris, 1815–17.

Corréard, Alexandre, and Henri Savigny. *Naufrage de la frégate la Méduse faisant partie de l'expédition du Sénégal en 1816,* 5th edition. Paris: Chez Corréard, Libraire, 1821.

Corréard, Alexandre et al. *A MM. les députés des départements. Réclamations des anciens condamnés politiques*. Paris, 25 juillet 1831.

Corréard, Alexandre. *Bases d'un projet de loi à intervenir dans l'intérêt des condamnés pour délits politiques sous les deux derniers règnes*. Paris, n.d. [1831].

Corréard, Alexandre. *Chemin de fer de Paris à Bordeaux, par Chartres. Pétition sur l'usurpation par les Ponts et chaussées du projet de chemin de fer de Paris à Bordeaux, pour la partie comprise entre Tours et Bordeaux, présentée à la Chambre des Pairs par Alexandre Corréard*. Paris, 1842.

Corréard, Alexandre. *Chemin de fer de Paris à Versailles, rive gauche. Causes de la ruine de l'entreprise et réponses critiques aux attaques de la Compagnie*. Paris: L. Mathias, 1839.

Corréard, Alexandre. *Élections des Représentants du peuple à l'Assemblée législative. Alexandre Corréard, Ingénieur (du Radeau de "La Méduse") aux électeurs du département Seine-et-Marne.* Batignolles, n.d.

Corréard, Alexandre. *Mémoire sur le projet d'un chemin de fer de Paris à Bordeaux.* Paris: Librairie Scientifique et Industrielle, 1838.

Corréard, Alexandre. *Mémoire sur les différents moyens qui peuvent être employés par l'État pour intervenir dans l'exécution des chemins de fer en France, contenant des renseignements sur l'affaire du chemin de Paris à Tours.* Paris: L. Mathias, 1837.

Corréard, Alexandre. *Pétition des membres de la commission des condamnés pour causes politiques, adressée aux deux chambres.* Paris, n.d. [1832].

Corréard, Alexandre. *Projet d'un barrage éclusé et mobile.* Paris, 1856.

Corréard, Alexandre. *Résumé pour le sieur Corréard.* Paris: n.d.

Courthion, Pierre. *Géricault raconté par lui-même et par ses amis.* Vésenaz-Genève: P. Cailler, 1947.

Critchley, MacDonald. *Shipwreck-Survivors, a Medical Study.* London: J. & A. Churchill, 1943.

Daget, Serge. "France, Suppression of the Illegal Trade, and England 1817–50," in *The Abolition of the Atlantic Slave Trade,* ed. Eltis and Walvin. Madison: University of Wisconsin Press, 1981.

Daget, Serge. "L'Abolition de la traite des noirs en France de 1814 à 1831," *Cahiers D'Études Africaines,* vol. XI, no. 41. Paris: École Pratique des Hautes Études, 1971.

Daget, Serge. *La répression de la traite des Noirs au XIX siècle.* Paris: Éditions Karthala, 1997.

Daget, Serge. *Répertoire des expéditions négrières françaises à la traite illégale (1814–1850).* Nantes: Centre de recherche sur l'histoire du monde atlantique: Comité nantais d'études en sciences humaines, 1988.

Dalyell, John Graham. *Shipwrecks and Disasters at Sea* (Edinburgh, 1812). London: George Routledge and Sons, 1866.

Dard, Mme., née Charlotte-Adelaide Picard. *La chaumière Africaine, ou Histoire d'une famille française jetée sur la côte de l'Afrique, à la suite du naufrage de la Frégate la Méduse.* Dijon: Noellat, 1824.

Darmon, Pierre. *La Rumeur de Rodez.* Paris: Albin Michel, 1991.

Daudet, Ernest. *La police politique: chroniques des temps de la Restauration 1815–1820.* Paris: Plon-Nourrit, 1912.

Daudet, Ernest. *Louis XVIII et le duc Decazes 1815–1820*. Paris: E. Plon, Nourrit et Cie., 1899.

Debien, Gabriel. "J. E. Morenas à Saint-Louis en 1818–19," *Bulletin de l'Institut Français d'Afrique noire,* series B, XXX, 2. Paris, April 1968.

Debord, Jean-François. "À propos de quelques dessins anatomiques de Géricault," in *Géricault, dessins et estampes des collections de l'École des beaux-arts.* Paris: École nationale supérieure des beaux-arts, 1997.

Delacroix, Eugène. *The Journal of Eugène Delacroix.* London: Phaidon, 1951; pbk. 1995.

Deslys, Charles. *Le naufrage de la Méduse.* Paris: G. Havard, 1859.

Déterville, H. *Le Palais-Royal ou les Filles en bonne fortune.* Paris: L'Écrivain, 1815.

Drujon, Fernand. *Catalogue des ouvrages, écrits, et dessins poursuivis, supprimés ou condamnés depuis le 21 octobre 1814 jusqu'au 31 juillet 1877.* Paris: Edward Rouveyre, 1879.

Dubaut, Pierre, and Claude Aubry. *Géricault dans les collections privées françaises.* Paris: Galerie Claude Aubry, 1964.

Dukay, Pierre. *Le Naufrage de "la Méduse."* Paris: Éditions Jules Tallandier, 1932.

Durand, Jean-Baptiste-Léonard. *Voyage au Sénégal.* Paris: Chez Henri Agasse, 1802.

Eitner, Lorenz. "Erotic Drawings by Gericault," *Master Drawings*, vol. XXXIV, no. 4. New York, 1996.

Eitner, Lorenz. "The Sale of Géricault's Studio in 1824," *Gazette des Beaux-Arts,* vol. LIII. Paris and New York: Presses universitaires de France, February 1959.

Eitner, Lorenz. *Géricault: His Life and Work.* London: Orbis Press, 1983.

Eitner, Lorenz. *Géricault, Sa vie, son oeuvre.* Paris: Gallimard, 1991.

Eitner, Lorenz. *Géricault's "Raft of the Medusa."* London: Phaidon, 1972.

Escudier, Denis. *L'affreuse vérité de M. Savigny: second chirurgien de la frégate la "Méduse," naufragé du radeau, miraculeusement sauvé par l'Argus, le 17 juillet 1816.* Saint-Jean D'Angely: Bordessoules, 1991.

Esquirol, Etienne. *Des maladies mentales considérées sous les rapports médical, hygiénique et médico-légal.* Paris, 1838.

Evans, Eric J. *Britain Before the Reform Act: Politics and Society, 1815–1832.* London and New York: Longman, 1989.

Falconbridge, Alexander. *An Account of the slave trade on the coast of Africa.* London: J. Phillips, 1788.

Faure, Claude. "La garnison européenne du Sénégal et la recruitement des premières troupes noires (1779–1858)," *Revue de l'histoire des colonies françaises,* no. 8, 3e trimestre. Paris: Société de l'histoire des colonies françaises, 1920.

Fellowes, William Dorset. *Paris During the Interesting Month of July, 1815, a Series of Letters.* London: Gale and Fenner, 1815.

Fournel, Charles. *L'hôpital Beaujon. Histoire depuis son origine jusqu'à nos jours.* Paris: Dentu, 1884.

Frye, Major W. E. *After Waterloo, Reminiscences of European Travel, 1815–19.* London: Heinemann, 1908.

Gallois, Léonard. *Promenade à Saint-Pélagie.* Paris, Leroux, 1823.

Geoffroy de Villeneuve, René-Claude. *L'Afrique ou Histoire, moeurs, usages et coutumes des Africains. Le Sénégal,* 4 vols. Paris: Nepveu, 1814.

Germer, Stefan. "'Je commence une femme, et ça devient un lion': On the Origin of Géricault's Fantasy of Origins," in *Géricault, Conférences et colloques du Louvre,* vol. 1. Paris: La documentation française, 1996.

Gilmore, Jeanne. *La République clandestine, 1818–48.* Paris: Aubier, 1997.

Girard, Louis. *Les Libéraux français, 1814–1875.* Paris: Aubier, 1985.

Giudicelly, Jean-Vincent. *Observations sur la traite des Noirs en réponse au rapport de M. Courvoisier sur la pétition de M. Morenas.* Paris: Chez les Marchands de Nouveautés, 1820.

Giudicelly, Jean-Vincent. *Réponse de M. l'abbé Giudicelly, ex-préfet apostolique du Sénégal et de Gorée, à une lettre de S. Exc. le Bon Portal, ministre de la marine, 30 Avril, 1821.* Paris: Impr. de Mme Jeunehomme-Crémière, 1821.

Gleyses, Chantal. *La femme coupable.* Paris: Éditions Imago, 1994.

Grandpré, Louis-Marie-Joseph Ohier, comte de. *Voyage à la côte occidentale d'Afrique fait dans les années 1786 et 1787,* 2 vols. Paris: Dentu, an IX [1801].

Grate, Pontus. "La critique d'art et la bataille romantique," *Gazette des Beaux-Arts,* vol. 54. Paris and New York: Presses universitaires de France, September 1959.

Grégoire, Henri. *On the Slave-Trade and on the Slavery of the Blacks and of the Whites, by a Friend of Men of all Colours.* London: Josiah Conder, 1815.

Griffon du Bellay, Jean. *Les Griffon pendant cinq cent ans*. Garnes: privately printed, 1979.

Grigsby, Darcy Grimaldo. *Extremities*. New Haven and London: Yale University Press, 2002.

Grocott, Terence. *Shipwrecks of the Revolutionary and Napoleonic Eras*. London: Caxton Editions, 2002.

Grunchec, Philippe. "L'inventaire posthume de Théodore Géricault," *Bulletin de la Société de l'histoire de l'art français*. Paris, 1976.

Guédron, Martial. *La plaie et le couteau: La sensibilité anatomique de Théodore Géricault, 1791–1824*. Paris: Kimé, 1997.

Gueye, M'Baye. "La fin de l'esclavage à Saint-Louis et à Gorée en 1848," *Notes d'histoire coloniale*, no. 102, extract from *Bulletin de l'I.F.A.N.*, vol. 28, series B, no. 3–4. Dakar, 1966.

Gueye, M'Baye. *L'Afrique et l'esclavage: une étude sur la traite négrière*. Romorantin: Éditions Martinsart, 1983.

Guilbaut, Serge. "Théodore Géricault: The Hoarse Voice of History," in *Théodore Géricault: The Alien Body: Tradition in Chaos*, ed. Serge Guilbaut, Maureen Ryan, and Scott Watson. Vancouver: Morris and Helen Belkin Art Gallery, 1997.

Hardcastle, Ephraim. *Wine and Walnuts or After Dinner Chit-Chat*. London: Longman, Hurst, Rees, Orme and Brown, 1823.

Harpaz, Ephraim. *L'Ecole libérale sous la Restauration, le Mercure et la Minerve, 1817–1820*. Genève: Droz, 1968.

Haydon, Benjamin Robert. *Life of Benjamin Robert Haydon, historical painter, from his Autobiography and his Journals,* ed. and completed by Tom Taylor. London: Longman, Brown, Green and Longman, 1853.

Henze, Hans-Werner, and Ernst Schnabel. *Das Floss der Medusa: oratorio volgare e militare in due parte*. Berlin: Deutsche Grammophon Gesellschaft, 1968.

Honour, Hugh. "Curiosities of the Egyptian Hall," *Country Life*, vol. CXV, no. 2973, 38–39. London, 7 January 1954.

Houssaye, Henri. "Un Maître de L'École française—Théodore Géricault," *Revue des Deux-Mondes*. Paris, 15 November 1879.

Huet, René-Paul. *Paul Huet d'après ses notes, sa correspondance, ses contemporains*. Paris: H. Laurens, 1911.

Hugues, Edmond. *Alexandre Corréard de Serres, naufragé de la 'Méduse'*. Gap, France, 1920.

Imbert, Auguste. *Biographie des imprimeurs et des librairies.* Paris, 1826.

Imbert, Auguste, and B. L. Bellet, *Biographie des condamnés pour délits politiques.* Brussels, 1827.

Jal, Auguste. *L'Ombre de Diderot et le bossu du Marais; Dialogue critique sur le Salon de 1819.* Paris: Corréard, 1819.

Jenkins, E. H. *Histoire de la marine française.* Paris: Albin Michel, 1977.

Jennings, L. C. "The Abolition of French Slavery," in *De la traite à l'esclavage. Actes du colloque international sur la traite des Noirs,* ed. Serge Daget (Nantes 1985). Paris and Nantes, 1988.

Jessop, Thomas. *Journal d'un voyage à Paris en septembre–octobre 1820,* ed. F. C. W. Hiley. Paris, 1928.

Joannet, Henri. *Le Radeau de la Méduse ou Comment un Serrois montre du doigt l'espérance au reste du monde.* Serres: Groupement d'action pour le développement de la vallée du Buèch: "Notre Pays," 1999.

Joannides, Paul. "The Raft of the Medusa," review of *Géricault's "Raft of the Medusa,"* by Lorenz Eitner, *Burlington Magazine,* vol. CXVII, no. 864. London, March 1975.

Johnson, Lee. "Géricault and Delacroix seen by Cockerell," *Burlington Magazine,* vol. CXIII, no. 822. London, September 1971.

Johnson, Lee. "'La grosse Suzanne' uncovered," *Burlington Magazine,* vol. CXXIII, no. 937. London, April 1981.

Johnson, Lee. "The 'Raft of the Medusa' in Great Britain," *Burlington Magazine,* vol. XCVI, no. 617. London, August 1954.

Jore, L. "La vie diverse et volontaire du Colonel Julien Désiré Schmaltz . . . Consul Général de France à Smyrne (Turquie) 1771–1827," *Revue d'histoire des colonies,* vol. XL, 2nd trimestre 1953. Paris, 1953.

Journal des débats et des décrets. Paris, 1814–24.

Knoch, Inken D. "Une peinture sans sujet? Étude sur les *Fragments anatomiques,*" in *Géricault, Conférences et colloques du Louvre,* vol. 1. Paris: La documentation française, 1996.

La Tynna, Jean de la. *Almanach du commerce de Paris, des départemens de la France et des principales villes du monde.* Paris: au bureau de l'Almanach du commerce, 1818 and 1822.

La Tynna, Jean de la. *Dictionnaire topographique, historique et étymologique des rues de Paris.* Paris, 1816.

Landow, George. "Iconography and Point of View in painting and literature; the example of the shipwreck," *Studies in Iconography* III. Highland Heights, Ky.: Northern Kentucky University, 1977.

Langeron, Roger. *Decazes, ministre du roi.* Paris: Hachette, 1960.

Langsdorff, Georg Heinrich freiherr von. *Voyages and Travels in Various Parts of the World during the Years 1803, 1804, 1805, 1806, and 1807.* London: Henry Colburn, 1813.

Lawrence, A. W. *Trade Castles and Forts of West Africa.* London: Jonathan Cape, 1963.

Le Maire, Jacques-Joseph. *Les Voyages du Sieur Le Maire aux Isles Canaries, Cap-Verd, Sénégal et Gambie.* Paris, 1695.

Le Pesant, Michel. "Documents inédits sur Géricault," *Revue de l'Art,* no. 31, 73–81. Paris: Flammarion, 1976.

Ledré, Charles. *La Presse à l'assaut de la monarchie, 1815–1848.* Paris: Armand Colin, 1960.

Legohérel, Henri. *Histoire de la Marine française.* Paris: Presses universitaires de France, 1999.

Lestringant, Frank. *Cannibals: The Discovery and Representation of the Cannibal from Columbus to Jules Verne.* Cambridge: Polity Press, 1997.

Lesur, C. L. *Annuaire historique universel Pour 1818.* Paris: Thoisnier-Deplaces, 1825.

Lodge, Suzanne. "Géricault in England," *Burlington Magazine,* vol. CVII, no. 753. London, December 1965.

Mainardi, Patricia. "Mazeppa," *Word & Image,* vol. 16, no. 4. London: Taylor & Francis, October 2000.

Mainardi, Patricia. "Husbands, Wives and Lovers. *Mazeppa* or Marriage and its Discontents in Nineteenth Century France," in *Géricault, Conférences et colloques du Louvre,* vol. 1. Paris: La documentation française, 1996.

Mainardi, Patricia. *Husbands, Wives, and Lovers.* New Haven and London: Yale University Press, 2003.

Mansel, Philip. *Louis XVIII.* Stroud: Sutton Publishing, rev. ed., 1999.

Mansel, Philip. *Paris Between Empires, 1814–1852.* London: John Murray, 2001; pbk. 2003.

Manson, Marie, and Henri de Latouche. *Mémoires de Madame Manson,* 7th edition. Paris: Pillet, 1818.

Martini, Eric. "Treatment for scurvy not discovered by Lind," *The Lancet,* vol. 364. London, December 18–25, 2004.

Martini, Michel. *La tuberculose ostéo-articulaire.* Berlin-Heidelberg, Springer-Verlag, 1988.

Marty, Paul. *Études Sénégalaise.* Paris: Société de l'Histoire des Colonies Françaises et Librairie Larose, 1925.

Masson, Philippe. *L'Affaire de la Méduse.* Paris: Tallandier, 1989.

Matteson, Lynn R. "Géricault and 'English Street Cries.'" *Apollo,* October 1977. London, 1977.

McLeod, John. *The Shipwreck of the Alceste, an English frigate in the straits of Gaspar; also the Shipwreck of the Medusa,* compiled from the papers of John McLeod and the narrative by Savigny and Corréard. Dublin: E. Tute, 1822.

McLeod, John. *Voyage of His Majesty's late ship "Alceste" along the coast of Corea to the island of Lewchew, with an account of her subsequent shipwreck in the straits of Gaspar,* compiled from the papers of John McLeod. London: John Murray, 1818.

Mellon, Stanley. *The Political Uses of History.* Stanford, Calif.: Stanford University Press, 1958.

Mercier, Roger. "Le Naufrage de "La Méduse"—Réalité et imagination romanesque," *Revue des Sciences Humaines,* fasc. 125. Lille: Université de Lille, Jan.–March 1967.

Michel, Régis, Bruno Chenique et. al. *Géricault.* Paris: Éditions de la Réunion des musées nationaux, 1991.

Michel, Régis, ed. *Géricault, Conférences et colloques du Louvre,* 2 vols. Paris: La documentation française, 1996.

Mishory, Alec. "Theodore Gericault's *A Paraleytic* (sic) *Woman,*" *Gazette des Beaux-Arts,* vol. CIIIV. Paris and New York: Presses universitaires de France, April 2000.

Mishory, Alexander. "Le 'reportage' réaliste d'un observateur objectif: le suite anglaise de Théodore Géricault," in *Géricault, dessins et estampes des collections de l'École des beaux-arts.* Paris: École nationale supérieure des beaux-arts, 1997.

Mollien, Gaspar. *Découverte des sources du Sénégal et de la Gambie en 1818.* Paris: C. Delagrave, 1889.

Mollien, Gaspar. *Travels in the Interior of Africa to the Sources of the Senegal and*

Gambia Performed by Command of the French Government in the year 1818. London: H. Colburn & Co., 1820.

Monestier, Alain, and Jacques Cheyronnaud. *Le Fait divers.* Paris: Éditions de la Réunion des musées nationaux, 1982.

Moncrieff, William. *The Shipwreck of the Medusa, or, The Fatal Raft!* London, 1830.

Morenas, Joseph Elzéar. *Pétition contre la traite des Noirs présentée à la Chambre des Députés le 14 juin 1820.* Paris: Chez Corréard, 1820.

Morenas, Joseph Elzéar. *Précis historique de la traite des Noirs et de l'esclavage colonial.* Paris, 1828.

Morenas, Joseph Elzéar. *Seconde Pétition contre la traite des Noirs, présentée à la Chambre des Députés le 19 mars 1821.* Paris, 1821.

Mullens, W. H. "William Bullock's London Museum," *Museums Journal,* no. 17. London: October, 1917.

Musée Renan-Scheffer. *La Nouvelle Athènes—le quartier Saint-Georges, de Louis XV à Napoléon III.* Paris: Musée Renan-Scheffer, 1984.

Nazarieux, Charles-Pierre de. *Mémoire pour la Société coloniale philanthropique, présenté à son excellence Mgr. le Ministre Secrétaire d'Etat de la Marine et des colonies par MM. les membres composant la Commission administrative de la Société coloniale.* Paris, 25 November 1816.

Néret, Jean-Alexis. *Histoire Illustrée de la Librairie.* Paris: Lamarre, 1953.

Nettement, Alfred M. *Souvenirs de la Restauration.* Paris: Jacques Lecoffre et Cie., 1858.

Newman, Edgar Leon. *Historical Dictionary of France from the 1815 Restoration to the Second Empire,* 2 vols. Westport, Conn.: Greenwood Press, 1987.

Nicolson, Benedict. "The 'Raft' from the Point of View of Subject Matter," *Burlington Magazine,* vol. CXVI, no. 617. London, August 1954.

Nochlin, Linda. "Géricault or the Absence of Women," in *Géricault, Conférences et colloques du Louvre,* vol. 1. Paris: La documentation française, 1996.

Noon, Patrick. "Colour and Effect—Anglo-French Painting in London and Paris," in *Crossing the Channel, British and French Painting in the Age of Romanticism,* ed. Patrick Noon. London: Tate Publishing, 2003.

Parson. *Premier rapport de M. Parson, chef de la délégation envoyée au Cap-Verd par la Société-coloniale-philanthropique à l'effet de reconnoître les lieux les plus propres à la fondation des colonies agricoles,* 2e édition avec des Notes par M. Sevigny. Paris: Au bureau de la Société coloniale philanthropique, 1817.

Pescay, François Fournier de. "Calenture," in *Dictionnaire des sciences médicales, par une société de médecins et de chirurgiens,* ed. Nicolas Philibert Adelon, vol. 2. Paris, 1812.

Pescay, François Fournier de. "Notice sur la Calenture, maladie particulière aux gens de mer," in *Annales des faits et des sciences militaires: faisant suite aux "Victoires et conquêtes des Français de 1792 à 1815,"* ed. Jean Denis Barbié du Bocage, 4 vols. Paris, March 1818.

Planta, Edward. *A New Picture of Paris, or The Stranger's Guide to the French Metropolis.* London: Samuel Leigh, July 1814.

Quotidienne, La. Paris, 1815–47.

Rabaroust, Marie Antoine. "Récit inédit du naufrage de La Méduse," *L'Intermédiaire des Chercheurs,* no. 45. Paris, 10 January 1902.

Rabbe, Alphonse. "Nécrologie, Géricault peintre d'histoire," *La Pandore, Journal des spectacles, des lettres, des arts, des moeurs et des modes,* no. 198. Paris, 29 January 1824.

Rang, Sander (Alexandre Rang des Adrets, *dit* Sander Rang). *Voyage au Sénégal, Naufrage de la Méduse.* Paris: Editions E.P.I., 1946.

Resnick, Daniel P. *The White Terror and the Political Reaction after Waterloo.* Cambridge, Mass.: Harvard University Press,1966.

Riding, Christine. "The Raft of the Medusa in Britain, Audience and Context," in *Crossing the Channel, British and French Painting in the Age of Romanticism,* ed. Patrick Noon. London: Tate Publishing, 2003.

Riley, James. *Loss of American Brig "Commerce" Wrecked on the Western Coast of Africa in the Month of August 1815.* London: J. Murray, 1817.

Robert, Louis. "Une odyssée atroce: le Radeau de la Méduse. La tragique origine d'une thèse de médecine," *La Presse Médicale,* no. 51. Paris: Masson, August 8, 1953.

Rosenblum, Robert. *Modern Painting and the Northern Romantic Tradition.* London: Thames and Hudson, 1975; pbk. 1978.

Rosenthal, Donald A. "Géricault's Expenses for the Raft of the Medusa," *Art Bulletin,* vol. LXII. New York: College Art Association of America, December 1980.

Ryan, Maureen. "Liberal Ironies, Colonial Narratives and the Rhetoric of Art: Reconsidering Géricault's *Radeau de la Méduse,*" in *Théodore Géricault: The Alien Body: Tradition in Chaos,* ed. Serge Guilbaut, Maureen Ryan, and Scott Watson. Vancouver: Morris and Helen Belkin Art Gallery, 1997.

Sagne, Jean. "Géricault et l'opinion libérale," in *Géricault, Conférences et colloques du Louvre*, vol. II. Paris: La documentation française, 1996.

Sagne, Jean. *Géricault*. Paris: Fayard, 1991.

Salgari, Emilio, and Luigi Motta. *Le Naufrage de "la Méduse."* Paris: J. Ferenczi et fils, 1926.

Savigny, J. B. Henry, and Alexandre Corréard. *Narrative of a Voyage to Senegal in 1816*. London: Henry Colburn, 1818.

Savigny, Jean-Baptiste-Henri, and Alexandre Corréard. *Naufrage de la frégate la Méduse, faisant partie de l'expédition du Sénégal, en 1816*. Paris, 1817.

Savigny, Jean-Baptiste-Henri. *Journal des débats*. Vendredi, September 1816.

Savigny, Jean-Baptiste-Henri. *L'affreuse vérité de M. Savigny: second chirurgien de la frégate la "Méduse," naufragé du radeau, miraculeusement sauvé par l'Argus le 17 juillet 1816*, documents assembled and presented by Denis Escudier. Saint-Jean D'Angely: Bordessoules, 1991.

Savigny, Jean-Baptiste. *Observations sur les effets de la faim et de la soif éprouvées après le naufrage de la frégate du roi "La Méduse" en 1816* (Paris 26 mai, 1818), in Denis Escudier, *L'affreuse vérité de M. Savigny: second chirurgien de la frégat: Bordessoules, la "Méduse," naufragé du radeau, miraculeusement sauvé par l'Argus le 17 juillet 1816*. Saint-Jean D'Angely: Bordessoules, 1991.

Savigny, Michel. "Henri Savigny," *L'Intermédiaire des Chercheurs*, no. 934, column 1010. Paris: 30 May 1901.

Scheffer, Charles-Arnold. *De l'État de la liberté en France*. Bruxelles: Demat, 1818.

Scott, John, of Gala. *Paris Revisited in 1815, by way of Brussels*. London: Longman, Hurst, Rees, Orme & Brown, 1816.

Sells, Christopher. "After the 'Raft of the Medusa': Gericault's Later Projects," *Burlington Magazine*, vol. CXXVIII, no. 1001. London, August 1986.

Sells, Christopher. "New Light on Géricault, his Travels and his Friends, 1816–23," *Apollo*, vol. CXXII, no. 292. London, June 1986.

Sells, Christopher. "Two Letters from Gericault to Madame Horace Vernet," *Burlington Magazine*, vol. CXXXI, no. 1032. London: March 1989.

Sévigny, P. H. J. *Mémoire au Conseil d'État pour la Société-coloniale-philanthropique de la Sénégambie, exposant les avantages politiques et commerciaux qui peuvent résulter pour la France de la fondation de cette nouvelle colonie, ainsi que les faits relatifs à l'établissement de la Société-coloniale.* Paris: Société-coloniale-philanthropique, 1817.

Shankland, Peter, and the Rt. Hon. Sir Michael Havers Q.C. *Murder with a Double Tongue.* London: Souvenir Press, 1990.

Shelley, Mary. *Frankenstein* (1818). London: Wordsworth Editions, 1993.

Simon, Robert. "Géricault and *l'affaire Fualdès,*" in *Géricault, Conférences et colloques du Louvre,* vol. 1. Paris: La documentation française, 1996.

Simon, Robert. "Géricault and the *fait divers,*" in *Géricault, Conférences et colloques du Louvre,* vol. 1. Paris: La documentation française, 1996.

Simpson, Brian A. W. *Cannibalism and the Common Law: The Story of the Tragic Last Voyage of the Mignonette and the Strange Legal Proceedings to Which it Gave Rise.* Harmondsworth: Penguin, 1986.

Spitzer, Alan B. *Old Hatred and Young Hopes: The French Carbonari against the Bourbon Restoration.* Cambridge, Mass.: Harvard University Press, 1971.

Spitzer, Alan B. *The French Generation of 1820.* Princeton, N.J.: Princeton University Press, 1987.

Stendhal (Henri Beyle). *Racine et Shakespeare.* Paris, 1823.

Sue, Eugène. *La Salamandre* (1845). Paris: Éditions des Autres, 1979.

Thomas, Hugh. *The Slave Trade.* London: Papermac, 1998.

Thompson, E. P. *The Making of the English Working Class.* New York: Vintage Books, 1963.

Times, The. London, 1816–22.

Titeux, Eugène. *Histoire de la Maison militaire du roi de 1814 à 1830.* Paris: Baudry, 1890.

Touches, Gicquel des. "Souvenirs d'un marin de la République," *Revue des Deux-Mondes,* parts I and II, vol. 28. Paris, 1905.

Tronchet, Louis. *Picture of Paris, being a complete guide to all the public buildings and curiosities in that metropolis.* London: Sherwood, Neely and Jones, 1815.

Tulard, Jean, and Louis Garros. *Itinéraire de Napoléon au jour le jour 1769–1821.* Paris: le Grand livre du mois, 2002.

Tulard, Jean. "Naufrage et cinéma," in *Le Naufrage—actes du colloque tenu à l'Institut catholique de Paris 28–30 Jan. 1998,* ed. Buchet and Thomasset. Paris: Honoré Champion, 1999.

Twyman, Michael. *Lithography 1800–1850.* London: Oxford University Press, 1970.

Vallery-Radot, Pierre. "L'anatomie et la psychiatrie dans la vie et l'oeuvre de Géricault," *La Presse médicale* 66, no. 27. Paris: Masson, April 5, 1958.

Vaughan, William. *Romantic Art*. London: Thames and Hudson, 1978.

Vayre, Pierre. *Les Larrey. Dominique, Hippolyte . . . et les autres*. Paris: Editions Glyphe, 2005.

Villeneuve, Roland. *Histoire du cannibalisme*. Paris, 1965.

Walvin, James. *England, Slaves and Freedom, 1776–1838*. London: Macmillan, 1986.

Werdet, Edmond. *De la librairie française: son passé, son présent, son avenir*. Paris: Dentu, 1860.

Whitney, Wheelock. *Géricault in Italy*. New Haven and London: Yale University Press, 1997.

Wright, Beth S. *Painting and History During the French Restoration, Abandonned by the Past*. Cambridge: Cambridge University Press, 1997.

Wrigley, Richard. *The Origins of French Art Criticism from the Ancient Regime to the Restoration*. Oxford: Clarendon Press, 1993.

Zelle, Carsten. "Théorie du naufrage: avant Géricault," in *Géricault, Conférences et colloques du Louvre,* vol. 1. Paris: La documentation française, 1996.

Index